T0323470

Strategic Taxation: Fiscal Capacity and Accountability in African States

Strategic Taxation

Fiscal Capacity and Accountability in African States

LUCY E. S. MARTIN

OXFORD
UNIVERSITY PRESS

OXFORD
UNIVERSITY PRESS

Oxford University Press is a department of the University of Oxford.
It furthers the University's objective of excellence in research, scholarship,
and education by publishing worldwide. Oxford is a registered trade mark of
Oxford University Press in the UK and in certain other countries.

Published in the United States of America by Oxford University Press
198 Madison Avenue, New York, NY 10016, United States of America.

Library of Congress Cataloging-in-Publication Data

Names: Martin, Lucy (Lucy Elizabeth Semple), author.
Title: Strategic taxation : fiscal capacity and accountability in African
states / Lucy Martin.
Description: New York, NY : Oxford University Press, [2023] | Includes
bibliographical references and index.
Identifiers: LCCN 2023007299 (print) | LCCN 2023007300 (ebook) | ISBN
9780197672631 (hardback) | ISBN 9780197672648 (paperback) | ISBN
9780197672662 (epub)
Subjects: LCSH: Taxation—Africa. | Finance, Public—Africa. | Government
accountability—Africa. | Public administration—Africa.
Classification: LCC HJ3021 .M37 2023 (print) | LCC HJ3021 (ebook) | DDC
336.20096—dc23/eng/20230216
LC record available at https://lccn.loc.gov/2023007299
LC ebook record available at https://lccn.loc.gov/2023007300

DOI: 10.1093/oso/9780197672631.001.0001
DOI: 10.1093/oso/9780197672648.001.0001

Contents

List of Figures

List of Tables

Acknowledgments

In 2011 I spent two months traveling around Northern Uganda, talking to NGOs and local leaders for a potential dissertation on foreign aid. Over the course of those interviews, taxation—and its lack—came up again and again. It became increasingly evident that taxation in modern developing countries, and especially in sub-Saharan Africa, had been largely neglected by political scientists, and that taxation was closely linked to governance more broadly. This book simply would not exist without the generosity of those who spoke to me that year, both elected village leaders and community organization workers, or without the dedication and intelligence of my research assistant that year, Emmanuel Ogonya.

Turning my intuitions about taxation into a fully formed book took over ten years, several interstate moves, becoming a parent, and surviving a global pandemic. I could not have finished it without the support of innumerable friends, colleagues, mentors, research colleagues, and family.

This project began during my time as a graduate student at Yale University. Kenneth Scheve, Christopher Blattman, Susan Rose-Ackerman, and Susan Stokes were an absolute powerhouse of a committee. They spent hours helping me to refine my ideas, develop research designs, and turn a vague project into a concrete and polished dissertation. They have also continued to provide support and advice as I turned the dissertation into the book. I am also grateful to the many other Yale faculty who generously gave me feedback and support throughout the dissertation process, including Peter Aronow, Kate Baldwin, Alexandre Debs, Thad Dunning, Greg Huber, Susan Hyde, and John Roemer.

During graduate school I received significant help and advice from a network of colleagues and advisors across universities. These include, Eric Dickson, Guy Grossman, Macartan Humphreys, David Laitin, Dan Posner, Michael Ross, Cyrus Samii, Georg Vanberg, and Jeremy Weinstein, all of whom gave invaluable advice at various stages of the project. I am also thankful for the feedback I received on parts of this project at the Leitner Workshop at Yale, WGAPE, CAPERS, MPSA, and APSA, as well as conferences at Princeton University, Duke University, and Harvard University.

Parts of this book were completed during a fellowship at Princeton University's Niehaus Center for Globalization and Governance. This included hosting a book conference for an earlier version of this manuscript. Thank you to Helen Milner and Pat Trinity for supporting and organizing this conference. I am eternally grateful to Guy Grossman, Kimuli Kasara, Laura Paler, and Michael Ross for carefully reading and considering my manuscript, and for giving me the insight and advice needed to make it stronger and more coherent.

This book was completed at UNC–Chapel Hill, which is perhaps the best place in the country to be an assistant professor. Thank you to my wonderful colleagues for their support and advice, especially my current and former department chairs, Mark Crescenzi and Evelyne Huber.

This book draws extensively on data collected in Uganda. This data collection was possible due to the large team of enumerators and research assistants at Innovations for Poverty Action in Uganda, as well as the fantastic support staff. Especial thanks to Esther Aganyira, Dean Buruhan, Robert Kalule, Vianney Mbonigaba, Joe Ndumia, Ezra Rwakazooba, and Gyagenda Solomon, without whose hard work and unlimited patience this project would not have been possible. Other data were collected in collaboration with Ignosi Research in Uganda. Thank you to Ivan Senkubuge, Ezra Rwakazooba, Vivienne Tibaberwa, and Denis Baliddawa for their work on this project, along with a large team of enumerators, translators, and support staff.

I am also grateful to my superb UNC research assistants, who worked on multiple iterations of data analysis and literature reviews. Thanks to Tyler Ditmore, Simon Hoellerbauer, Eric Parajon, Ayelen Vanegas, and Mitchell Watkins.

Parts of this book draw on co-authored work. Special thanks to Adam Dynes, and to Brandon de la Cuesta, Helen Milner, and Daniel Nielson for allowing me to incorporate our joint work into this book. It has been a true pleasure working with you all.

Data collection for this book was funded in part by the Leitner Program at Yale University, the Yale Lindsay Fellowship, the MacMillan Center at Yale, Princeton University, and a Vanguard Charitable Trust. Thank you for your support.

At Oxford University Press, I am grateful to my editor, David McBride, my project editor, Sarah Ebel, and my production manager, Thomas Deva. Two anonymous reviewers provided incredibly thoughtful, constructive, and detailed feedback that improved the book's contribution, clarity, and statistical rigor.

I became a political scientist in large part due to the outstanding teaching and mentorship I received as an undergraduate at Kenyon College. Fred Baumann, Pamela Camerra-Rowe, John Elliot, Laurie Finke, Joe Klesner, Marla Kohlman, David Rowe, and Steve Van Holde helped me to develop a love of rigorous, thoughtful research. Special thanks are due to Carol Schumacher, for teaching me how to write proofs.

Finally, I would like to thank my family. My parents for creating a family environment in which education was valued above all other pursuits; for loving and raising me. My sister, Violet Martin, for pushing me as siblings are wont to do. To my husband, Cameron Ballard-Rosa, who has been not only a loving and equal partner for over 15 years, but has also helped me to think through knotty problems and develop my ideas. And to my son, Michael, for bringing unmeasurable joy into my life.

1

Introduction

By almost any metric, Africa is booming. Average GDP per capita, which was largely stagnant in the 1980s and 1990s, has grown from $2,100 in 2000 to over $4,000 today.[1] In 2000, only 15 African countries had reached lower- or upper-middle income status; by 2019 this had increased to 39. While the COVID-19 crisis has reduced some of these gains, there are hopes for a rebound. Politically, too, there has been progress. Eleven countries have instituted multi-party elections since 2000, and elections have become more free and fair in many countries. Citizens have successfully fought election-fixing, as happened in Malawi, or forced long-term autocrats out of office, as in Burkina Faso.

Yet, in some areas of state development African countries show little improvement. In contrast to the progress cited above, some countries, like Uganda, have seen an increase in repression and more authoritarian rule. More generally, Transparency International's Corruption Perceptions Index shows no improvement for African countries, on average, between 2000 and 2021. State bureaucracies are weak and understaffed. Crucially, government revenues are lagging. The fraction of GDP African governments collect in taxes has increased only slightly in 40 years. It hovered around 11% throughout the 1980s and 1990s, then saw slow and intermittent progress to 14% or 15% in recent years (ICTD/UNU-WIDER 2020).[2]

Without more taxation, it will be difficult for African countries to continue to grow. Improving health and education systems will be needed to support a healthy, educated workforce. There is a critical need for more investment, too, in infrastructure like roads, electricity, and internet, to support growing economies. Foreign aid is simply not sufficient to fill the financing gap. Rising debt burdens in the wake of COVID-19 make domestic revenues even more important for avoiding defaults like the recent one in Ghana. Ultimately, sustainable development will require more domestic revenue from taxation.

[1] Numbers are taken from the World Bank (2020), PPP measure. In contrast, average GDP per capita increased by only US$90 between 1980 and 2000.
[2] Numbers from recent years are hard to interpret due to the significant economic shock of the COVID-19 pandemic.

Strategic Taxation: Fiscal Capacity and Accountability in African States. Lucy E. S. Martin.
Oxford University Press. © Oxford University Press 2023. DOI: 10.1093/oso/9780197672631.003.0001

Higher fiscal capacity could potentially help solve many African countries' governance problems, as well. European state development, including the development of representative institutions, was driven in part by rulers' revenue demands (Tilly 1992). The need to raise taxes forced monarchs to bargain with wealthy elites, granting policy concessions or political representation in return for paying taxes (North and Weingast 1989; Bates and Lien 1985). Revenue demands also led to the development of a professional bureaucracy, with positive benefits for overall levels of state capacity and professionalization (Moore 2004). This suggests that, if African governments expanded taxation, it could have positive spillovers for other areas of state development.

So, why does fiscal capacity remain low in so many African countries? Standard theories of taxation tend to view governments as revenue-maximizing, so as countries become richer, why are governments not taking more of this new wealth for their budgets? In this book, I argue that existing theories of state development—especially those based on the European experience—are insufficient to explain the dynamics of taxation and fiscal capacity in modern developing states. In early modern Europe, the exigencies of war and national defense created a pressing need for revenue, and states that survived were those that could develop steady sources of revenue and strong bureaucracies. Taxes, and strong states, developed because the alternative was oblivion. State development looks very different today, especially in the post-colonial states of sub-Saharan Africa. This book develops a new theory to explain why modern developing countries may systematically under-invest in fiscal capacity, and what will be needed to change this.

1.1 What Makes Taxation Special?

Governments can raise revenue from a number of sources. These are typically divided into "unearned" revenues—like natural resources and foreign aid—and "earned" resources, namely taxation. Borrowing provides a third route. This book follows a long line of research arguing that taxation plays a special, outsized role in the functioning of the state. As Schumpeter famously wrote (quoting Rudolf Goldscheid), "the budget is the skeleton of the state, stripped of all misleading ideologies" (Schumpeter 1991).

Relative to other revenues sources, taxation differs along two dimensions that grant it its special status. First, collecting taxes typically requires more state capacity than collecting other types of revenue. Receiving foreign aid requires almost no state capacity—in fact, it is countries with low capacity who typically receive the most aid money. Donors typically require some kinds of systems in place to monitor and audit how funds are spent, but these require little information about actual citizens. Natural resource rents may require slightly more capacity in order to monitor extraction, but is still possible when state capacity is low. Even rebel groups are able to extract significant resource rents (Sánchez De La Sierra 2020). In contrast, governments need detailed information on citizens, and their sources of income, in order to implement many forms of taxation. Once governments have this information, it can have positive effects on other areas of the bureaucracy, as detailed economic and demographic data can be used to plan public services or professionalize other areas of the bureaucracy (Moore 2004; Bräutigam, Fjeldstad, and Moore 2008).

Second, taxation differs in the extent to which it is *earned*. While aid and resource rents are often considered "windfalls," mass taxation creates a sustained point of contact between citizens and their governments. As I show in this book, this has significant implications for the demands these citizens will place on their leaders. Taxed citizens will require more public goods and services, and potentially even more democratic forms of government, and this has the potential to drastically reshape the state.

Combined, these differences suggest that taxation should advance state development, while non-earned revenues like aid and oil will have much smaller or even negative effects—even when aid is expressly directed towards such development. A vast political economy literature backs this up. Work on the resource curse suggests that access to oil and other natural resources is associated with poor governance (Ross 1999, 2001; Mehlum, Moene, and Torvik 2006; Ross 2012; Sandbu 2012). Much of the research on foreign aid suggests that it too may lead to higher corruption or hurt the quality of democracy (Bräutigam and Knack 2004; Morrison 2009, 2015; Djankov et al. 2008). However, this view is not universal: other scholars have argued that, especially in the post-Cold War period, aid is not subject to the resource curse (Bermeo 2015; Dunning 2005).

In contrast, taxation is associated with higher levels of democracy (Ross 2004) and lower corruption (Baskaran and Bigsten 2013). Prichard (2015) finds similar patterns for a broader set of countries using updated data. Timmons (2005) finds links between the tax base and who benefits from public policy. At the subnational level, local governments that rely on own revenues as opposed to central transfers are have lower corruption and provide more public goods (Gadenne 2017; Brollo et al. 2013; Fisman and Gatti 2002).

Thus, understanding taxation is critical to understanding state development. And yet we still lack a strong understanding of why so many developing countries are reluctant to increase taxation despite a desperate need for revenue. Saying simply that many African countries' citizens are too poor to pay taxes doesn't hold up. While formal levels of poverty do remain high in many African states, it does not follow that there is no tax base. When one talks (as I have done in both Uganda and Malawi) with small business owners and average citizens, many express a strong willingness to pay more in taxes, provided that the government spends the money wisely. Even among poorer countries, there is significant variation in the ability and willingness of governments to tax citizens. Poverty is not a compelling explanation. Similarly, arguments that the post-colonial borders of African states, combined with a lack of interstate war, makes low state capacity forordained (Herbst 2000) are likewise insufficient. As I discuss more in subsequent chapters, countries can face existential threats and a strong need for taxation even when borders are fixed. Patterns of taxation also do not reflect the type of geography. Even states with similar geographies have a wide range of tax extraction.

1.2 A New Theory of Taxation and Statement Development

How, then, should we think about taxation and state development in modern developing countries? To answer this question, I separate this book's theory into two parts. First, I argue that taxation fundamentally changes citizen-state relations, leading citizens to make more demands on their government. Second, I examine how this affects the willingness of governments to tax. I show that in some cases the accountability effects of taxation result in a paradox: if taxation increases accountability, governments will avoid taxing citizens in order to minimize the citizen pressures they face.

The first part of the theory examines how the act of paying taxes affects citizens' ability and willingness to hold leaders accountable by punishing poor performance. I argue that taxation, by removing earned income from citizens, induces a sense of loss in taxpayers. Eager to recover the lost income, citizens care more about government spending and increase the demands they place on leaders. This makes them more upset when demands are not met, and therefore more likely to punish leaders through voting, protests, and other forms of political action. Extensions to the theory show that this logic holds even when citizens face barriers to holding officials accountable, or when citizens and governments interact over many periods. The key implication of the theory is that, when citizens are taxed, they will be more willing to punish wrongdoing by leaders. This wrongdoing could take the form of poor public services, or high levels of rent-seeking. Fundamentally, taxation increases the demands citizens make of their leaders.

The second part of the theory takes as given that taxation increases citizens' demands, and examines how this will affect when and how governments tax citizens. As a starting point, I assume that governments are *rent maximizing*. This is subtly different than the standard assumption that governments are *revenue maximizing* (Levi 1989). The key difference is that a rent-maximizing government wishes to extract as much revenue as possible only to the extent that it allows them to increase spending for their own priorities and consumption. Rulers may, in this formulation, not wish to increase revenue if it does not either increase their short-term rents or prolong their tenure in office (thus securing long-term access to rents). This can occur if leaders do not get much (or any!) direct utility from revenues they must spend on citizens' priorities, instead having their own preferences. These could be spending on private consumption through embezzlement, or spending in ways that maintain their political support in the medium- or long-term.

While the rent-seeking assumption may seem intuitive for autocrats, it is not a standard assumption for democratic governments, which are typically assumed to represent citizens' preferences (see e.g. (Acemoglu and Robinson 2006)). However, many new democracies simply do not fit this approach. In a number of cases, particularly in sub-Saharan Africa, formal transitions to multi-party elections have not resulted in changes to the executive. President Museveni of Uganda has survived the onset of multi-party politics, as has Paul Biya in Cameroon and executives in a number of other countries. Even when there has been regime change and a theoretical shift to more democracy, the new rulers are often former members of the ruling party, and it is not clear that they have preferences that are actually more in line with citizens than the incumbents they defeated or ousted. For example, after Robert Mugabe was ousted in a coup, a former member of his ruling coalition became president of Zimbabwe. In Burkina Faso, the main opposition to President Blaise Compaoré was comprised by former members of his ruling coalition. This is borne out in continuing high levels of corruption and patronage in many areas, even when autocrats lose power. It therefore seems reasonable to assume that rulers and citizens in these contexts may have different spending priorities, and that rulers care primarily about rent extraction.

Given the rent-maximization assumption, I develop a formal model in which a government considers the short- and long-term benefits and costs of taxation, and decides whether it wishes to tax. The model first considers autocracies in which citizens cannot remove the leader from office, and then a democracy in which citizens have more power. If a government does choose to tax, it must choose whether to do so through coercion or tax bargaining. Coercive taxation uses the power of the state to monitor citizens and enforce penalties for non-compliance. It is costly for rulers, but ensures that all citizens pay the tax. Under tax bargaining, the government negotiates with citizens and agrees to provide policy concessions (here, higher public goods provision) if citizens pay the tax without coercion (Levi 1989). This reduces the costs of collection, but commits rulers to spending concessions in the future. If a government chooses to tax, it can lead to higher accountability (measured by the degree of rent-seeking) in two ways. First, if the government bargains with citizens successfully, it will agree to provide citizens with a certain level of their desired public good in each period. This will improve public goods provision relative to the revenue system that would exist without the bargain. Even if bargaining cannot be sustained, it is still possible for taxation to improve accountability if taxation makes citizens more likely to punish poor government performance. However, while bargaining (where citizens' leverage comes from the ability to withhold tax revenue) can occur in autocracies and democracies, the second mechanism requires citizens to have enough political freedom that they can use protests or elections to sanction poor performance under taxation.

A key finding of this book is that when taxation increases accountability demands, governments may respond by decreasing taxation, rather than improving accountability. And, this is more likely under democracy than autocracy. This occurs because democracy makes taxation less important for extracting accountability. While democratization gives citizens a credible way to punish rulers—thus making it more likely that rulers keep tax bargains—it also gives citizens a method of holding governments accountable even when they are not paying taxes. This effectively makes tax bargains less valuable to citizens, as they can extract some concessions from government even when taxation is zero. While many early democracies were a direct result of taxation, in many modern cases they are more likely to be the result of complex processes that are heavily influenced by international norms: it is now credible for citizens to keep democracy but not taxation. Thus, democracy makes it more likely that leaders keep a tax bargain, but less likely that citizens will; depending on which effect predominates, democracy could therefore increase or decrease taxation.

My theory predicts that when state capacity is high, democracy will tend to increase taxation; the opposite will hold in low-capacity states. This is because public goods are expensive to provide relative to revenues in low-income, low-capacity states, and so citizens are less likely to value taxation. Thus, in modern developing countries, which are typically low capacity, there will be few incentives to invest in higher fiscal capacity. In high-capacity states, governments will be better able to meet citizens' demands with available revenues, and this will make taxation more likely under democracy.

This book also provides new insights on when taxation is likely to lead to more accountable governments in the form of lower rent-seeking by politicians. Like other theories of taxation and accountability, I expect that higher levels of taxation will generally be associated with lower levels of government corruption and mismanagement. However, my theory provides additional implications for when this relationship is likely to hold, and when it will be strongest. I show that while taxation can lead to better governance in both autocracies and democracies, we should expect this relationship to be stronger in democracies. Drawing on co-authored work with Brandon de la Cuesta, Helen Milner, and Daniel Nielson, I also show that direct taxes are more likely to generate accountability dividends than indirect taxes.

1.2.1 Empirical Approach

This book relies on a mixed-methods approach to better understand the linkages between taxation, democracy, and good governance. The theory introduced above, and developed over the course of this book, is based on over a year of research conducted in Uganda. This research included not only the experiments described below but also extensive interviews and focus groups with citizens, politicians, bureaucrats, and non-governmental organizations (NGOs). I supplemented this work with additional qualitative research and data collection in Malawi and Ghana. While I draw most heavily on the qualitative research in Chapter 7, it was critical to building my understanding of the political dynamics surrounding taxation. I also use statistical analysis of both experimental and observational data to test the implications of my theory, and to better understand the mechanisms at work.

To test the first part of my theory—that taxation will lead to higher citizen demands on government—I use a mix of experimental and observational data. To clearly identify the causal effect of taxation on political behavior, I developed and ran a set of laboratory experiments in Uganda. These experiments allow me to precisely isolate the effects of taxation from other aspects of politics, and to test my proposed loss-aversion mechanism against several alternatives. To confirm that the results are not driven by the abstract nature of the experiments, and to explore the scope conditions of the theory, I ran additional experiments in both Uganda and Ghana. I then draw on Afrobarometer survey data on taxation and political action to show that the results hold outside of a lab setting.

The second part of the theory has a number of implications. I use cross-national panel data to test two key implications. First, I show that democracy will only lead to higher taxation when states are sufficiently high-capacity. This finding is supported by additional data on the size of the tax net in African states. Second, I show that while taxation can lead to lower rent-seeking in both autocracies and democracies, the effect is stronger for democracies, and for direct taxes.

Finally, to further examine how governments structure taxation to reduce accountability demands, and how democratization affects this process, I use the case of Uganda. Drawing on original survey data, interviews with government officials, and the secondary literature, I examine how government willingness to tax varies across different groups of citizens and tax types, and show that my theory can explain the government's strategic choices. The case studies balance the crossnational data, testing pieces of the theory that are not easily amenable to large-N quantitative analysis.

1.3 Plan of the Book

The rest of the book develops the core argument in more detail and provides extensive evidence for the theory's predictions. Chapter 2 sets the stage for the argument by dissecting the differences between the European experience of state formation, and the experience of modern African countries. The chapter focuses on three key differences. First, while European states were driven by the existential threat of interstate war, modern states are more likely to face internal threats. This can alter revenue incentives significantly, especially if raising taxes can create more domestic opposition. Second, while early European states had limited access to non-tax revenues, modern states have several alternative sources of revenue available, in particular foreign aid and resource rents. These "non-earned" resources reduce the need for taxes and allow states to be more strategic in how and when they rely on taxation. Finally, while the development of representative government in Europe was often a direct result of rulers' revenue needs, this link is significantly weaker in modern states. The wave of African democratizations in the 1990s was driven by a mix of domestic and international factors that often had little relation to taxation. Critically, African states typically democratize when state capacity is still low, while in Europe democratization happened further along in economic and state development. Combined, these differences highlight the need to revise our understanding of the relationship between taxation, state-building, and democracy.

Chapter 3 introduces a new theory to explain why and how taxation increases the accountability pressures governments face. It develops the argument introduced above in more detail. I argue that citizens expect to receive their earned income, and that taxation induces a sense of loss. Theories of loss aversion imply that, when individuals are in the realm of losses, their utility functions are more sensitive to changes. We should therefore expect that citizens care more about the level of public goods provided, and will be more upset if government misspends tax dollars. If citizens' willingness to engage in political actions like voting or protesting is linked to this perception of losses and the negative emotions they can generate then taxed citizens should be more likely than untaxed citizens to demand better performance from leaders, and to take action when dissatisfied. The chapter appendix presents the formal model on which the chapter is based.

Chapter 4 shows how government incentives to tax are affected when taxation increases accountability pressures. I develop a formal model of taxation in which a government, who cares primarily about rent extraction, must decide whether to tax a group of citizens. If it does tax, it must decide between using coercion and engaging in tax bargaining. The government and citizens then engage in an infinitely repeated game. I develop two versions of the model. In the first, there are no elections and so citizens' only leverage on the government comes from their ability in the bargaining game to withhold tax revenues. I then introduce elections, and examine how the equilibria are affected when citizens can vote a leader out of office. The model produces new predictions regarding when and how governments are likely to tax. I find that while taxation can lead to higher accountability, this is not always the case. There are conditions under which governments will prefer short-term extraction and subsequent electoral losses to providing citizens with higher public goods provision. There are also cases where leaders are simply willing to forgo tax revenues if doing so lowers the accountability demands they face. Critically, I find that while democracy can make taxation more sustainable under certain conditions, it can also have a negative effect on both coercive taxation and tax bargaining, leading to lower taxation overall. The model also reproduces many existing findings from the tax bargaining literature—such as the importance of the government's discount rate and the necessity of gains from trade for tax bargaining to be sustained.

Chapter 5 tests the micro-foundational theory developed in Chapter 3. To isolate the effect of taxation on willingness to punish leaders, I introduce a set of laboratory-in-the-field experiments, conducted in Uganda. The experiments show that a randomized treatment in which citizens lose real money to a simulated tax increases willingness to punish low transfers from a leader, even when punishment is costly and has no economic benefit. Qualitative data, combined with survey results, shows that respondents did treat the lab experiments as simulating taxation and political engagement. I then use additional experiments to show that the results cannot be attributed to alternative mechanisms such as fairness norms, and that losses do drive willingness to punish. The lab experiments also allow me to document that, as predicted by the theory, individuals do get expressive (i.e. non-economic) benefits from punishing leaders. Extensions of the experiments show that the effect of taxation persists, and even increases, when there are additional barriers to punishment. Additional experiments show that taxation is most likely to generate citizen accountability pressures for visible taxes, and that indirect consumer taxes are typically not visible to citizens. Finally, to provide external validity for the lab findings, I use Afrobarometer survey data from 31 countries to show that taxed citizens are more likely to engage in a range of political actions. Combined, this evidence provides strong support for the book's main assumption: that taxation increases the accountability demands leaders face from citizens.

Chapter 6 tests the predictions from Chapter 4 regarding when governments will choose to tax, and when doing so is likely to lead to better governance and lower corruption. Using a cross-national panel dataset, I show that democracy is only strongly associated with higher taxation in higher-income countries. In low-income countries, the effect is null or even negative. Indeed, political liberalization is associated with a significant average *decrease* in tax-to-GDP ratios in following years. I then use data from Afrobarometer to construct a cross-sectional measure of tax net size in a sample of African states and show that the tax net is smaller in democracies. Finally, I show that taxation is associated with lower rent-seeking, as measured by corruption, as predicted by the model. As predicted I also find that taxation has a more pronounced effect on corruption for democracies in which citizens' demands can translate into policy more easily. Finally, I show that direct taxes have a stronger relationship with corruption than indirect taxes, following the results in Chapter 5.

To further test the book's theory, Chapter 7 uses a case study of taxation in Uganda to show how my theory can explain the government's tax decisions. Uganda's revenue system has undergone substantial changes since elections were reintroduced in the 1990s. As the political system liberalized between 1996 and 2006, the government has significantly altered taxation. Some new taxes have been introduced, while others have been eliminated. Some taxes have also been kept, but have gone from being coercive to more closely resembling tax bargaining. I show that the expansion of democracy led to elimination of several key forms of taxation, as predicted by the model, and that the contraction of political competition has led to the introduction of new, often unpopular, taxes. Critically, the government has consistently changed the structure of taxation to minimize the accountability demands it faces from citizens, despite the revenue shortfalls it faces.

Chapter 8 concludes. It discusses the implications of the theory, and outlines an agenda for future research.

1.4 Implications

As African countries grow, they will need to strengthen government revenues and infrastructure to sustain growth and improve the lives of citizens. This will only be possible if governments are willing, and able, to increase taxation. Yet, fiscal capacity remains low in many countries. Outside observers often assume that taxation in Africa is low either because most people are too poor to pay taxes, or because governments lack the capacity to collect taxes efficiently. This book argues that the problem is, at its heart, a political one. Taxation creates new pressures on governments, and leaders will only tax if they are willing and able to meet those demands and constrain rent-seeking. Otherwise, leaders will prefer to maintain lower capacity and revenues in order to keep citizens' demands low.

This book makes several contributions to our understanding of taxation and state development. First, it provides a strong theoretical foundation for when, and how, taxation will increase citizens' accountability demands. By applying insights from behavioral economics, I show that taxation will increase the transfers citizens demand from governments. This can lead to higher political engagement when those demands are not met. The mechanism also helps us understand when taxation will have this effect: when taxes are not visible, or when the costs of political action are prohibitively high, taxation will have little impact. While I test this theory in sub-Saharan Africa, the theory itself is general and should apply to taxpayers in all geographic regions.

Second, this book provides a new framework for analyzing when and how governments will tax their citizens. This framework was designed to be applicable to a wide range of political environments. While I focus here on its predictions for low-capacity states, it can also be used to think through the likely impacts of taxation in other regions of the world. For sub-Saharan Africa, and low-income states more generally, this theoretical model generates a number of novel implications that expand our understanding of when taxation is sustainable. Most importantly, I show that the relationship between taxation and democracy is more complex than many theories predict. While standard median voter theories argue that democracies should tax at higher rates than autocracies, I argue that this will only be the case for high-capacity states where citizen demands can be efficiently met. If these conditions do not hold, than democratization can lead to lower, not higher, taxation. This book joins other recent work in challenging the presumed positive link between democratization, taxation, and state capacity. For example, Bastiaens and Rudra (2018) argues that democracies will have a harder time replacing revenue that is lost to lower trade taxes during globalization, and Suryanarayan (2021) argues that franchise extensions in India lead elites to "hollow out" the state to avoid redistribution. This book makes a related but broader argument about fiscal capacity across regime types more generally.

The theory also generates a number of additional predictions that, while not explicitly tested here, can help us better understand when taxation is politically feasible, and when it will lead to lower government rent-seeking. Some of these replicate existing findings from the literature on taxation. I show that tax bargaining will be more likely when rulers have long time horizons; when coercive taxation is costly; and when citizens share preferences for a public good. However, other predictions are new. While previous work has focused on the importance of long time horizons for leaders, I show that citizens' time horizons are also important. I also show that tax bargaining will be difficult to sustain when public goods are relatively expensive to produce relative to the revenues raised through taxation, even when citizens agree in theory on which public goods they want.

The findings presented here also have implications for how to best build state and fiscal capacity. It suggests that purely economic interventions, or attempts at capacity-building in isolation, will likely be ineffective. Rather, taxation in sub-Saharan Africa, and developing countries more generally, needs to be treated as a political problem, not a purely administrative or economic one.[3] This approach contributes to a broader shift towards viewing state capacity, not as exogenous, but as something that governments can—at least in part—control. If donors and governments can work together to simultaneously increase public goods and tax capacity, and to strengthen ties between citizens and leaders, it may be possible to generate a self-reinforcing equilibrium in which a strong fiscal state is combined with an accountable government. However, this will require overcoming hesitancy of both politicians and citizens.

[3] For work on political barriers to taxation in Latin America, see Flores-Macias (2019).

2

Understanding Fiscal Capacity

2.1 Introduction

In early modern Europe, the need for revenue to fund war and state defense led leaders to bargain with elites, and ultimately to grant significant representational concessions in return for funding the state. In the nineteenth and twentieth centuries, this provided the foundation for modern states to take an increasingly important role in the economy, both in terms of taxation and spending. In the pre-colonial period in sub-Saharan Africa, dynamics started to emerge that were similar to those in early Europe. However, European colonization of Africa interrupted that process, setting up new institutions and borders that persisted after independence. In the post-colonial period, key differences have emerged between modern developing states and their European predecessors. The survival incentives of leaders are very different; combined with new revenue sources like foreign aid and natural resources, taxation has become less central to state survival. Similarly, patterns of democratization are very different today than in pre-modern Europe, less tied to taxation and driven more by other international and domestic forces. And, while economic development preceded democratization in Europe, this is not the case in many African countries. Combined, these differences have led to a different sort of state, with different concerns and revenue needs. In some cases existing theories of taxation and state capacity still apply, but many dynamics are simply not explained by existing theory.

This chapter goes through each stage of this history in more detail. It shows why a new theory of taxation in modern developing countries is necessary, and how the nature of taxation is likely to be different, given the different constraints and incentives faced by rulers.

Strategic Taxation: Fiscal Capacity and Accountability in African States. Lucy E. S. Martin.
Oxford University Press. © Oxford University Press 2023. DOI: 10.1093/oso/9780197672631.003.0002

2.2 The Old Story: Taxation and State-Building in Early Europe

In early Europe, taxation played a key role in building strong states. Monarchs who wished to remain in power and implement their preferred policies needed to maximize revenues, primarily in the form of taxes. This need for taxes, in turn, drove other changes in the structure of the state. Studies of taxation in Europe grant a special role to interstate conflict—and its accompanying existential threat—in pushing monarchs to build the state institutions necessary to extract large amounts of revenues (Tilly 1992; Bates and Lien 1985; Stasavage 2011). Facing the frequent threat of invasion, rulers needed to raise the revenues necessary to pay soldiers, buy weapons, and otherwise wage war. While monarchs in the sixteenth and seventeenth centuries often had their own sources of revenue, typically from crown lands, they also taxed wealthy elites or forced them to give the crown loans (Bates and Lien 1985; Tilly 1992). While these revenues could directly fund war, they were often slow to collect and insufficient for the needs of monarchs. Thus, taxation also played an indirect role in improving rulers' access to credit: states that could generate a steady stream of tax revenues were better able to borrow money, and at better rates. Stasavage (2011) argues that it was ultimately access to credit that determined state survival.

This need for higher tax revenues had two impacts on state development: it created incentives for the state to develop the capacity to track citizens and potential revenue sources, and it (at times) forced rulers to strike bargains with taxpayers, granting them policy and institutional concessions in return for tax compliance. Many states originally developed professional bureaucracies in part to increase tax revenues (see discussion in Moore (2004) and Seelkopf et al. (2021)). Historically, a common method of extracting revenues was tax farming, in which a private company (or individual) paid a fixed sum in return for the right to collect a certain tax (Kiser and Karceski 2017). While this approach guaranteed the state a steady revenue stream, it also had serious disadvantages. If the price of the tax tender was set too low, the tenderer grew rich while the state receives few revenues. Compounding this problem, tax farmers often turned to coercive extraction, using threats and even violence to increase their profits. This could lead to tax resistance, including riots, that threatened the ruler's stability.

An alternative is for governments to collect taxes themselves. This means that revenues will vary more given economic circumstances, but also means that the government can control revenue collection more closely—including the level of coercion—and benefit when revenues increase. It also gives rulers an incentive to collect a maximum of tax revenues at the least possible cost. One way to do this is to increase the information government officials have about the tax base and the performance of tax collectors. This is not a trivial task, often requiring detailed information about the population and its sources of income. Early states typically turned to fixed, immobile assets for tax revenues, although these still required significant bureaucratic resources to collect.[1] As revenue needs increased, rulers started to collect from sources that required more and more state capacity. This need led in many cases to the development of a bureaucracy based on merit, rather than political patronage (Kiser and Karceski 2017).[2]

This increased capacity has potential benefits for other state functions. Demographic and economic information originally collected for tax purposes can often be used to plan efficient public goods provision and infrastructure investments. Roads can be planned to connect population centers, and a good census will help governments decide where to place schools, hospitals, and other services. The data also create a more sophisticated picture of the nation's economic well-being, which can guide economic policy. Because the health of the economy, and future economic growth, directly affect the amount the government can collect in taxes, rulers now have incentives to pursue policies that increase economic growth and promote investment. If rulers' time horizons are sufficiently long, they will avoid over-extraction in order to maintain access to a higher long-term stream of revenues (Bates 2015).

Increasing bureaucratic capacity thus allowed rulers to decrease the costs of tax collection, and increase the costs of tax evasion; this then had benefits for other areas of state development. However, while this approach made it harder for citizens to evade some taxes, and successfully increased tax revenues, other forms of taxation were harder to enforce, especially those that taxed less visible assets or income. For these taxes to be collected, taxpayers had to be willing to give up a portion of their income at least somewhat voluntarily.

---

[1] Consider for example England's window tax, introduced in 1696, which required local agents to count the number of windows in each dwelling in order to assess the correct tax burden, then mechanisms for collecting this revenue.

[2] See Brewer (2002) for a description of this process in England.

The other tactic that emerged as a way to improve revenue collection was tax bargaining. The classic example of this dynamic comes from early English history. As the crown shifted from taxing land to taxing more mobile assets, elites whose assets could be easily hidden or removed from the country found it easy to avoid paying taxes. When the monarch desperately needed funds to wage war, he allowed the creation of Parliament, granting it some control over taxation as well as additional policy concessions (Bates and Lien 1985). North and Weingast (1989) expand the English story to the Glorious Revolution. By the seventeenth century the original tax bargain with elites had broken down, and the crown often engaged in forced "loans" (that were never repaid) and other abuses by the crown. Ultimately new institutions were needed that granted taxpayers control over both taxation and spending in order to produce an enforceable bargain. North and Weingast (1989) argue that this was possible in part because the Glorious Revolution had given taxpaying elites a credible threat against the crown: even without a democratically elected head of state, there was a real threat of violence against a monarch who reneged on the bargain.

Early tax bargains had several specific qualities, most linked to the fact that the taxed subjects were typically elites. First, the relatively small numbers of taxpayers meant that rulers could bargain with a limited number of individuals who had relatively similar preferences. This reduced the cost of bargaining, especially in a time when communication and travel were difficult and expensive, even across short distances. Second, the monarch and the elites had similar preferences: Moore (2004) argues that a strong British navy was of value to all parties. For the throne, it helped to wage war and secure British sovereignty. For elites—who were increasingly engaged in the wool trade— the navy secured shipping routes against piracy and other threats. Finally, successful taxation in this context helped regime survival only indirectly. A steady stream of tax revenues was critical in lowering the costs of obtaining loans for warring monarchs, allowing them to quickly access credit when needed to wage war (North and Weingast 1989; Stasavage 2011).

In her seminal book, Margaret Levi develops a more nuanced theory of tax bargaining, which also helped to explain when taxation is likely to occur more generally (Levi 1989). She argues that rulers, whether in democracies or autocracies, maximize revenues subject to the constraints implied by their discount rates, bargaining power with respect to their constituents, and the transaction costs of successful taxation and bargaining. While in some cases rulers will be able to extract revenues strictly through coercion, typically they will have to offer something in return. This creates contracts between rulers and different groups of citizens. Where citizens are relatively powerful, or the transaction costs of coercive taxation are high, bargains will be more likely to favor citizens. Over time, rulers will also invest in institutions or state capacity that will lower these transaction costs and, when possible, shift the balance of power away from citizens. The existence of bargains, however, is only possible given certain conditions, including that there are potential gains from trade; that each side has a credible punishment should the bargain fail; and that each side can effectively monitor the bargain.

Levi also stresses that, even under tax bargaining, compliance is at best "quasi-voluntary." She argues that continued compliance depends in part on perceptions that the tax system is fair. Because many bargains result in the provision of public goods that all can benefit from regardless of compliance, free-riding becomes a serious concern. If there are too many free-riders, compliance will break down as citizens view the system as unfair. Rulers can avoid a breakdown of the bargain by effectively punishing non-compliers; this signals to others that compliance is high, and increases the costs for citizens of reneging on the bargain. Even with some level of coercion in place, and checks on the rulers' power, Levi argues that bargains will likely need to be periodically renegotiated as circumstances change.

Tax bargaining is thus credited with the development of parliamentary democracy in seventeenth- and eighteenth-century Europe. Where assets were mobile, successful states struck bargains where rulers traded policy and institutional concessions in return for compliance. There is also an implicit threat in tax bargains: if rulers concede democracy to citizens based on tax payments, sufficient non-compliance with taxation may lead to democracy breaking down.

2.3 The Evolution of Modern Tax Systems in Europe

While these early European states were "strong" in many ways, they are a far cry from modern understandings of high state capacity. While they could (sometimes) defend their borders, government budgets still accounted for only a small fraction of GDP. They also still relied heavily on non-tax forms of revenue, including borrowing, seizing, and selling assets (as France did to church lands in the 1790s), extracting wealth from colonies, and in some cases simply printing money (Bordo and White 1991; Kiser and Karceski 2017). This started to change with the industrial revolution in the nineteenth century, but up until World War I, the modern state remained relatively small and constrained (Kiser and Karceski 2017; Wilensky 2002). In 1880 the British government extracted only 7.5% of GDP in taxes, which barely increased to 7.9% in 1900 (Piketty 2013). By 1920 the United Kingdom had managed to extract 20% of GDP in taxes, but countries like France and Sweden still raised less than half of that (Piketty 2013). It is not until World War II that Western European states started to raise taxes equivalent to a third or more of GDP, and the modern welfare state emerges. As Boix (2001) states, "Excluding war times, government expenditure remained constant around 10 percent of GDP during the nineteenth century.... In OECD nations, total current public revenue had risen to 24 percent of GDP in the early 1950s. Thirty years later it had stabilized at around 44 percent" (p. 1).

The structure of taxation also did not "modernize" until the twentieth century in many cases. The United Kingdom was an early adopter of the permanent income tax (as opposed to one that was levied only during war) in 1842, as was Prussia in 1850 (Seelkopf et al. 2021). However, other countries did not adopt an income tax until the twentieth century—in France, not until 1914 (Seelkopf et al. 2021). Even once income taxes were introduced, they often did not initially comprise a large fraction of revenues (Flora, Alber, and Kraus 1983). Progressive taxation, in which the rich pay a much larger share of income in taxes than the poor, did not become prevalent until after World War I (Scheve and Stasavage 2010).

In the nineteenth and early twentieth century, then, tax systems and state capacity continued to develop, and by the middle of the twentieth century looked more like modern governments that raise significant revenues and account for significant fraction of economic consumption. Over this period the electoral franchise greatly expanded in many European states, the Industrial Revolution reshaped economic and political power, and modern taxes like the income tax became permanent for the first time. Scholarship on the politics of taxation in this period suggest a more complicated story than the early state development period, which is instructive for understanding modern state development.

On the surface, the story looks simple. Over the course of the 1800s and early 1900s, many states expanded suffrage to a wider range of men, and over the same period tax revenues increased, and several governments introduced the income tax. This would seem to suggest that, once again, democracy and taxation are moving hand in hand. However, the story here is more complicated.

First, while the first country to introduce the permanent income tax (Great Britain) was democratic, this pattern does not hold more generally. Mares and Queralt (2015) argues that in autocracies, a limited franchise made it easier to strike bargains between manufacturing and agricultural elites to introduce the income tax. The logic is that the small selectorate will accept more taxation in return for limiting the power of the poor and the rising middle class. In the twentieth century, progressive taxation was closely linked not necessarily to the franchise, but to the "equal sacrifice" of capital and labor during wartime (Scheve and Stasavage 2016).

The role of war in state-building also became more complicated in the nineteenth and twentieth century. Queralt (2022) shows that while wartime borrowing led to higher taxation in early Europe, the same does not hold once international finance becomes available. When bondholders are international instead of domestic, the incentives to raise taxes to pay back loans are lower. This, in turn, weakens the need for increasing fiscal and state capacity to raise more revenue. For European states who already had strong fiscal capacity this was less important, but for other parts of the world it hindered the relationship between war and state development.

2.4 Taxation in Africa

The sections above examined the history of state development in Europe, focusing on the role of taxation and fiscal capacity more generally. This section provides a brief overview of the comparable time period in sub-Saharan Africa. I focus on the extent to which there are parallels and differences between the two regions. The next section then examines in more detail the ways in which theories based on Europe may or may not help us explain the path modern developing countries will follow.

2.4.1 Pre-colonial Taxation

Prior to colonization, the state-building process in sub-Sarahan Africa was not so different from that in Europe, including the mix of larger empires and smaller states. Likewise, taxation played a prominent role in many of these states. For example, in West Africa, the Hausa states of modern-day Nigeria levied taxes on many citizens, although exempted some Muslim subjects. In the same area, the Caliphate that emerged by the 1820s relied on a system of tribute from subordinate Emirs (Iliffe 2017). Iliffe further describes the system of taxation as highly coercive, with nobles granted rights to collect taxes from peasants. These taxes helped to support the large slave-trading empires in Western Africa.

Taxation was also present in much smaller states. By the late eighteenth century, the Acholi people of Northern Uganda had started to develop a degree of political centralization. In his history of the Acholi, Atkinson (2015) describes a system of about 70 small states, each comprising lineages ranging from 500 to 15,000 people. Membership in a chiefdom was established through paying tribute, which typically consisted of a portion of any game killed; iron tools (from blacksmiths); and in-kind labor in the *rwot* (king's) fields. The *rwot* would use tribute as a means of increasing his own wealth and power, but also as a form of redistribution: tributes of meat could be used to feast subjects, and various forms of wealth could be gifted to lineage heads in order to maintain support (Atkinson 2015). Importantly, the state-building process in this area resembled that of Europe, with progressively larger polities emerging as population density increased and borders began to clash.

As in most of sub-Saharan Africa, this process of state development was interrupted and in many cases destroyed by the process of European colonization. The 1884 Berlin Conference officially divided up Africa between the great European powers, and by 1914, only Liberia and Ethiopia were still independent; the rest of the continent was under European rule. In many cases, colonial powers were able to draw on existing political institutions, including systems of tribute and taxation, to support the colonial project.

2.4.2 Taxation in Colonial Africa

The colonial period in Africa led to expanded systems of coercive taxation. As metropole governments pushed their colonies to become self-financing, colonial administrations began to develop ways to extract revenues from the subjugated population. Indirect taxes on trade and consumption were paid by both white settlers and Africans, but fell far more heavily on Black

Africans.[3] Likewise, marketing boards imposed heavy export taxes on African farmers (Bates 1981). Income and poll (head) taxes were levied on both Europeans and Black Africans, but in percentage terms fell much more heavily on non-Europeans (Gardner 2012). Poll taxes were particularly coercive; as they could only be paid in cash they forced many subsistence farmers into the cash economy, thus providing a pool of labor for plantations and mines (Jamal 1978).

The result of the overall taxation system was that while both Black Africans and white colonials paid taxes, the burden was extremely unequal. Jamal (1978) estimates that, in Uganda, by the 1940s a Black African would pay about 50% of his income in taxes, compared to only 6% for whites. Colonial tax systems were also fundamentally coercive: Black Africans had no political representation, and any resistance was put down ruthlessly. Under the British system of indirect rule, colonial authorities deputized appointed chiefs to collect revenues on their behalf; provided a chief met his revenue targets and kept the peace, he had wide leeway to rule however he wished (Mamdani 1996). French colonies, while they used direct rule and (in theory) recognized existing systems of chiefs, had similar tactics (Mamdani 1996).

The main limit on colonial taxation was the threat of rebellion. Rebellion could be extremely costly, requiring colonial administrators to send in troops and disrupting economic activity. The threat of violence was primarily a concern with direct taxes, rather than customs duties. For example Gardner (2010) documents concerns in Nyasaland and Northern Rhodesia in which colonial leaders stress the importance of only taxing to the extent that "there is no fear of disturbance arising in consequence of it" (Gardner (2010), 224).

Colonial tax systems suggest several points of interest. First, there were attempts at tax bargaining between white settlers and colonial governments, with some improvements to governance and representation granted in return for paying taxes (Tarus 2004). This is very much in line with standard tax bargaining stories where a relatively small elite succeeds in extracting concessions. At the same time, taxation of Black Africans remained

---

[3] Jamal (1978) shows that, in Uganda, goods used by wealthy Europeans were taxed much more lightly than those consumed by the Black majority. For example, candles (used by poor Africans) faced import duties of 24%, compared to only 3% for electric light bulbs (used by wealthy Europeans). Coarser common salt was taxed at twice the rate of refined table salt; and used clothing was taxed more heavily than new.

extremely coercive, with no political representation at all. However, while explicit bargaining did not take place, contemporary documents do still suggest that colonial governments were concerned with the possibility of rebellion, and actively attempted to provide at least some services in return for the taxes Black Africans paid. Yet this was not bargaining in any real sense of the word: many of the services were chosen sole based on the priorities of whites.

The other striking attribute of colonial taxation is the degree to which it was based on taxing rural areas. In recent times, tax revenues in many African countries have been heavily centered around urban areas, as I discuss further below. Rural taxation is often assumed to be difficult due to the logistical challenges and relatively low incomes. Colonial governments demonstrate that it is still possible to raise significant revenues from rural areas. However, doing so required a high degree of coercion, and a tax system that heavily distorted the incentives for agricultural production through export taxes and marketing boards.

2.4.3 Taxation in Modern African States

Following independence, African countries faced a monumental challenge: how to create new states despite few trained bureaucrats and in the face of overwhelming demands for fast economic development and political change. The need for development created a strong appetite for revenues, and led many countries to keep colonial tax systems relatively intact after independence. This included forms of poll and hut taxes, agricultural taxes implemented by marketing boards, and many excise and trade taxes.[4] However, progress in many countries has been slow.

Patterns of taxation and revenue in sub-Saharan Africa show substantial variation, but also some commonalities. First, taxation is important to all budgets. The degree to which a government's budget is comprised of taxes (rather than non-earned revenues) is often referred to as tax reliance. Using data from the ICTD's Government Revenue Database (GRD), Figure 2.1 depicts average tax reliance in sub-Saharan Africa from 1980 to 2015.[5] For most countries, taxes form a significant fraction of government budgets,

---

[4] For example, versions of the hut and poll taxes often survived as "graduated taxes" where even the poorest citizens were required to make a fixed payment in cash each year.

[5] Tax reliance is calculated by dividing total taxes by the sum of total revenue, including non-grant revenue and grants.

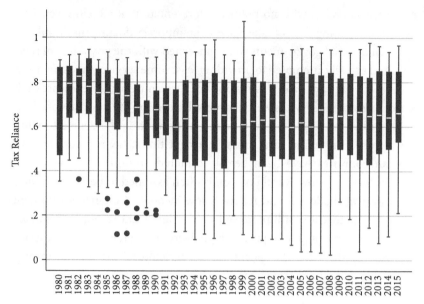

Fig. 2.1 Average tax reliance in SSA, by year. Data are from ICTD's GRD database and are unimputed.

averaging 60% to 80% of revenue. However, there is significant variation. While some countries depend almost entirely on taxes, in a few countries taxes account for less than 20% of revenues. These are typically resource-dependent states. In Equatorial Guinea, for example, resource rents have made up over 80% of revenues every year this century. Interestingly, on average there is limited variation in tax reliance over time. While median tax reliance does decrease slightly in the 1980s, rebounding again in recent years there are few clear continent-wide trends. In all years, at least 75% of African countries receive more than 40% of their revenues from taxes: taxation is consistently a key source of government revenue.

Second, there is also significant reliance on non-earned revenues, both for resource rents and foreign aid. This variation is present both for aid and resource revenues as a fraction of the total economy, and in terms of how important each type of windfall revenue is for budgets. There is also significant variation in access to foreign aid. In many countries, aid is larger than the entire government budget; this is especially the case in weak states like the DRC and Central African Republic. However, other countries are significantly less aid reliant. In middle-income countries like Kenya and Ghana, total ODA is less than a third of government spending.

Thus, African governments rely heavily on taxation, but in many cases have access to significant non-earned revenues. Next, consider the patterns of taxation itself. On average, African countries rely much more heavily on indirect, relative to direct, taxes. Average direct taxes as a fraction of GDP are about 5% in the ICTD GRD database, compared to an average of 10% for indirect taxes. These percentages have changed very little over the past 40 years, suggesting a reasonable amount of stability. However, there have been some shifts, particularly in which forms of indirect taxation have dominated. In 1980, African countries raised an average of 6% of GDP through trade taxes, compared to 2.8% from taxes on goods and services. Over the next 20 years trade taxes gradually decreased, while taxes on goods and services increased to compensate, particularly as VAT was introduced. By the year 2000 African countries raised approximately 4% of GDP for each source of indirect tax, and in 2015 the position has flipped: trade taxes were 2.4% of GDP, compared to 6.7% for taxes on goods and services.

2.5 Comparing Europe and Africa

The classic European state development story has several core elements: the role of war in driving fiscal capacity; the limited availability of non-tax revenues; and the importance of democracy for state development. Given the significant revenue needs of modern developing countries, and newly independent governments looking to cement their rule, we might expect that similar dynamics would lead to strong states in post-colonial Africa. However, states remain relatively weak, even when they raise revenues similar to those of early twentieth-century European states.

This section examines the extent to which we should expect the European story to travel to modern African states. I focus on whether three key factors can explain the persistent low state capacity in many countries. First, the types of threats leaders face are very different, given the rarity of interstate war. Second, governments have access to a different set of revenue instruments. For many countries, foreign aid and resource rents are attractive alternatives to taxation. Even taxation itself looks different, with more sophisticated forms of indirect taxation taking the place of many direct taxes. Finally, the process of democratization—and when it occurred in the process of economic development—looks very different today than in Europe. Many countries democratized, not as a result of tax bargaining, but rather in response to a mix of economic crisis, international pressures, and domestic unrest. Together, these differences point to the need for a new theory of taxation and state development.

2.5.1 The Nature of Survival Incentives

State development in early Europe was driven in large part by the need to survive. Interstate war was common, and polities that could not raise sufficient revenues to fund their defenses did not survive (Tilly 1992). This led to the rise of tax bargaining and limited government, as described above. However, since independence, the borders of sub-Saharan Africa have been relatively fixed, despite being exogenously imposed by colonial powers, rather than arising through a more endogenous process of state formation (Alesina, Easterly, and Matuszeski 2011). Even when one country invades another—such as Rwanda invading the Democratic Republic of Congo, or Tanzania intervening in Uganda—the aim has typically been to pursue security objectives in the other country, rather than to claim territory. Borders may be porous, and internal conflicts have frequently turned into regional ones, but the threat that a country will be subsumed by another is rare. This has been driven in part by strong international norms against changing borders.

One way to interpret the relatively fixed nature of borders is that it will hinder state development. When a large army is not required, the need for taxation will on average be lower. This allows rulers to be more strategic about the taxes they impose, and therefore the degree to which they invest in state capacity. For example, Chowdhury (2017) argues that this lack of interstate war makes it difficult for modern states to develop capacity. Likewise, Herbst (2000) posits that in many cases, the states that resulted from colonial borders have large hinterlands or other low-density areas that leaders have few incentives to control. Even when interstate war does exist, Queralt (2022) shows that it may not lead to higher tax capacity when international financing is available. And Centeno (1997) argues that weak states are particularly unlikely to engage in state-building in response to war, as taxation is too expensive relative to alternative revenue sources.

However, a lack of existential threat to a country's survival does not mean that the *regime* currently in power does not face threats. Civil war can likewise be a threat to leaders, as can conflicts and rebel groups that spill across borders. Several countries have faced secession threats, which in both Sudan and Ethiopia have been successful. Coups have been relatively frequent since independence, and have often superceded other methods of transferring power. Likewise, regional conflicts can still be a threat to states, as can other forms of intrastate threats (Thies 2005), including ethnic rivalries over who will control a state (Thies 2007). Frizell (2021) finds that both civil wars and interstate wars make the introduction of new direct taxes more likely in a cross-national historical dataset. Other work suggests that civil war in particular can lead to higher taxation (guez Franco 2016; Kisangani and Pickering 2014).

This means that rulers who wish to stay in power do still consider survival threats, and at least some of these may generate revenue demands and higher taxation. The threats rulers face also depend in part on regime type. Autocracies must worry about rebellion and coups, which are more likely to arise from urban areas (Ballard-Rosa 2020). In many African countries, limited economic development also means that economic elites and political elites overlap to a large degree: this may make it especially hard to tax elites, who are necessary to maintain a grasp on power. However, one contention of this book is that modern leaders must also consider that raising taxes can actually increase, rather than decrease, the degree to which leaders face threats. More generally, rulers may be able to appease citizens and stay in power through means other than raising revenue.

Democratic leaders, in contrast, must consider the threat of losing power via elections. Standard median voter models predict that, as the median voter in most countries has income below the mean, that tax rates will be high in democracies (Meltzer and Richard 1981). However, as in autocracies, the small nature of the elite, and the degree to which it is typically tied to ruling parties, may make this difficult. Mass taxation provides an alternative, but as I show in the next chapter, it may also make citizens demand more from leaders, lessening taxation's appeal. Thus, democracies, too, may not have the same incentives to raise taxes as their early modern counterparts, despite facing some threats.

2.5.2 Available Revenue Streams

Even if a country faces threats and wishes to raise revenue, it does not necessarily follow that we should expect higher taxation in many modern states.

In contrast to some earlier periods, many modern developing countries have access to significant sources of non-tax revenues other than debt, in particular foreign aid and resource rents.

In the former colonial states of sub-Saharan Africa, foreign donors have played a significant role in budgets since independence. While some states receive very little aid relative to the size of the economy—such as Botswana, Nigeria, and South Africa—other states remain heavily reliant on aid; for example, in Liberia aid comprises over 20% of GNI (World Bank 2020). The median country gets almost 5% of GNI as aid, comparable to direct taxation in many countries (World Bank 2020). While some of this aid flows directly to government budgets, donors are increasingly funneling at least some ODA through non-government actors like local and international NGOs. Still, even off-budget ODA still reduces reliance on taxation in that it provides key public services without citizens' financial involvement.

An increasing number of African countries also have access to resource rents as an important source of non-tax revenues. These include oil, but also natural gas, coal, minerals, and forest rents. While some countries receive little in rents, in others rents form over 20% of GDP (World Bank 2020). In several countries this number is likely to go up in coming years. In Uganda, for example, significant oil deposits have been discovered but have yet to start flowing. In some cases these revenues are technically generated via taxes on natural resource extraction, but differ significantly from normal tax revenues in that they are not paid by citizens.

The prevalence of both aid revenues and natural resource rents has allowed many governments to maintain a relatively high level of funding despite low levels of taxation. This in turn may make raising taxes less attractive, especially when doing so is potentially politically costly. While many earlier European governments were able to extract some revenues from natural resources, they did not play the dominant role in the economy that they do today.

Even when modern governments tax, they can choose from a much wider set of fiscal instruments than their early European counterparts. Early monarchs typically taxed small groups of elites, or narrow types of assets. For example, the English window tax was levied on each glass window a house had, while the taxes at stake in some of the early tax bargains were on wool exports. This made tax bargaining easier, as the group of taxpayers was relatively small, was well organized, and had similar interests. By the time mass taxation emerged, the bureaucratic state was already developed, and state capacity was fairly strong. Modern governments have engaged in much more mass taxation at a lower level of capacity. This is due in part to relatively new tax instruments, like the Value Added Tax, which are levied on almost all citizens in a country. According to the Tax Introducction Dataset, in 1979 Cote d'Ivoire was the only African country with a VAT; by 2014 83% of African countries had introduced the VAT. Because the VAT levies a relatively low tax on a large tax base, it is preferred by international economists and promoted heavily by international donors and financial institutions.

But it is not clear that VAT, which is paid indirectly as goods are purchased, should have similar effects on state capacity, and on accountability, as more traditional forms of taxation. Its self-enforcing nature requires relatively less state capacity to collect, compared to an income tax. It also may be less visible to citizens, and harder to avoid, making it less likely to be a source of tax bargaining or other accountability demands. Together, these different revenue streams paint a picture of a very different state. In contrast to the European case, where governments relied heavily on taxing small groups of elites, many modern African governments have access to substantial sources of non-tax revenue, and to tax instruments that sidestep elite bargaining.

2.5.3 The Sequencing of Democracy and Development

Early theories of taxation and accountability focused on the rise of representative government and (albeit limited) forms of democracy. These institutional changes were typically extremely limited in scope: a small group of male elites were given representation and some form of suffrage in return for partial control over government revenue and spending (North and Weingast 1989; Bates and Lien 1985). Over the nineteenth and twentieth century the franchise expanded in many European countries, typically gradually. In some cases, elites were able to limit mass suffrage in return for paying taxes, and direct taxes only expanded when suffrage was sufficiently broad (Mares and Queralt 2015; Aidt and Jensen 2009b,a).

There are certainly modern cases where bargains for limited forms of representation do still occur, as Eubank (2012) shows in Somaliland.[6] However,

---

[6] Note that Somaliland is a rare case of a country that lacks international recognition and faces existential threats that are close to the European case.

overall democratization in Africa has looked very different, as has the sequencing of democracy and state development. I argue that this may change the relationship between taxation, democracy, and state-building.

First, consider what European and African countries looked like at the time of universal suffrage. In Europe, universal suffrage came at a period when bureaucracies were established, and both local and national governments were relatively strong. This meant that, when suffrage expanded, the state was able to meet the new demands placed on it. The state was also sufficiently well developed that higher levels of progressive taxation through the income tax, which is typically fairly resource-intensive, was feasible. In sub-Saharan Africa, the wave of democratizations in the 1990s occurred in a period when many states were weak, and only beginning to emerge from economic and political crises of the 1980s. The wave of democratization in the 1990s is typically attributed in part to international pressures that were absent from early European democratization. Democratization also often occurred in times of economic crisis, or when elite cohesion broke down, rather than as a result of the revenue imperative (Van de Walle 2001). Democratization also occurred much faster than in Europe, with a shift to universal suffrage the norm.

As a result, the process of democratization in modern Africa has largely been delinked from taxation. While—as Prichard (2015) shows—it can still play an indirect role, democratization is less likely to occur as a direct result of taxation. Likewise, a decrease in taxation is unlikely to result in the revoking of the franchise. This raises the question of whether democracies will in fact tax more than autocracies, and how democracy will affect the types of taxes we see. Indeed, in the modern period the link between taxation and democracy is weak. While some studies have found that democracies tax more than autocracies, others find little relationship (Easterly and Rebelo 1993; Bird, Martinez-Vazquez, and Torgler 2008; Profeta, Puglisi, and Scabrosetti 2013; Mulligan, Gil, and Sala-i Martin 2004; Boix 2001; Fauvelle-Aymar 1999; Thies 2005). In Chapter 4, I return to the relationship between taxation and democracy in more detail.

2.6 Conclusion

Modern Africa is not seventeenth-century Century Europe: the survival incentives, revenue streams, and political structures are all profoundly different. This raises the question—should we expect taxation to still lead to state-building and democracy in modern developing countries? Taxation and state capacity are both low in many African countries, but African states are quite good at extracting some kinds of taxes. Modern European countries raise about 15% of GDP in indirect taxes, while African governments average about 10%. A few countries, like Kenya, raise almost as much in indirect taxes (8.23% of GDP) as the United Kingdom (11.42% of GDP in 2015).

When it comes to direct taxation, African governments are more clearly behind wealthier parts of the world. Average direct taxation in Europe in 2015 was 10% of GDP, compared to just over 5% of GDP for African countries. However, African governments do not raise significantly less in direct taxes than other low- and middle-income countries, and even raise more in taxes than many oil-producing states.

One thing is clear: the revenues of African governments are not sufficient to fund the public goods and services that citizens often want, and that are necessary for development. While European states have government budgets averaging 36% of GDP, African governments spend only 19% of GDP on average (World Bank 2012). Low tax revenues are due to a mix of low tax rates and poor enforcement of many existing taxes. Raising additional revenues could significantly boost citizen well-being, reduce aid dependence, and, as this book argues, improve accountability. Why, then, does taxation remain low? One answer is that citizens in many African countries are simply too poor to pay taxes. Yet, anecdotally, many citizens I have talked to in Uganda and Malawi express a strong willingness to pay more—provided they think the money will be spent wisely. Afrobarometer data backs this up: across 34 countries, close to half (44%) of respondents expressed support for a new tax to fund health care, and in eight countries a strict majority would support the tax (*Afrobarometer Data, Round 5* 2011).

An alternative explanation is that taxation is simply not attractive to many governments, especially politicians concerned with survival. If taxation increases citizens' demands on the state, and this interferes with rent-seeking or other government priorities, taxation will not be in the best interests of the state. And this is especially true when governments have access to other sources of revenue (aid, oil) that allow rent-seeking even in the absence of other revenues. The rest of the book develops this thesis in more detail, starting with how taxation changes citizens' demands of government, and then examining when taxation will be in the best interests of governments, given these demands.

3

How Taxation Increases
Accountability Demands

A fundamental claim of this book is that taxation affects how citizens interact with the government, and that this impacts how and when governments will tax citizens. This chapter introduces a theory for how taxation affects the demands citizens make of leaders, making them more likely to monitor government actions and punish corruption or other forms of poor performance. The next chapter then develops a theory of how this affects when, and how, a government will wish to tax its citizens. In examining how taxation affects accountability demands, the implied counterfactual is a state in which the government relies on non-earned revenue instead of taxation, typically aid or oil. As discussed in Chapter 2, governments that rely on non-tax revenue are typically less democratic, more corrupt, and less accountable to citizens than ones that rely on taxation.[1] This chapter first discusses a more general theory of why citizens might demand accountability, then shows how paying taxes can affect that process.

While the notion that taxation increases accountability demands fits with the intuition of many observers, there is surprisingly limited evidence regarding whether—and why—it is actually the case. In fact, there are many reasons to doubt that citizens might be more willing to punish government malfeasance for misuse of tax revenues. The standard tax bargaining story argues that taxation grants citizens an additional form of leverage over governments in the form of non-compliance with taxation: it says nothing about whether citizens should be more likely to use other forms of accountability pressures, like elections or protests, to hold officials accountable. Indeed, a rational citizen may realize that she would be much better off if non-earned revenues like aid, oil, or central transfers were used properly, and thus be willing to punish malfeasance for all types of revenues. Consistent with this

---

[1] Alternately, we can consider a state in which government relies on a mix of taxes and non-earned revenues, but a sizeable fraction of citizens pay no taxes.

Strategic Taxation: Fiscal Capacity and Accountability in African States. Lucy E. S. Martin.
Oxford University Press. © Oxford University Press 2023. DOI: 10.1093/oso/9780197672631.003.0003

story, several recent studies have found quite high willingness to monitor aid and oil windfalls (see e.g. Paler (2013); de la Cuesta et al. (2019)).

It is also not clear precisely why or how taxation might affect citizens' preferences or willingness to punish. Understanding the mechanism is not merely an academic question. If, for example, taxation increases citizens' demands due to some kind of societal norm regarding how different types of funds should be spent, it suggests that public education campaigns to change norms could be extremely valuable. It also suggests that, provided the government's revenue comes from taxes, the exact type of tax may not matter. If, however, taxation's effect is created only by the specific act of paying taxes and losing earned income—as this chapter argues—then it may be much more difficult to achieve similar accountability pressures for aid or oil revenues. It would also suggest that only highly visible taxes will create accountability dividends, while more "hidden" taxes (for example many consumer taxes) will have smaller accountability dividends.

Finally, it is not clear how strong such an effect of taxation on preferences might be. Perhaps the effect exists, but is too small to have a substantial impact on actual government behavior. Or, perhaps taxation makes citizens *want* to punish more, but in reality there are so many barriers to punishing leaders that citizens are unable to act on their desires. In either case, taxation will only affect equilibrium levels of accountability if leaders recognize that taxation affects citizens' demands, and does so in way that makes responding to said demands incentive-compatible.

This chapter uses insights from cognitive psychology and behavioral economics to develop a theory of how and why taxation changes the way citizens interact with their leaders. I first discuss the steps necessary for citizens to successfully demand improved performance from leaders, then outline how taxation could affect each step of the accountability process. The rest of the chapter focuses on a single step in this process: how taxation affects the way citizens evaluate information about government performance. Citizens who are taxed have lost a portion of their income, and if they do not recover those losses in the form of public goods they will suffer more from corruption or poor performance, compared to citizens who are not taxed.

This chapter is based on a game-theoretic model of citizen behavior. To improve readability, I have put the formal model, including proofs and extensions, in the chapter appendix. Less technical readers, or those not concerned with the minutiae of the model, are welcome to skip this appendix.

3.1 A Theory of Accountability

Accountability is a complex process. For citizens to effectively make demands on their leaders, a number of steps need to occur. First, citizens need good information about what their government has actually done. This can be information that citizens garner through observing the level of public goods the government has provided, or information that is collected by the media or other groups and disseminated to citizens. Much of the previous work on increasing accountability has focused on this step (see e.g. Dunning et al. (2019)). However, the empirical evidence suggests that simply giving citizens information is not sufficient to generate accountability pressures (Dunning et al. 2019). Citizens must also *evaluate* this information and translate it into a decision about whether to sanction or reward the government. If they observe that the government has built ten new schools, is this good or bad? If citizens decide that ten schools is not good, is it sufficiently bad that they wish to protest, vote for the opposition, or otherwise take action against the incumbent government? A number of factors may affect this process, including expectations about what government could be providing, and how much each citizen values the public good. Finally, if citizens decide government performance is sufficiently bad, they must actually engage in some kind of collective action; this may entail its own set of barriers and problems.[2]

If all of the steps just described are functioning properly—citizens have access to information, know how to interpret it, and can overcome collective action problems—then they can credibly threaten to sanction poor government performance. However, each step can break down in a number of different ways, and if even one part of the process breaks down it will be difficult or impossible for citizens to demand good government performance.

This chapter focuses on how taxation affects the middle stage of the process, in which citizens evaluate information and decide whether to take action. I argue that taxation changes how citizens evaluate information by increasing the perceived benefits of punishing non-accountable leaders, relative to the costs. This will make taxed citizens more likely to sanction a given level of low government performance (or high corruption), relative to non-taxed citizens. It also has implications for citizens' ability to overcome

---

[2] While I focus on citizens' demand for accountability in this chapter, the next chapter discusses the government's response in this process.

the collective action problem, especially if citizens realize that others are also paying taxes. To understand how taxation affects willingness to act, we first need a theory of how citizens evaluate information more generally. When citizens receive information about government performance, they must decide whether to take action to reward or sanction the government for its actions. I focus here on the decision of whether to sanction. If a citizen takes to the streets to protest; lobbies the government for change; or takes part in electoral opposition movements, she must compare the costs of doing so to the expected benefits.

The costs of taking political action include both opportunity costs and collective action costs. Opportunity costs include loss of income if taking action requires taking time off work, or simply forgoing leisure time. Collective action costs include the extra time and effort needed to organize with other citizens. In autocratic environments, the costs also include the possibility of government reprisals, including the risk of physical violence, against those who take action. These costs are relatively fixed for a given individual in a given political system, and in some cases may be substantial. If the costs are sufficiently high then citizens may never make demands on their leaders, and citizens simply will not demand accountability. This is the case in absolutist states. However, in most cases the costs are low enough that at least some citizens will act when government performance is sufficiently bad.

Given that political action is costly, citizens will only act if they also expect to receive some kind of benefit. There are two types of possible benefits: economic and psychological. First, if political action succeeds in either removing a low-performing incumbent or incentivizing existing leaders to change their behavior, citizens may expect better policy in the future. This means that political action can be beneficial to citizens because it increases their future expected economic utility. This is consistent with models of prospective voting in which citizens attempt to select politicians based on who will provide their preferred policies (Fearon 1999).

While citizens certainly often desire government change for economic gain, it is harder for economic benefits to explain when a given individual citizen will take action. The outcome of an election, or the success of a protest, is rarely determined by a particular individual's choice of how to vote or whether to participate. In these cases, rational individuals should let others protest or vote, reaping the benefits of successful action while avoiding the cost: this is the class free-rider problem defined by Olson (1965).

For this reason, Olson and others have argued that collective action is most likely when participants also receive some kind of private benefit that is not available to non-participants (Kuran 1997). One possible source of such benefits is if citizens receive psychological, or expressive, utility from taking part in political action—or that citizens pay psychological costs if they fail to take action (Aytaç and Stokes 2019; Pearlman 2013). An extensive literature in psychology and behavioral economics has demonstrated that there are many settings where individuals are willing to punish others even when there are no economic benefits from doing so (Henrich et al. 2006; Fehr and Gächter 2002). Punishment relieves the negative emotions that individuals experience when they believe that someone has acted unfairly or violated norms (Fehr and Gächter 2000). Because negative emotions are stronger for more egregious violations, expressive benefits are also higher when punishing such behavior. This view also points to the potential role of expectations: whether an individual is upset at behavior may depend on what they believe should happen.

So, when citizens take action to punish a government for poor performance, they expect to pay some kind of costs and, in return, to receive a mix of economic and psychological benefits. As government performance worsens, both types of benefits will increase relative to the costs. Economic benefits increase because there is more room for future improvement if sanctions against the government succeed. And, some research suggests that the expressive utility individuals receive from punishing is increasing in the severity of the offense being punished (Fehr and Gächter 2000, 2002). Thus, citizens should also receive higher expressive benefits from political action as government performance decreases.

This suggests a threshold model of citizen punishment. When government performance (measured by policy decisions, public goods provision, or levels of corruption) is relatively high, the costs of sanctioning are high and the benefits are low or non-existent. As performance gets worse, the benefits increase while the costs remain constant; at a certain point the benefits begin to exceed the costs, and citizens will punish poor performance. This is the punishment threshold.

Economic and psychological benefits suggest two ways of looking at these thresholds. Economic benefits suggest a prospective voting model, in which citizens punish to increase future utility. Psychological benefits suggest a more retrospective model, in which political action relieves negative emotions generated by low previous performance. Because psychological benefits more closely match the type of private benefits to collective action that we think are more likely to drive engagement, I focus for the rest of the chapter on the retrospective model, in which citizens evaluate information about prior government performance. I show below that, to the extent that prospective voting considerations are also present, they will tend to reinforce the effect of taxation in the retrospective model.

3.2   How Do Citizens Set Thresholds?

Simply knowing that citizens have thresholds tells us little about how citizens actually evaluate information about performance and decide whether it crosses the threshold for taking punitive political action. To better understand this process, it helps to consider one key aspect of government policy: how the budget is allocated and spent. All governments must divide available resources among different priorities; once money is allocated governments must also actually carry out the desired projects. If governments perfectly implement citizens' preferences, they will allocate the money to citizens' preferred goods and services and then spend the funds without engaging in patronage or corruption.[3]

Once the budget has been allocated and spent, citizens receive some signal of what has been achieved using the money. This could be through observing the level and quality of public goods provision, or through information they receive from the media, accountability groups, or even friends and neighbors. Citizens could also receive information indicating that government officials have stolen funds, overpaid contractors, or otherwise not spent money wisely. Citizens must now *evaluate* this information and decide whether performance was good or bad and, if bad, whether it is sufficiently severe that political action is warranted.

There is growing evidence that individuals evaluate performance not in a vacuum, but relative to some kind of expectations (see e.g. Gottlieb (2016); de Kadt and Lieberman (2020)). Thus, two citizens with varying expectations may interpret the same level of performance very differently. Consider a local government that builds five new wells. A citizen who expected no new wells may view this as very good performance; a citizen who expected five new wells may view performance as just adequate; and a citizen who

---

[3] This concept closely follows the definition of accountability in Fearon (1999).

expected ten new wells may suspect the government of malfeasance and be very upset. One way to think about this process is that citizens consider how well off they would be be under the "best possible" performance they think the government could achieve, and compare it to how well off they are given the outcomes they actually observe. The key to this approach is that citizens are effectively considering how much utility they have "lost" due to any lack of accountable government behavior. This means individuals' evaluations of performance may vary widely based on their perceptions of government, including capacity and how funds should be spent. It also means that thresholds will be affected by a citizen's beliefs about what the government could do if it wanted to. While this latter point could certainly have a large impact on punishment, for the purposes of understanding taxation's effects on citizen behavior I hold it constant.

What this framework implies is that two citizens can evaluate the same level of government performance differently, even if both have full information, if their utility functions look different. What could affect this utility loss? One possibility is the value that citizens place on public goods; a citizen who relies on government-provided health care will lose more utility, and be more upset, from poor health care provision than another citizen who has access to a private health-care system. Another possibility, which I focus on here, is that citizens' utility is affected by their personal economic well-being before considering government performance. There is substantial evidence that individuals consider their own utility not in absolute terms, but relative to their own expectations or *reference point*, as proposed by Kahneman and Tversky (1979) (see also Kőszegi and Rabin (2006) and Abeler et al. (2011)).

This reference point approach can explain why citizens who are taxed may be more willing to punish a given level of government performance, relative to untaxed citizens. First, consider how citizens evaluate their own utility relative to expectations. Individuals tend to have some "level" of utility that they expect to reach. This is typically based on expectations, prior experiences, and what seems normal (Kőszegi and Rabin 2006; Abeler et al. 2011). For example, consider someone who is making US$50,000, and has made that amount for some time. They "expect" to receive that much as a salary. If their salary increases, they will feel good and view it as a gain. If it goes down, they will feel unhappy and view it as a loss. This implies that two individuals receiving the same salary may view it very differently. Someone who goes from making $25,000 per year to making $50,000 will likely be fairly happy with the outcome, while someone who used to make $100,000 might be deeply unhappy at the pay cut.

In 1979, Kahneman & Tversky introduced the related concepts of prospect theory and loss aversion. While the full theory has a number of implications, key for this work is the idea that gains and losses can affect both subjective utility and behavior very differently. Theories of loss aversion posit that the utility individuals receive from an unexpected gain is smaller in absolute terms compared to the disutility suffered from a loss. If I give you $10, you feel better but only a little, but if I take $10 away from you, you are much more upset. This leads to an "S-shaped" utility function around an individual's reference point, as shown in Figure 3.1 below. Since its introduction, prospect theory has spawned a large body of work on the conditions under which losses may "loom larger than gains," and the extent to which reference points affect how individuals make decisions (Rieger, Wang, and Hens 2011; Abeler et al. 2011; Gal and Rucker 2018; Yechiam 2019). In Section 3.5 I discuss recent challenges to prospect theory, focusing on why I expect loss aversion to affect perceptions and behavior in the case of taxation.

3.3 How Taxation Affects Willingness To Punish

To see how taxation fits into loss aversion, consider a typical worker. This worker earns wages, and this amount serves as a natural reference point, as I discuss more below. Each year the worker gets a stable income and spends it on her preferred goods and services. Imagine that the government introduces a tax on income. The worker now takes home less than she did before, and thus can no longer afford her preferred bundle of goods and services: she is in the realm of losses. It is possible for the government to replace these losses if it spends her tax payments on public goods or other policies that make her better off. But if they don't, she will be worse off than she was before the tax, and will be upset.

Another way to approach the intuition is to consider two citizens who have equal salaries and identical policy and spending preferences. One pays no taxes, while the other faces an income tax rate of 20%. The first citizen expects to receive—and indeed does receive—full income. If the government provides any public goods, these are treated as a bonus gain on top of her expected utility. The second citizen also expects to receive their income, but instead only receives 80% of it. Unless the government spends their tax payments (and those of other citizens) on public goods that they value, they will be in the realm of losses. Now, say that the government provides some public goods, but spends the rest on its own priorities, which bring no benefits to citizens. The untaxed citizen is still above her reference point: she has her pre-tax income plus some public goods. If the government had not appropriated the rest of the budget she would be even better off, but she is still better off than she was with just her salary. In contrast, the taxed citizen is below their reference point, and could be much better off if the whole budget was spent on public goods. Due to the fact that the utility function is steeper below the reference point, this implies that the taxed citizen has lost more utility compared to their ideal point, and thus should be more upset and more likely to punish: taxation increases willingness to punish.

To see this more clearly, consider a stylized model of taxation and punishment (see chapter appendix for formal model). Take a country consisting of a unified government and a group of citizens. I compare two versions of the world: one where the government relies on taxation, and one where it relies on a non-earned windfall. In both cases the government's budget is exactly the same size. In the "windfall" regime, the government does not levy a tax and is funded solely by non-earned revenues like foreign aid or oil. In the "Tax" regime the government collects a proportional tax on each citizen's income. In both regimes the government must choose how much of the budget to spend on citizens' preferred public goods, such as education, health care, infrastructure, or any other good valued by citizens. Any money not spent on the public good is extracted by the government in the form of rents.

If citizens and the government have identical preferences, then taxation will not affect government behavior. However, in many cases government leaders have different preferences than citizens, especially if leaders wish to extract private rents. If this divergence in preferences exists, then we can examine whether taxation makes citizens more likely to push government to spend money on public goods. I will collectively refer to any money not spent on the public good as "rent-seeking"; this encompasses corruption but also any other non-optimal spending.

I assume that citizens care about their own economic well-being, but also about the costs and expressive benefits that result from taking punitive action against the government. Economic well-being is determined by earned income (minus any taxes), as well as any public goods that the government provides. Following the discussion above, I assume that citizens evaluate their economic well-being in relation to their expectations (reference point), rather than in absolute terms. In particular, I assume that citizens expect to receive at least their pre-tax income. When post-tax income plus public goods makes a citizen better off than just getting non-taxed income alone, a citizen's economic payoff exceeds his reference point: he is in the realm of gains. When this is not the case the citizen is below his reference point and is in the realm of losses.

A critical assumption of this theory is that citizens have utility functions that met the three criteria of loss-averse functions defined by Kahneman & Tversky (1979).[4] One such function is illustrated in Figure 3.1. When citizens get exactly as much economic utility as they expect, they are at the origin on the graph. When they get more than they expect, they are in the realm of gains; otherwise, they are in the realm of losses.

To understand when citizens are in the realm of losses or gains, we need to fix their reference point. Prior work suggests that reference points are determined by a mix of recent utility and expectations (Kőszegi and Rabin 2006; Abeler et al. 2011). I argue that a natural reference point is that citizens evaluate their utility in reference to pre-tax income assuming no public goods are provided: they expect to get their wages. This will map onto the empirical tests in Chapter 5, but is also in line with work suggesting that individuals feel ownership over their pre-tax income (Murphy and Nagel 2002). If citizens are not taxed they expect to receive only their private income, regarding utility from any public goods as an unexpected "gain." However, if citizens are taxed, their utility when no public goods are provided is now below the reference point.

The second component of a citizen's utility is determined by their decision of whether or not to punish the government. If the citizen decides to punish the government through taking part in protests, voting for the opposition, or otherwise taking punitive action, they must pay a cost, which includes any collective action and opportunity costs. They then receive in return a psychological, non-economic benefit. I assume that this benefit is in turn comprised of two components. One part is an individual-specific factor that represents a given citizen's underlying propensity for political engagement.

---

[4] First, citizen utility $u(x)$ is monotonically increasing, where x is the individual's reference point, and $u(0) = 0$. This normalizes citizens' utility to be 0 when they are exactly at their reference point. Second, $u(x)$ is concave for all $x > 0$, and convex for all $x < 0$. That is, individuals are risk-averse in the realm of gains and risk-seeking in the realm of losses. Finally, utility is not symmetric around zero: the utility an individual gets from a gain is smaller in absolute terms from the amount of disutility from a comparable loss, and the utility curve is overall steeper below the reference point.

This reflects that some individuals may care more about accountability, or simply enjoy engaging in political action. This individual factor is then amplified by the degree to which the citizen has lost economic utility due to government rent-seeking. This, in turn, can be understood as the gap between citizens' economic utility given the government's actual public goods provision and the level of utility citizens would receive if the entire budget was devoted to public goods provision. So, a citizen's expressive benefit will be higher when they have a higher propensity for engagement, and when personal utility losses from corruption or rent-seeking are higher. A rational citizen will punish only when her losses from rent-seeking are sufficiently high that the benefits of punishment exceeds the costs.

If the costs of taking action are extremely high (perhaps due to government repression) or if an individual does not care about politics (i.e. receives very low expressive benefits from taking action), it may be the case that the citizen will not punish even if no public good is provided. For such citizens the results below will not hold: taxation will have no impact on accountability pressures at all. Consider now the universe of cases where the costs of taking action are not prohibitively high, and where individuals do receive at least some utility from political engagement. When the level of public good is very low, these citizens will take action to punish the government. When the level of public good is high, and rent-seeking is low, most citizens will not punish. In between, there is some threshold level of public goods (government performance) at which a given citizen is indifferent between punishing and not punishing. This implies that citizens have a *punishment threshold* that represents the lowest level of public goods the government can provide and still avoid punishment by that citizen. This is the key variable that taxation may affect.

3.3.1 Taxation's Effect on the Punishment Threshold

As citizens expect to receive at least their reference utility of pre-tax income, taxation pushes citizens into the realm of losses. Recall that a citizen's utility function is by assumption steeper below the reference point. This means that a taxed citizen loses more utility from a given level of rent-seeking compared to a non-taxed citizen. This directly implies that taxation increases the punishment threshold: citizens demand higher government transfers when they are taxed.

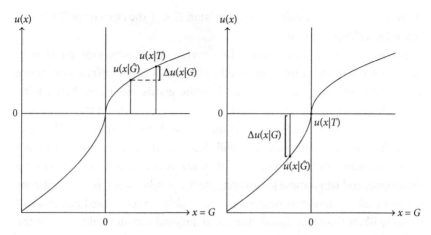

Fig. 3.1 Economic utility for taxed and non-taxed citizens. The left-hand graph shows utility for a non-taxed citizen; here the origin represents utility when $G = 0$. The right-hand figure depicts a taxed citizen. Now for all $G < T$ the citizen is in the realm of losses. On both graphs the two points mark utility if $G = T$—full public goods provision—and utility given that the government actually provides $G = \hat{G}$. The vertical distance between the two points is $\Delta u(x|\hat{G})$, the economic utility a citizen loses from rent-seeking.

To see this more clearly, Figure 3.1 graphs citizen utility with and without taxation. In each graph, the origin represents utility when the citizen receives exactly her pre-tax income y. When the x axis is positive, the citizen is above her reference point and is in the realm of gains. When the x axis is negative, the citizen is in the realm of losses and has negative utility. Each graph marks citizen utility at two key points. First, the higher point marks utility when the government is providing the maximum level of public goods G possible given a budget of T (denoted $u(x|T)$). The lower point marks citizen utility given that the government actually provides some lower level of public good $\hat{G} < T$ (denoted $u(x|\hat{G})$). The horizontal distance between these two points represents the level of rent-seeking and is constant across the two graphs.

The vertical distance between $u(x|\hat{G})$ and $u(x|T)$ on each graph represents the citizen's utility loss from rent-seeking, denoted $\Delta u(x|\hat{G})$. In the graph on the left, the citizen is not taxed and if the government provides no public goods (i.e. sets $G = 0$) the citizen's utility is at the origin. Any positive level of the public good represents a gain; utility is highest when $G = T$. The graph on the right depicts citizen utility under taxation. Now $u(x|T)$ is at the origin, as the citizen requires full public goods provision to regain his loss from paying taxes. For any partial public goods provision $G < T$ the citizen's utility is still below the reference point.

The graphs show that, because loss-averse utility functions are steeper below the reference point (compared to above), a taxed citizen loses more utility from any given level of partial public goods provision than a non-taxed citizen. The chapter appendix contains a formal proof that this holds more generally. Because the loss from rent seeking decreases as the level of public good increases, citizens will demand more transfers, and have a higher punishment threshold, when they are taxed. Thus, when citizens are loss averse, and when these losses increase the psychological benefits citizens get from taking action against non-accountable leaders, taxed citizens will be more likely than non-taxed citizens to demand accountability. This is the first key prediction of the theory.

3.3.2 Taxation and Variation in the Propensity for Punishment

The theory's second prediction concerns the degree to which taxation will increase a particular citizen's willingness to punish rent-seeking. Recall that a higher punishment threshold indicates that the government must provide a higher level of public goods to the citizen in order to avoid punishment. This occurs because the expressive benefits of punishment are higher, relative to the costs. Each citizen's punishment threshold is a function in part of taxation, but also that particular citizen's propensity for civic engagement. As this propensity increases, a citizen's expressive benefit from punishing the government increases; this raises the punishment threshold. However, there is also an interaction effect between the two, and so the degree to which taxation increases willingness to punish will be a function of a citizen's underlying propensity for engagement. The formal model predicts that, as propensity for engagement increases and citizens care more about punishment, taxation will at first have an increasingly large effect on citizens' willingness to punish, but at some point the effect of taxation will peak, and among citizens with a higher propensity to punish a further increase in this propensity leads to a smaller effect of taxation on punishment, although the effect always remains positive. There is a formal proof of this pattern in the chapter appendix.

The graph on the left in Figure 3.2 visualizes this logic by plotting a citizen's punishment threshold, with and without taxation, as a function

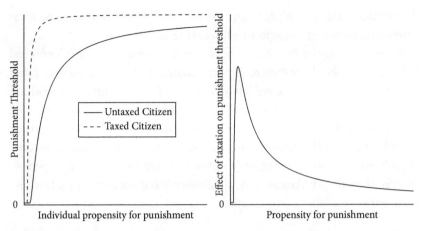

Fig. 3.2 Heterogeneity in taxation's effect on punishment. The graph on the left shows citizens' punishment thresholds with and without taxation, as a function of an individual's propensity for engagement. The graph on the right depicts the estimated effect of taxation on punishment as a function of this propensity. These graphs were generated based on the model in the chapter appendix.

of her individual propensity for punishment. The punishment threshold is increasing in this propensity, and is always higher under taxation. However, the vertical distance between the two curves—the effect of taxation on a citizen's punishment threshold—is not constant.

The right side of Figure 3.2 graphs the difference between a citizen's punishment threshold with and without taxation, as a function of their personal propensity for punishment. For a given individual, this is the vertical distance between the two lines in the graph on the left. Citizens with a very low propensity never punish with or without taxation: here taxation has no effect on punishment. The next segment of the parameter space represents individuals with slightly higher propensity for punishment: without taxation they never take action against leaders, but with taxation they will punish when government performance is sufficiently bad. As propensity for punishment increases further, the effect of taxation on punishment increases, meaning the gap in punishment thresholds between a taxed and non-taxed citizen gets larger. Past a certain threshold of propensity for punishment, a citizen will punish at least some levels of malfeasance with or without taxation. In this part of the parameter space the effect of taxation on the punishment threshold is at first increasing in an individual's propensity for punishment. However, it soon reaches a threshold such that, for all individuals with higher propensities, the effect of taxation *decreases* as propensity increases, asymptoting towards zero.

When we consider the likely effect of taxation on an individual's political behavior, we should therefore expect taxation to have the highest effect on citizens who are not completely disengaged from politics, but also not already highly engaged. A natural interpretation of this is that those who care strongly about rent-seeking (high propensity for punishment) already punish even small deviations by leaders, so taxation moves them only slightly, while those who care very little about rent-seeking (low propensity for punishment) are likewise difficult to move; it is those in the middle whose behavior is most affected by taxation.

3.4 Complicating the Model

The theoretical model just developed is simple, but generates several insights into how taxation will affect citizens' accountability pressures. However, one might be concerned that the theory has been simplified too far, and that the results might not hold once additional nuances are introduced. This section considers two issues. First, I discuss scope conditions for the model, focusing on the types of taxes for which we should expect it to hold. Second, I discuss a number of extensions to the model, which are further developed in the chapter appendix, showing that the effect of taxation holds, or is even increased, once we consider more long-term dynamics; uncertainty; or collective action problems.

3.4.1 Tax Modality and Scope Conditions

The theory so far has considered a generic tax that is proportional to income. While this closely resembles the classic income tax, it looks very different than many other common taxes, especially indirect taxes like value-added tax (VAT), excise taxes, and sales taxes. In many low-income countries, such indirect taxes reach a much larger segment of the population than direct taxes do. This makes it critical to understand how tax modality may affect the extent to which taxation generates accountability pressures from citizens. In ongoing joint work with Brandon de la Cuesta, Helen Milner, and Daniel Nielson, we develop a theory of tax modality and accountability (de la Cuesta et al. 2020). We follow Bräutigam, Fjeldstad, and Moore (2008) in arguing that, to generate accountability dividends, a tax must be *visible* to citizens. More particularly, we argue that:

> While indirect taxes are often visible when first introduced, over time citizens acclimate to the higher prices such taxes cause, much as consumers adjust to normal rates of inflation. This reduces tax visibility and therefore dampens indirect taxation's long-run effect on citizens' demands for political accountability. In contrast, direct taxes are highly visible both when introduced and years after their introduction. Individuals transfer their earned income directly to the government consciously and annually, maintaining the tax's salience.

In short, we should expect that highly visible taxes, including most direct taxes, to have a strong influence on citizen behavior. However, when a tax is less visible, taxation will have only a muted effect on citizens' accountability demands. In general, we should expect direct taxes to have a large impact on accountability demands and subsequent citizen behavior. Indirect taxes may have a short-run effect when first introduced, but this will dissipate over time as the tax becomes less visible.

3.4.2 Model Extensions

Even for direct taxes, there are several potential challenges to the theory presented above. First, while the theory considers a single interaction between leaders and citizens, politics is typically a repeated game. The main change when considering a repeated interaction is that citizens may now punish not only because they receive expressive benefits, but also because they anticipate economic benefits in the future. This is perhaps easiest to conceptualize in a democracy: after the government implements a chosen level of public goods provision, citizens observe it and decide whether to re-elect the incumbent or vote for a challenger. In this case a citizen's "punishment threshold" is the level of public goods below which they vote for the opposition. If the challenger is, in expectation, the same as the incumbent, then there are no anticipated economic benefits of punishment, and the prediction is the same as the single-period model. If however there is at least some chance that the challenger will provide more public goods than the incumbent—for example because the challenger prefers public goods to rent-seeking—then citizens may expect economic benefits from punishment; that is, citizens consider both prospective and retrospective concerns when making their vote. A multi-period extension of the model shows that, when punishment can generate economic benefits in a future period, the effect of taxation is even larger. Thus, in a repeated game we should expect taxation to have an even stronger effect on willingness to punish, relative to a single-shot game. This occurs because citizens who are in the realm of losses have steeper utility functions, and so anticipate more economic utility from increasing public goods provision in the future.

A second concern is that the theory abstracts away from very the real challenges citizens face in sanctioning government officials. In some cases, citizens may try to sanction the government (for example through protest movements or election campaigns) but the targeted leaders survive without paying a significant cost. I examine how two such challenges affect the taxation-accountability relationship: uncertainty over punishment, and collective action problems.

First, consider uncertainty. Citizens often face at least some uncertainty when they decide whether to take political action. Perhaps citizens pay the costs of organizing around or campaigning for the opposition, but the government steals the election and nothing changes. Or, perhaps elections are fair but the incumbent manages to survive because the opposition simply didn't muster enough support. Another possibility is that there is uncertainty about whether enough citizens are willing to engage in collective action that the incumbent government will be forced to step down or make changes. In any of these cases, citizens still pay the costs of taking punitive action against the government, but it may not succeed.

A failed action has implications for both economic and psychological benefits of punishment. Economic benefits are clear: citizens will only receive them if government behavior changes, and thus if the political action fails then no economic benefits are received. The effect on psychological benefits depends on whether they come from simply taking action and expressing ones' displeasure with the government, or whether they depend on the action's success. The exact form that these benefits take is beyond the scope of this work, but it seems plausible that at least some expressive benefits will be lost if punishment is not successful.[5] This suggests that citizens will be less

---

[5] If benefits only come from successful action, then uncertainty over whether punishment succeeds will reduce the expected psychological benefits of punishment. If expressive benefits are

willing to punish when punishment is risky. However, it does not necessarily follow that this will wipe out the effect of taxation.

In the chapter appendix, I extend the loss-aversion model to examine how citizen behavior changes when there is uncertainty over whether punishment will succeed. The extended model shows that taxation will still increase punishment, even in the presence of uncertainty. In fact, the loss-aversion theory has another implication: taxation's effect will actually *increase* when punishment's success is uncertain. This occurs in part because, when citizens have reference-dependent utility, they are more willing to take risks when they are in the realm of losses. Intuitively, individuals who have suffered a loss are willing to take on more risk and more uncertainty in order to recover their standing or avoid future losses; this is central to the model developed in Kahneman and Tversky (1979), and acknowledged even by loss-aversion skeptics (Gal and Rucker 2018). Thus, even if there are barriers to successful punishment, we should still expect taxation to lead to higher citizen demands.

Finally, consider one particular form of uncertainty: the collective action problem. Most forms of political action require citizens to work together in order to be effective. Even elections, in which citizens make individual decisions, may rely on citizens' ability to coordinate on an opposition candidate, campaign, or otherwise take costly actions that are only successful if others also participate. One way to understand this uncertainty is to think of citizens as having variation in their underlying propensity to engage in political action, as discussed above. If there is variation in propensity for punishment, most citizens will be more willing to punish under taxation, but there will be substantial variation in citizens' exact thresholds. Thus, if a citizen wants to take action, he must consider whether he thinks others are also willing to take action, or whether they have not yet reached their threshold for action.

There are theoretical reasons for expecting taxation to increase accountability pressures even in the presence of collective action problem. For example, taxation could foster collective action either by increasing the private expressive benefits citizens receive from such actions, or by making citizens believe that others are also more likely to take action, raising the perceived probability of an action's success. Both increase the expected private payoff a citizen receives from taking action, which Olson (1965)

---

entirely driven by the act of attempted punishment, rather than by success, then the expressive benefits will be unchanged.

argues should help citizens overcome free-riding. Taxation could therefore serve as a coordination device such that taxation decreases the collective action problem for citizens.

The appendix models this as a game in which two citizens must coordinate on punishment, and each citizen is unsure about whether their fellow citizen wants to punish. The model shows that multiple equilibria are possible. If all citizens believe that no one else is willing to act, it is possible to get stuck in a "low-accountability" equilibrium in which taxation increases citizens' underlying willingness to take action, but no citizen is willing to act because they believe the action has no possibility of success. This is consistent with the point made above that, if the costs of action are sufficiently high (or collective action capacity is too low), then citizens will never punish even when there is taxation. However, there are also equilibria of the model where taxation means that collective action can be sustained with a higher punishment threshold than is possible without taxation: taxation can lead citizens to demand more collectively, as well as individually.

3.5 Alternative Mechanisms and Related Issues

By applying research from psychology and behavioral economics, the previous sections showed how the concept of loss aversion can explain how taxation changes citizens' demands on leaders. This section examines potential challenges to the theory. I first discuss debates about whether loss aversion is a real phenomenon, and why we should expect it to apply in the case of taxation. I then turn to a discussion of three other potential mechanisms through which taxation could affect citizens' accountability demands. Finally, I discuss how the loss-aversion theory fits into theories that taxation improves overall accountability not by increasing citizens' willingness to act, but through a different path such as sending a signal about government budgets, or by inducing tax bargaining.

3.5.1 Is Loss Aversion Real?

In recent years, a number of prominent psychological theories have failed to hold up under closer scrutiny and replication attempts (see e.g. Klein et al. 2014, 2018). Among these are a number of articles announcing that loss aversion "fails to replicate" and challenging the concept of prospect theory more generally (Gal and Rucker 2018; Yechiam 2019). However, a nuanced look at the evidence suggests a more measured story. Both of the papers most broadly cited as sounding the "death knell" for loss aversion do, upon a closer reading, support the notion that losses loom larger than gains in some settings. Gal and Rucker (2018) write that "our review suggests the need for a more contextualized perspective whereby losses sometimes loom larger than gains, sometimes losses and gains have similar psychological impact, and sometimes gains loom larger than losses" (498). Similarly, Yechiam (2019) argues that while loss aversion is not universal, "What appears to be a robust finding is an aversion to high-stakes losses, and gain/loss neutrality for small-to-moderate losses" (1329).

Thus, the consensus is increasingly that losses *can* loom larger than gains, and that individuals *can* be more risk-seeking in the realm of losses—as predicted by prospect theory—but that this effect is context-dependent. A natural question is, therefore, whether taxation is a reasonable setting to expect to find loss aversion. Evidence reviews by loss-aversion skeptics typically argue that the size of the loss matters (Gal and Rucker 2018; Yechiam 2019). For example, studies in the United States typically involve either very small losses (i.e. 50 cents) or thousands of dollars. When the loss is small, about 50% of respondents typically display loss aversion, while when stakes are high a much larger fraction of individuals are loss-averse (Yechiam 2019). As many forms of taxation involve larger sums that are significant to those paying the tax, this suggests that the losses from taxation may indeed activate loss aversion. Even when losses are smaller, the studies cited challenging loss aversion still agree that up to half of experimental subjects exhibit loss aversion even for small losses. Thus, even for taxes that are paid in small increments, we may still expect a significant fraction of taxpayers to view the tax as a loss and respond accordingly, raising aggregate citizen demands on the government.

Another reason to expect that loss aversion is relevant for studying taxation is that several papers have found that, even when losses do not loom larger than gains in an abstract way, they may be processed differently, leading to a differential effect of losses on *behavior*. For example, Yechiam and Hochman (2013) shows that losses and gains can differentially affect behavior in some settings. This is noted explicitly in Gal and Rucker (2018), who give this effect of losses on behavior as an explanation for phenomena like how dissatisfied customers are more likely to leave negative reviews than happy customers are to leave positive reviews. As the theory developed here is about how the gain/loss framing of public goods provision may affect citizens' political behavior, this again suggests that loss aversion is still a useful framework.

3.5.2 Increasing Action without Loss Aversion?

There are three main alternative ways that taxation could increase citizens' political engagement other than the loss-aversion theory. First, behavioral economics has shown that individuals punish behavior that is perceived as unfair (Fehr and Schmidt 1999; Fehr and Gächter 2000), and that fairness norms play a role in explaining when citizens punish. It seems clear that the loss-aversion theory does not require us to deny that fairness might affect punishment thresholds. However, it does suggest that fairness norms do not *systematically differ according to the type of revenue being spent.* For fairness to constitute an alternative mechanism to loss aversion, it would need to be the case that many societies have a stricter societal fairness norm regarding how tax dollars should be spent.

While such a fairness mechanism would also predict that citizens will be more likely to punish when they are taxed, there are areas where the two mechanisms generate competing predictions. The loss-aversion theory predicts that an individual will only be more willing to punish when they have personally lost earned income to taxation. In contrast, the fairness model predicts that a non-taxed citizen should still be more willing to punish when they see someone else's tax funds being misused, because the same societal fairness norm should apply. Additionally, the loss-aversion model's second implication regarding heterogeneity in taxation's effect does not hold: while the loss-aversion model predicts that the effect of taxation first increases then decreases as a citizen's propensity for punishment increases, the fairness model predicts a monotonically decreasing effect of taxation over the same range. Chapter 5 tests both the loss-aversion and fairness mechanisms.

A second alternative mechanism is that the theory above is correct except that citizens are not reference-dependent and instead utility functions are globally concave; this follows many standard utility models in which individuals receive declining marginal utility in income. If this model is correct, then taxation will also increase punishment. However, like the fairness mechanism, a globally concave utility function does not predict the heterogeneity discussed in Section 3.6. Thus, while there are potential alternative characterizations of citizens' utility and behavior that can explain some of the loss-aversion model's predictions, other predictions will help separate out the precise mechanism at work.

Finally, in co-authored work with Brandon de la Cuesta, Helen Milner, and Daniel Nielson, we show that the loss-aversion mechanism is complementary to a third mechanism: a sense of psychological ownership over the government's budget (de la Cuesta et al. 2022). In our research, we draw on work in psychology to argue that citizens will be more likely to sanction poor government performance when they feel a sense that the government budget "belongs to them." We also argue—and show using lab experiments—that paying taxes increases citizens' sense of budget ownership, and accounts for at least part of the effect of taxation on citizens' accountability demands. This makes it important to understand how loss aversion differs from ownership, and from related concepts like the endowment effect. In many ways, taxation only increases ownership through loss: loss aversion is causally prior to ownership. It is through feeling a loss from taxation, and then *seeing one's earned income transferred to the government* that taxation induces higher ownership. Mechanism tests in Chapter 5 confirm that the loss-aversion mechanism is separate from the ownership one, and thus both are important.

3.5.3 Alternative Paths to Accountability

Finally, it is important to understand how the theory proposed here fits into other arguments linking taxation to higher accountability without relying on a change in citizens' willingness to punish. While such alternative pathways would not invalidate the loss-aversion theory, it is important to consider how and when these mechanisms may interact.

One branch of research argues that the act of paying taxes affects the information available to citizens. Moore (2004) argues that government funds are more easily hidden when they are derived from a few concentrated sources, such as oil rents, than when they come via taxes paid by many citizens. Gadenne (2017) makes a similar argument; the presence of taxation may signal the size of the government budget to citizens, making them more aware of corruption when it occurs. This argument also appears in Sandbu (2006) and Brollo et al. (2013). Rodden (2005) argues that taxation provides information to citizens in a different manner: when multiple, often overlapping levels of government are responsible for public goods provision, citizens can use taxation as a cue for which level of government should receive blame or credit for government performance. A large literature suggests that such clarity of attribution is important for electoral accountability to function properly (see e.g. Powell Jr and Whitten 1993). In an extension of the information theory, Paler (2013) uses a set of experiments in Indonesia to show that individuals in a "taxed" condition are more willing than untaxed citizens to take a costly action to seek information about government performance: taxation seems to increase citizens' willingness to monitor and seek information. And more recently, Weigel (2020) argues that taxation signals to citizens that state capacity is higher than previously believed, increasing citizens' expectations and demands.

If citizens are truly uncertain about whether the government has any funding, then it seems feasible that taxation does provide information to citizens. If citizens pay taxes to the local government, they know that the government has at least some funds. This is consistent with Weigel's work on local property taxes in the Democratic Republic of Congo (Weigel 2020). More generally, however, the degree to which taxation actually provides information to citizens is not clear, and to the best of my knowledge there are no empirical tests of whether taxation inherently provides a credible signal to citizens about the size of the budget. The arguments by Paler and Rodden have more empirical support but explain only when citizens will have the necessary information to hold governments accountable, rather than when citizens are actually willing to do so. This suggests that there are limits to the ability of taxation to increase accountability through providing information.

The second alternative mechanism is that of tax bargaining. Normally, citizens can put pressure on government officials by protesting or, in democracies, threatening to vote against the incumbent in the next election. In some cases, taxation also grants citizens a unique form of leverage: the ability to withhold tax revenues from the government. This is the basis of the tax bargaining theories discussed earlier. However, this mechanism can only function when taxation is not overly coercive, and when it is feasible for citizens to effectively hide taxable income from the government.

These two alternative mechanisms are in many ways more limited than the one presented here. Tax bargaining requires a credible threat of tax non-compliance, which is not always possible. The information mechanism may be applicable in some cases, but suggests that taxation should only affect accountability when citizens' baseline level of information about state capacity and the budget is low: that is, taxation should only affect accountability in non-transparent, low-capacity states. This is especially true of cases like that in Weigel (2020), where taxation is signaling state capacity. If, in contrast, the loss-aversion theory is correct, then taxation should increase citizens' demands in a wide range of contexts.

Finally, Prichard (2015) argues that, to generate accountability dividends, taxes need to be *salient* to citizens, defining a salient tax as one that is "visible and broadly felt." Previous work has suggested that salience will be higher when media coverage and historical legacies make a tax more contentious, and when taxes are perceived as unfair or when they are paid frequently (Prichard and Leonard 2010; Martin and Gabay 2018). The loss-aversion theory does not deny the importance of salience. Rather, it provides an explanation for how a visible tax affects citizen utility and behavior. It also suggests that taxes that induce greater perceived losses may be more politically salient and, thus, more likely to generate accountability demands.

3.6 Conclusion

One way to explain the empirical relationship between taxation and accountability is that taxation makes citizens more likely to hold government officials accountable. This chapter proposes one mechanism that could explain this effect: taxation, by removing earned income, pushes citizens into the realm of losses. Eager to recover these losses, taxed citizens are more upset than non-taxed citizens when they lose out because the government has stolen funds or spent them in ways that citizens do not value. This makes citizens more willing to impose sanctions on leaders they see as providing insufficient benefits, and more generally leads taxed citizens to demand more from leaders.

The theory presented above generates several implications that are tested in Chapter 5. The most important of these is that, all else equal, a taxed citizen should demand higher transfers from leaders than an untaxed citizen. We should also see that the effect of taxation is smallest for citizens with a very low or very high propensity for civic engagement, and largest for those citizens in the middle. Finally, we should see that taxation's effect is a product of the losses citizens feel from taxation, and the psychological benefits they receive from sanctioning poor government performance.

Understanding not only why but how taxation affects accountability pressures is critical to a broader understanding of government accountability. First, the loss-aversion mechanism suggests that there may be a crucial difference between simply reducing citizens' tax burden, and eliminating it entirely. Provided citizens pay even a small amount of tax, they will want to recover those losses and demand more from leaders. This would not necessarily follow from something like tax bargaining, where small tax payments effectively reduce citizens' ability to threaten government revenues through non-compliance. The loss-aversion mechanism also implies that it may be difficult to fully replicate taxation's effect for non-earned revenues. Taxation effectively serves as a self-reinforcing mechanism for increasing citizen action. In contrast, assuring that citizens demand accountability for how non-earned revenues like aid and oil are spent may require more sustained support and campaigns to avoid complaisance.

One additional question is what types of taxes should be most likely to generate accountability demands from citizens. In joint work with Brandon de la Cuesta, Helen Milner, and Dan Nielson, we argue that taxes will be most likely to affect citizen behavior when they are *visible* (de la Cuesta et al. 2020). This accords well with the loss-aversion theory, in that for citizens to feel a loss from a tax, they need to be aware that they have paid it. This suggests a natural distinction: direct taxes should be generally visible, while indirect taxes may be less visible. Indirect tax visibility, in turn, is lower because it is typically paid as part of a purchase in which the citizen receives something of value in return at the same time. In many cases, like VAT, the tax is simply built into the purchase price, again reducing visibility. We should therefore expect that direct taxes—like income and property taxes—will tend to generate higher accountability pressures, while indirect taxes—like VAT and excise taxes—will have a smaller effect on citizens. Chapters 5 and 6 draw on this distinction when testing the theory presented here.

A casual observer of history will note many cases where governments are able to extract high levels of taxes while providing few (if any) benefits in return. Indeed, taxation is much older than democracy or accountability more generally. This suggests that there are scope conditions on when taxation will increase citizens' willingness to punish, and when taxation will increase equilibrium levels of accountability. These scope conditions depend in part on the costs citizens must incur in order to demand accountability. If these costs are too high—perhaps because government repression is severe, or because citizens are spread out over rural areas where collective action is difficult—then taxation is unlikely to be a sufficient impetus for citizens to incur these costs. In such cases, a taxed citizen will be more upset about poor government performance than a non-taxed citizen, but she will not be able to act on that anger to punish the officials involved. Only when the costs of action are sufficiently low will taxation affect observed willingness to punish.

Additionally, citizen demands are only part of the story. If government leaders recognize that taxation will generate higher demands, then they can respond in multiple ways. One is to keep the tax in place, but provide citizens' preferred policies or public goods in order to avoid punishment. Another is to simply accept the costs of punishment; for example, a corrupt leader could decide to keep stealing tax funds and accept that he will lose office soon. Finally, if the government has access to other forms of revenue, it could decide that taxation is not worth the effort: perhaps it is better to have lower government revenue but in return face fewer demands from citizens. The next chapter explores these dynamics in more detail.

Appendix

Appendix: A Model of Taxation and Punishment

This appendix presents a formal model that more precisely presents the theory introduced in Chapter 3. Assume there is a state consisting of a unified government and a group of citizens, with the citizens represented as a continuum of mass one. I compare two versions of the world: one where the government relies on taxation, and one where it relies on a non-earned windfall. In the taxation regime the government collects an exogenously chosen proportional tax, τ, on each citizen's income, y. Citizens cannot evade the tax. Taxation is non-distortionary and collection is costless. In the windfall regime, $\tau = 0$; the government is funded solely by non-earned sources such as foreign aid or oil. In both regimes the government receives total revenue T and must allocate it between a public good, G, and a private good, p, with $G + p = T$. The private good p represents money extracted by the government as rents; this could represent corruption, or other non-optimal spending. I assume that citizens only receive utility from the public good, while the government receives utility only from the private good. The results presented here will also hold in less extreme cases provided citizens prefer G to p, while the government prefers p to G.

The citizens' utility function includes their economic payoff, and their payoff from any punitive action taken against the government. Citizens evaluate economic well-being in relation to their expectations (reference point); we can write a citizen's economic utility as $u(x)$, where $x = y(1 - \tau) + G - r$; y is citizens' pre-tax income; τ is a proportional tax; G is the level of the public good; and r is the citizen's reference point. When $x > 0$, a citizen is in the realm of gains. When $x < 0$ the citizen is in the realm of losses.

The function $u(x)$ must meet the three criteria of loss-averse functions defined by Kahneman & Tversky (1979). First, $u(x)$ must be monotonically increasing, with $u(0) = 0$. Thus, individuals' utility is increasing in both income and public goods, and utility is normalized to 0 at the reference point. Second, $u(x)$ must be concave for all $x > 0$, and convex for all $x < 0$. This implies that individuals are risk-averse in the realm of gains and risk-seeking in the realm of losses. Finally, it must be that $u(x) < -u(-x)$ for $x > 0$, and $u'(x) < u'(-x)$ for $x > 0$. This says that utility is not symmetric around 0: the utility an individual gets from a gain is smaller in absolute terms from the amount of disutility from a comparable loss, and the utility curve is overall steeper below the reference point.

I argue that a natural reference point (r) is y: citizens evaluate their utility in reference to pre-tax income assuming no public goods are provided. If citizens are not taxed they expect to receive only their private income, regarding utility from any public goods as an unexpected "gain." However, if citizens are taxed, their utility when no public goods are provided ($G = 0$) is now below the reference point. A citizen's full utility function is

$$V_C = u(x|G, r, \tau) + s_i(\beta_i * \Delta u(x|G, r, \tau) - c). \qquad (3.1)$$

The first term is economic utility given the reference point r, the level of public good G, and tax rate τ. The second term represents utility derived from punishing the government. The citizen's decision of whether to punish the government is denoted $s_i \in \{0, 1\}$. If the citizen decides to punish the government through taking part in protests, voting for the opposition, or otherwise taking punitive action, $s_i = 1$; otherwise $s_i = 0$. If $s_i = 1$ the citizen pays a cost c that includes any collective action and opportunity costs. They then receive in return a psychological, non-economic benefit $\beta_i * \Delta u(x|G, r, \tau)$. The first part of the benefit, $\beta_i > 0$, is an individual-specific factor drawn from some distribution $F(\cdot)$. Citizens with higher values of β_i can be understood as having a higher propensity for political engagement, either because they care more about accountability, or because they simply enjoy engaging in political action. This individual factor is then multiplied by $\Delta u(x|G, r, \tau)$, the *amount of economic utility the citizen has lost due to rent-seeking*. This loss is defined as

$$\Delta u(x|\hat{G}, r, \tau) = u(x|T, r, \tau) - u(x|\hat{G}, r, \tau), \qquad (3.2)$$

which can be understood as the gap between citizens' economic utility given the government's actual public goods provision $G = \hat{G} \in [0, T]$ and the level of utility citizens would receive if the entire budget was devoted to public goods provision (i.e. $G = T$). In equilibrium, each citizen will punish (set $s_i = 1$) only when his losses from rent-seeking are sufficiently high that the benefits of punishment exceeds the costs, i.e. when $\Delta u(x|G, r, \tau) > \frac{c}{\beta_i}$.

If the costs of taking action (c) are extremely high, or if β_i is very low, citizens will not punish even when $G = 0$. This occurs if $\Delta u(x|G, r, \tau) < \frac{c}{\beta_i}$ even when $G = 0$ and $\tau > 0$. For such citizens the results below will not hold: taxation will have no impact on accountability demands. Consider now the universe of cases where the costs of taking action (c) are not prohibitively high, and β_i is not extremely low. For these individuals there will be some point $G^* \in (0, T)$ at which a given citizen is indifferent between punishing and not punishing. This occurs when $\Delta u(x|G^*, r, \tau) = \frac{c}{\beta_i}$.

As $\Delta u(x|G, r, \tau)$ decreases as G increases, this directly implies that, given indifference point G^*, a citizen will prefer to punish the government only if $G < G^*$. I define this cut-point value G^* as the *punishment threshold*.

Taxation's Effect on the Punishment Threshold

As citizens expect to receive at least their reference utility $r = y$ (pre-tax income), taxation pushes citizens into the realm of losses. Recall that the utility function $u(x)$ is by assumption steeper below the reference point. This means that a taxed citizen therefore loses more utility from a given level of rent-seeking compared to a non-taxed citizen— formally, for any $G < T$, $\Delta u(x|G, r, \tau)$ is higher under taxation. This directly implies that taxation increases the punishment threshold G^*: citizens demand higher government transfers when they are taxed. This holds true for any loss-aversion function $u(x)$ and any level of public goods $G \in [0, T]$. As the loss from rent seeking ($\Delta u(x|G, r, \tau)$) decreases as G increases, citizens will demand more transfers, and thus have a higher punishment threshold, when they are taxed: $G_\tau^* > G_0^*$.

Proof Recall that citizens punish the government if and only if $\Delta u(x|G, r, \tau) > \frac{c}{\beta_i}$. Assume that $\Delta_\tau u(x|G = 0, r, \tau) > \frac{c}{\beta_i}$, and so $G_\tau^* > 0$, where $\Delta u(x|G^*, r, \tau) = \frac{c}{\beta_i}$. As $\Delta u(x|G, r, \tau)$ is decreasing in G, taxation will increase the punishment threshold G^* if, for all $G \in [0, T)$, $\Delta u(x|G, r, \tau)$ is larger for a taxed citizen: $\Delta_\tau u(x|G, r, \tau) > \Delta_0 u(x|G, r, \tau)$.

These parameters are defined as:

$$\Delta_0 u(x|G) = u(y + T - y) - u(y + G - y) = u(T) - u(G) \tag{3.3}$$

$$\Delta_\tau u(x|G) = u(y(1 - \tau) + T - (y(1 - \tau) + T)) - u(y(1 - \tau)$$
$$+ G - (y(1 - \tau) + T)) = u(0) - u(G - T). \tag{3.4}$$

The condition for taxation to increase G^* is therefore

$$u(0) - u(G - T) > u(T) - u(G). \tag{3.5}$$

Note that the horizontal difference is the same for both sides of the equation: $T - G$. If the first derivative with respect to G is larger for every point on the left-hand side of the equation, this implies that the total utility difference on the LHS is also larger. From the characteristics of loss-averse utility functions, $u'(x) < u'(-x)$. Therefore $u(-T) - u(-G) > u(T) - u(G)$.

For all $x < 0$, $u(x)$ is strictly convex, and so, $u'(-T) < u'(-T + G)$, and $u'(-G) < u'(-G+G)$. The same holds for all values in between. Therefore $u(-T) - u(-G) < u(-T + G) - u(-G + G)$.

Together this implies: $\Delta_0 u(x|G) < u(-T) - u(-G) < \Delta_\tau u(x|G)$ and so $\Delta_\tau u(x|G) > \Delta_0 u(x|G)$ for all $G < T$ and $G_\tau^* > G_0^*$ for all individuals with $\beta_i > \frac{c}{-u(-T)}$.

Taxation and Variation in the Propensity for Punishment

The punishment threshold G^* is partly a function of taxation, but is also affected by β_i, a citizen's personal propensity for civic engagement. As β_i increases, so does the punishment threshold G^*. However, there is also an interaction effect between taxation and β_i, and so the degree to which taxation increases willingness to punish will be a function of a citizen's underlying propensity for engagement. This section proves that, as β_i increases and citizens care more about punishment, taxation will at first have an increasingly large effect on citizens' willingness to punish, but at some point the effect of taxation will peak, and among citizens with a higher propensity to punish an increase in β_i leads to a smaller effect of taxation on punishment, although the effect always remains positive.

First, consider low β_i such that the citizen never punishes the leader even when taxed and $G^*_\tau = G^*_0 = 0$. This implies that $G^*_\tau = u^{-1}\left(-\frac{c}{\beta_i}\right) + T \le 0$, or: $\beta_i \le \frac{c}{-u(-T)}$. For this range of β_i, $\Delta G^* = 0$.

Next, consider β_i such that $G^*_0 = 0$ but $G^*_\tau > 0$. Over this range, an increase in β_i implies an increase in G^*_τ while G^*_0 remains at zero, and so $\frac{\partial \Delta G^*}{\partial \beta_i} > 0$. As $G^*_0 = u^{-1}\left(u(T) - \frac{c}{\beta_i}\right)$, this holds when $\frac{c}{-u(-T)} < \beta_i \le \frac{u(T)}{c}$.

Finally, consider all $\beta_i > \frac{u(T)}{c}$; here both taxed and non-taxed citizens punish at least some level of corruption. Note that

$$\Delta G^* = G^*_\tau - G^*_0 = u^{-1}\left(-\frac{c}{\beta_i}\right) + T - u^{-1}\left(u(T) - \frac{c}{\beta_i}\right) \tag{3.6}$$

For this range,

$$\frac{\partial \Delta G^*}{\partial \beta_i} = \frac{c}{\beta_i^2} * \left((u^{-1})'\left(-\frac{c}{\beta_i}\right) - (u^{-1})'\left(u(T) - \frac{c}{\beta_i}\right)\right) \tag{3.7}$$

which by the properties of inverse functions is equivalent to

$$\frac{c}{\beta_i^2} * \left(\frac{1}{u'(u^{-1}(-\frac{c}{\beta_i}))} - \frac{1}{u'\left(u^{-1}(u(T) - \frac{c}{\beta_i})\right)}\right). \tag{3.8}$$

Substituting back in G^*_τ and G^*_0 using the above definitions:

$$\frac{c}{\beta_i^2} * \left(\frac{1}{u'(G^*_\tau - T)} - \frac{1}{u'(G^*_0)}\right). \tag{3.9}$$

Therefore $\frac{\partial \Delta G^*}{\partial \beta_i} > 0$ only when $u'(G^*_\tau - T) < u'(G^*_0)$.

First, consider the threshold case where $G^*_0 = 0$, $G^*_\tau > 0$ and so Equation 3.9 is positive, as $u'(0) > u'(G^*_\tau - T)$. As $u'(x)$ is continuous, this implies that $\frac{\partial \Delta G^*}{\partial \beta_i} > 0$ for some range of sufficiently small $G^*_0 > 0$, and so for some portion of this range, the effect of taxation is still increasing in β_i.

Next, consider the case where $G^*_0 \ge \frac{T}{2}$, and so $G^*_\tau > \frac{T}{2}$. From the properties of loss averse functions, the following inequalities must hold:

$$u'(G^*_\tau - T) > u'(-\frac{T}{2}) > u'(\frac{T}{2}) \ge u'(G^*_0) \tag{3.10}$$

and so $\dfrac{\partial \Delta G^*}{\partial \beta_i} < 0$ when $G_0^* \geq \dfrac{T}{2}$. By the intermediate value theorem, there must therefore be some $\hat{\beta}_i$ such that $\dfrac{\partial \Delta G^*}{\partial \beta_i}$ is zero at $\hat{\beta}_i$, positive below $\hat{\beta}_i$, and negative above $\hat{\beta}_i$. This inflection point must occur at some $G_0^* \in \left(0, \dfrac{T}{2}\right)$.[6]

The above shows that the effect of taxation, $\Delta G^* = G_\tau^* - G_0^*$, has the following characteristics:

1. For all $\beta_i \leq \dfrac{c}{-u(-T)}$, taxation has no effect because $G_\tau^* = G_0^* = 0$.

2. For all $\beta_i \in \left(\dfrac{c}{-u(-T)}, \dfrac{u(T)}{c}\right]$, the effect of taxation is positive and *increasing* in β_i.

3. For $\beta_i \geq \dfrac{u(T)}{c}$, the effect of taxation is positive. There exists $\hat{\beta}_i^*$ such that the effect of taxation is *increasing* for $\beta_i \in \left[\dfrac{u(T)}{c}, \hat{\beta}_i^*\right)$ and *decreasing* for all $\beta_i > \hat{\beta}_i^*$.

Taxation in a Repeated Game

Consider a two-period game similar to that introduced above. In the first period, the government chooses a level of G to provide. Citizens observe this decision, then decide whether to pay a cost to remove the government from office; this could entail collective action costs, facing the possibility of repression, or opportunity costs. A new leader is then chosen, but during the election their type is uncertain. With probability α they are "good" and have the same preferences as the citizens. With probability $1 - \alpha$, they are "bad" and favor rent extraction over public goods. Following the election the incumbent or challenger take office in period 2, and choose a new level of G to provide. The game then ends. Let G_t be the level of public good provided in period $t \in \{1, 2\}$. I solve for subgame-perfect equilibria.

Recall that the total budget (with or without taxation) is T. In period 2, any rent-seeking type will always set $G_2 = 0$, and any good type will always set $G_2 = T$.

The citizen must make a punishment decision for every possible $G \in [0, T]$. For any given G, the citizen's whole-game utility from keeping the rent-seeking incumbent (i.e. not punishing) is:

$$u(x|G_1) + \delta * u(x|G_2 = 0) \tag{3.11}$$

And the expected utility from punishing is:

$$u(x|G_1) + \beta_i * \Delta(u(x|G_1)) - c + \delta(\alpha * u(x|G_2 = T) + (1 - \alpha) * u(x|G_2 = 0)) \tag{3.12}$$

The citizen will therefore punish when:

$$\beta_i * \Delta(u(x|G_1)) - c + \delta(\alpha * u(x|T) + (1 - \alpha) * u(x|0)) > \delta * u(x|0) \tag{3.13}$$

---

[6] This holds if ΔG^* is single-peaked over the range of β_i such that $G_0^* > 0$.

Which simplifies to:

$$\Delta u(x|G_1) > \frac{1}{\beta_i} * (c - \alpha\delta[u(x|T) - u(x|0)]) \tag{3.14}$$

As in the original model, this leads to a cutpoint strategy for citizens. Let $G_1 = G^*$ be the value that makes the above equation an equality. Then the citizen's strategy will be:

$$s_i = \begin{cases} 1 & \text{if } G < G^* \\ 0 & \text{otherwise} \end{cases} \tag{3.15}$$

Now consider how taxation affects citizens' willingness to punish. In this version of the model, taxation affects the punishment threshold in two ways. First, as before, for any $G_1 \in [0, T)$, $\Delta u(x|G_1)$ will be higher under taxation (see proof in previous sections). However, taxation now has a second effect: by the same logic, it will increase $u(x|T) - u(x|0)$. This increase will thus lower the necessary condition on $\Delta u(x|G_1)$; again, taxation makes citizens more willing to punish. This second effect can be understood as follows: loss aversion also means that citizens gain more future utility from replacing a bad type with a good type.

Uncertain Punishment

This section shows that taxation will still increase citizen demands even when punishment is not certain. While uncertainty will decrease citizen demands overall, this decrease will actually be *smaller* for taxed, relative to untaxed, citizens.

Now, consider a version of the model above that differs only in that punishment is now uncertain: if a citizen chooses to punish they always pay a cost c, but they only receive the expressive benefit $\beta_i * \Delta(u(x|G)$ with probability q; with probability $1 - q$ the attempted sanctions fail. This could be due to failure of other citizens to also act, risks of reprisals, or other sources of uncertainty. This model assumes that expressive benefits are derived wholly from sanctions' efficacy. Thus, a citizen's expected utility from punishing, conditional on government transfer G, is:

$$-c + q * \beta_i * \Delta u(x|G, r, \tau) \tag{3.16}$$

For a given G, the citizen's optimal punishment rule as a function of β_i is therefore:

$$s_i = \begin{cases} 1 & \text{if } \beta_i > \beta^* = \frac{c}{q*\Delta u(x|G,r,\tau)} \\ 0 & \text{otherwise} \end{cases} \tag{3.17}$$

As $q \in (0, 1)$, adding uncertainty therefore increases β^* and decreases the range of β_i that will punish. Therefore, uncertainty will decrease punishment thresholds, implying lower accountability demands under uncertain punishment.

Punishment is also, as before, affected by the level of public good G provided. In particular, the range of β who will punish increases when $\Delta u(x|G, r, \tau)$ increases. This increase in $\Delta u(x|G, r, \tau)$ could be caused by a decrease in G. However, the previous section shows that $\Delta u(x|G, r, \tau)$ is also higher when $\tau > 0$. Therefore, even under uncertainty, taxation should increase the range of β_i who punish; likewise, conditional on β_i, individuals will demand higher transfers when taxed.

The final prediction of the "uncertainty" model is that, while the range of citizens who punish a given level of transfers G will always decrease with uncertainty, this decrease will be *smaller* when citizens are taxed.

To see this, let β^N be the cutoff value of β^* when there is no uncertainty ($q = 1$) and let β^R be the cutoff of β^* when punishment is risky/uncertain, i.e. when $q < 1$. Holding G constant, we can therefore define the decrease in punishment due to uncertainty as:

$$\beta^N - \beta^R = \frac{c}{\Delta u(x|G, r, \tau)} - \frac{c}{q * \Delta u(x|G, r, \tau)} = \left(1 - \frac{1}{q}\right) \frac{c}{\Delta u(x|G, r, \tau)} \qquad (3.18)$$

That is, individuals with $\beta_i \in \left[\frac{c}{\Delta u(x|G,r,\tau)}, \frac{c}{q*\Delta u(x|G,r,\tau)}\right)$ will no longer punish once uncertainty is introduced.

Notice that, as $\Delta u(x|G, r, \tau)$ increases, the range of types who no longer punish due to uncertainty decreases. As taxation increases $\Delta u(x|G, r, \tau)$ for any given $G < T$, this directly implies that while taxation will reduce the drop in punishment due to uncertainty: taxed citizens are less affected by uncertainty, relative to untaxed citizens.

This final implication could also hold because of a factor not included in the model: loss aversion dictates that citizens who are in the realm of losses are risk-seeking, while those in the realm of gains are risk-averse. As taxation pushes citizens into the realm of losses, it should also affect their risk preferences, making them more willing to punish under uncertainty.

Taxation and Collective Action

This section demonstrates that taxation can still increase citizens' accountability demands when punishing the government requires coordination between citizens. Multiple equilibria of the collective action model are possible, including some where no punishment takes place. However, I show that taxation increases the range of possible equilibria, and makes it feasible to sustain higher levels of punishment.

Consider a model in which there are now two citizens and one leader. The level of G provided by the government is received by each citizen. After the government selects $G \in [0, T]$ the citizens play a simultaneous game of incomplete information in which each citizen simultaneously decides whether to punish (pick $s_i \in \{0, 1\}$). In this version of the model, each citizen's utility function is:

$$V_i(G, r, \tau) = u(x|G, r, \tau) + s_i(s_j * \beta_i * \Delta u(x|G, r, \tau) - c) \qquad (3.19)$$

Thus, if the citizen punishes ($s_i = 1$) the cost c is paid, but the expressive benefit $\beta_i * \Delta u(x|G)$ is only received if the other citizen also punishes ($s_j = 1$).[7]

---

[7] This assumes that the expressive benefit is derived solely from successful punishment. If instead some or all of the expressive benefit comes from simply voicing one's displeasure with the government's decision, the model will more closely resemble the original model.

Now let $\beta_i \in \{\beta_L, \beta_H\}$, with $\beta_L < \beta_H$: each citizen receives either a high or low expressive benefit from punishment. Each citizen knows her own type, but does not know the type of the other citizen, only that it is high with probability z. I now solve for the possible Bayesian Nash equilibria for each feasible $G \in [0, T]$.

Define $G^i \in \{G^L, G^H\}$ as the threshold at which each type of citizen would wish to punish if they could decide on it unilaterally. This occurs when:

$$\Delta u(x|G^i) = \frac{c}{\beta_i} \tag{3.20}$$

Thus, if they knew the other citizen would punish, low types wish to punish any $G < G^L$, while high types wish to punish any $G < G^H$.

Pooling Equilibria

In equilibrium a number of possible pooling strategies are possible. Consider the following strategy: for some $\hat{G} \leq G^L$, for $i \in \{1, 2\}$ and $\beta_i \in \{\beta_L, \beta_H\}$, let

$$s_i(\beta_i) = \begin{cases} 1 & \text{if } G < \hat{G} \\ 0 & \text{otherwise} \end{cases} \tag{3.21}$$

This will always constitute an equilibrium strategy. For any $G < \hat{G}$, citizen i knows that citizen j will punish, and because $\hat{G} < G^L$, regardless of i's type, he also wishes to punish conditional on $s_j = 1$. For any $G > \hat{G}$, citizen i knows that citizen j will not punish, and so the unique best response is to likewise not punish.

Therefore, there are a set of Bayesnian Nash equilibria in which both types punish up until some threshold less than G^L, and don't punish otherwise. This includes an equilibrium in which $\hat{G} = 0$ and punishment never occurs; it also includes equilibria in which punishment does occur. However, for all cases with $\bar{G} < G^L$, both types would punish more in the absence of a collective action requirement.

Separating Equilibria

There are also equilibria in which the high type is more willing to punish than the low type. Consider a strategy profile in which the low type for each player plays the following strategy:

$$s_i(\beta_L) = \begin{cases} 1 & \text{if } G < G^L \\ 0 & \text{otherwise} \end{cases} \tag{3.22}$$

and where the High type plays:

$$s_i(\beta_H) = \begin{cases} 1 & \text{if } G < \bar{G} \\ 0 & \text{otherwise} \end{cases} \tag{3.23}$$

where $\bar{G} \in [G^L, G^H]$. Note that this strategy is optimal for the Low type: they always successfully punish for the full range of G at which they wish to punish, and never punish otherwise.

Is there a $\bar{G}$ that is optimal for the High type? If $G < G^L$, both types punish and thus punishment is optimal for the High type. If citizen i punishes some $G > G^L$, the probability that the punishment is successful is the probability that they are playing another High type; this is equal to z as defined above. Therefore, the expected payoff of type H from punishing $G > G^L$ is:

$$z * \beta_H * \Delta u(x|G) - c \qquad (3.24)$$

Which means punishment is optimal for $G < \bar{G}$, with

$$\Delta u(x|\bar{G}) = \frac{c}{z * \beta_H} \qquad (3.25)$$

if $\bar{G} > G^L$, there is a possible separating equilibrium for every $G \in (G^L, \bar{G}]$. If $\bar{G} \leq G^L$, only the pooling equilibria are possible. Separation is more likely when z or β_H are high.

In contrast to the original model, the collective action game has many possible equilibria. Depending on the relative values of β_L and β_H, and the value of z, there may or may not be a separating equilibrium. Even within pooling equilibria, there are cases where no punishment occurs, and cases where all $G < G^L$ are punished; there is no theoretically informed way to tell which of these will occur.

Taxation's Effect Under Collective Action

How does taxation affect punishment in the presence of collective action problems? For both types of citizen, taxation affects punishment by increasing $\Delta u(x|G)$ for all $G \in [0, T)$. Therefore, we can expect that taxation will increase both G^L and G^H. For both pooling and separating equilibria, this expands the values of G that are punished.

For pooling equilibria, there is still a pooling equilibrium for all $G \leq G^L$; as taxation increases G^L, there are now higher-punishment pooling equilibria that were not feasible before. However, any pooling equilibrium with $\hat{G} < G^L(\tau > 0)$ will still be viable. If a separating equilibrium is possible, the highest possible punishment threshold for High types is likewise now higher, again increasing the range of G under which the government faces a risk of punishment under some equilibrium.

Taxation can therefore increase punishment even when citizens face collective action problems. However, as numerous equilibria are possible in both cases, it is less clear when these higher-punishment equilibria will be chosen; more empirical and theoretical work is needed on this topic.

4

A Model of Taxation and Accountability

4.1 Introduction

The previous chapter argues that citizens feel a sense of loss from paying a tax, and that this makes them more upset by poor government performance, and more willing to take political action, than non-taxed citizens. One implication of this theory is that governments who tax may be willing to provide higher levels of accountability in order to avoid citizen sanctions. However, this positive equilibrium is not a foregone conclusion: if citizen demands are high, then a rent-seeking government might decide that they would rather forgo tax revenue altogether. Or, the ruling party might be willing to accept losing office next year if it means they can extract more rents this year. It is also possible that taxation's effects on citizen demands interact with other ways of demanding accountability, like tax bargaining or elections. This chapter develops a framework for thinking through these issues. I show that the higher accountability demands of tax-paying citizens can lead rent-seeking governments to deliberately limit fiscal capacity in an effort to limit those demands, and that this is especially likely in low-capacity democracies.

While existing models have produced a number of key insights into the political economy of taxation, democratization, and electoral politics, they are insufficient for exploring how modern developing countries make tax policy. First, many models assume that taxation takes the form of a single proportional tax rate that is collected and then redistributed as a lump-sum transfer to each citizen (see e.g. Acemoglu and Robinson (2006); Meltzer and Richard (1981)). In such a setting citizens can only recoup their tax payments if they have below-average incomes. Yet, even higher-income citizens may support taxation when it can be used to fund valued public goods. Many of these models also assume away issues of tax compliance, focusing instead on other aspects of tax policy (Acemoglu and Robinson 2006; Meltzer and Richard 1981; Boix 2001). Models that do examine tax compliance either

Strategic Taxation: Fiscal Capacity and Accountability in African States. Lucy E. S. Martin.
Oxford University Press. © Oxford University Press 2023. DOI: 10.1093/oso/9780197672631.003.0004

assume a quasi-voluntary compliance or "tax morale" approach—in which citizens pay so long as the government is providing their preferred policies— or a cost-benefit approach in which citizens pay when the threat of audit and punishment is sufficiently high; for canonical works on these approaches, see Torgler (2007) and Allingham and Sandmo (1972). Besley and Persson (2014) models both compliance decisions and public goods provision, but does not consider rent-seeking governments, nor the effects of taxation on citizens' political preferences. I am aware of no model that considers the core claim of this book: that taxation affects the demands citizens place on governments, and that this affects government behavior.

This chapter develops a formal model in which a government must choose whether and how to tax a group of citizens when doing so may increase the accountability pressures leaders face. The model adds nuance to existing theories of taxation. Starting with a few basic assumptions, I show that multiple tax equilibria are possible, and explain when each is most likely to occur. When citizens can credibly threaten government interests, governments will only tax if they can meet those demands and still extract rents. In other cases, they will prefer to forgo taxation to maintain access to rents from existing revenues. I show that while democracy can—as standard theories predict—lead to higher taxation in high-capacity states, in low-capacity states democracy can lead to lower taxation.[1] This approach joins other recent work in arguing that state capacity may be artificially limited by political concerns; see for example Flores-Macias (2019); Suryanarayan (2021); and Beramendi, Dincecco and Rogers (2019).

In the model, a government makes a two-stage decision in which it first considers whether to tax a particular group of citizens. If the government does tax, it must decide whether to tax coercively, or bargain with citizens for quasi-voluntary compliance. It then must decide how to actually spend any funds raised through the tax. In a democracy, the government must consider how these decisions will affect political survival. The model can be interpreted in two ways. First, as a government choosing whether, and how, to tax a particular group of citizens, for example when a government is deciding whether to bring a new group into the net. It can also be understood as modeling broad-based taxes like the income tax. The next two sections

[1] For work arguing that democracy leads to higher taxation, see discussion in Acemoglu and Robinson (2006); Meltzer and Richard (1981); Boix (2001).

consider some of the factors that might affect when a government will introduce a new tax, and the ways in which it can generate tax compliance. I then introduce a formal model of taxation, first an autocratic model in which citizens cannot remove the incumbent regime, then a democracy in which citizens have additional leverage over the government. The model produces a number of testable implications for when governments will invest in fiscal capacity, and the conditions under which taxation will lead to improved government accountability.

4.2 Why Tax?

Governments may wish to raise tax revenues for a number of reasons. These can be divided into raising revenues "for their own benefit" versus "for the benefit of citizens." Leaders who are altruistic, or who share citizens' preferences, spend taxes on providing public goods and services, developing the economy, or alleviating poverty. Rent-seeking governments extract funds for their own personal use, or spend revenues to improve their own economic or political standing, for example by subsidizing industries in which they have a stake or hiring their political supporters. In some cases these reasons overlap: subsidizing an industry may primarily help political elites but also generate jobs for citizens, and leaders may still derive utility from investing in public sanitation or improving the electricity grid.

The decision to raise taxes can also affect leader survival. In the classic state development literature, European states raised taxes because it *increased* their probability of survival: facing the threat of interstate war, states that could extract higher tax revenues had better access to credit and so could quickly raise the money necessary to pay an army, buy munitions, and otherwise survive in a hostile environment (Tilly 1992; Stasavage 2011). Interstate war is relatively rare in modern African states, but conflicts do spill over borders, and states may still face threats from internal conflict; Frizell (2021) shows that both internal and external modern conflicts can lead to higher taxes, and other work has shown mixed effects of war on fiscal capacity (see for example the debate on war and state capacity in Latin America by Centeno (1997) and Thies (2005)). Queralt (2022) shows that, in the modern era when international finance is available, states can borrow for security needs without needing to tax citizens. I argue that, on average, modern leaders are more likely to consider how taxation could have a *negative* effect on leader survival. If taxation increases citizens' willingness or ability to demand accountability from leaders, levying a new tax may expose leaders to the threat of losing office, particularly in democracies.

4.3 How to Tax?

Once a government decides to levy a tax on a particular group of citizens, it must consider how best to ensure that citizens actually pay what they owe. The two main approaches to compliance are coercion and tax bargaining. In its most extreme form, coercive taxation involves the government forcibly removing assets from citizens. This, however, is relatively rare, although it does happen: under Uganda's graduated tax, the police rounded up non-payers and even collected taxes at gun-point during community events like weddings (Therkildsen 2006). More commonly, coercion involves dedicating significant resources to tracking citizen income and collecting and monitoring taxes so that the costs of evasion are higher, and increasing the penalties for non-compliance. There is experimental evidence that increasing perceptions of the audit rate or penalties for non-compliance increase tax payments by citizens in many cases (see e.g. Coleman (1996); Del Carpio (2013); Castro and Scartascini (2015)).

Coercive taxation is appealing because the government does not need to negotiate with citizens over payment. However, it can also be extremely costly. For example, a government that collects taxes on small businesses via coercion may need to invest in better information about the number of businesses, hire more tax collectors, audit business owners' tax receipts, and potentially use the police to shut down the shops of tax evaders. If citizens riot or otherwise resist taxation, the government will have to increase repression or law enforcement, potentially at great cost. These measures will increase overall compliance, but also reduce the fraction of revenues that the government has available after the costs of coercion are paid. The costs of collection will likely be higher when taxpayers are geographically dispersed; when income is less visible; and when the government lacks good information about the population of taxpayers. In extreme cases, the costs of collection from a particular income source could even exceed the revenue the government could hope to collect—at that point taxation is simply not profitable.[2]

In many cases, governments have an alternative to coercion: they can bargain with citizens for quasi-voluntary compliance. Quasi-voluntary compliance implies that while there are penalties for non-compliance, taxpayers are paying at least somewhat voluntarily in return for benefits from the government. Early theories of tax bargaining assumed an explicit bargaining process, in which citizens agree to pay taxes voluntarily, and in return the government promises policy and, potentially, institutional concessions. This explicit bargaining model does fit some cases, both historical and modern, quite well. However, it is possible—especially in the presence of a democratically elected legislature—that bargaining can occur more indirectly, with legislators representing the interests of citizens when they make policy decisions. Indirect tax bargaining may also happen over a period of time, as the government and citizens gradually reach agreement on policy (Prichard 2015); in these cases citizen groups and protests often play a role. As with coercion, there is significant evidence that citizens are more likely to comply with taxation when they feel that government is spending money wisely (Levi, Sacks, and Tyler 2009; Picur and Riahi-Belkaoui 2006).

Tax bargaining is attractive to governments because it decreases the costs of revenue collection: citizens are willing to pay taxes provided the government keeps its side of the bargain, and so the government can reduce the coercive apparatus and free up additional funds for its own priorities. However, tax bargaining can also have significant drawbacks for governments. While more revenue reaches the government, it has less control over spending, as maintaining a bargain necessitates spending some fraction on citizens' priorities. Second, the bargaining process itself may be costly in some cases. If citizens are not well organized, or if they have diverse preferences, it may be difficult to reach agreement on what exactly citizens require in return for quasi-voluntary compliance. It may also be difficult to sustain bargains: both citizens and government must not only keep their side of the bargain, but be able to credibly punish the other side for deviating. This could mean that the government can credibly return to coercion if

---

[2] While this seems unrealistic, it does occur in some cases. There are areas of Uganda that spent more collecting the graduated tax than they received in revenues; in Kasungu district in Malawi the government recently owed salary arrears to some market fee collectors because revenues are lower than salaries.

citizens stop paying voluntarily, or that citizens can enact political costs on the government if it stops providing public goods.

To understand when governments will invest in tax capacity, we therefore need to understand both the decision to tax, and when they will choose bargaining over coercion.

4.4 A Note for Readers

The following sections develop a game-theoretic model of taxation. Such models are almost by definition quite abstract: they take a complex, messy political environment and reduce it to a set of symbolic actors who can make only a handful of choices in a constrained setting. The goal is not to fully emulate reality, but to make a few reasonable assumptions and then see what follows logically from those assumptions. This theory-building exercise generates a set of implications that the researcher can then test. For readers who are familiar with such models, I recommend skipping to the next section and reading the model in its entirety. For readers without such a background, the rest of this section lays out the intuition for what follows below. The reader can then skim the development of the model in sections 4.5 and 4.6, picking up again with section 4.7, which discusses the model's key implications. I still recommend skimming the modeling sections because I discuss many of the model's core assumptions there.

Consider a group of citizens and their government. Every year, the government takes its budget and decides how much of it to spend on public goods that the citizens want, and how much to spend on other priorities or simply steal through corruption. Now, imagine that one year the government is deciding whether to impose a tax on the citizens. If it decides to tax, one possibility is taxing through coercion: the government simply declares that everyone must pay the new tax, and uses the power of the state to enforce the tax as far as they are able. Of course, such a tactic is costly, and so for every dollar paid in the new tax, the government loses some fraction to the costs of monitoring the citizens and extracting tax payments. The alternative is for the government to strike a bargain with citizens where citizens agree to pay the tax voluntarily, and in return the government pledges to spend a certain fraction of the funds on public goods every year. This can be better for the citizens if they get more public goods than they would have without a bargain, as well as a less coercive state. The bargain can also benefit the government if they spend less on taxing coercively, and still get to extract some rents from the process.

So, the government must choose whether it should tax at all, and if so whether to seek a bargain with citizens or tax coercively. If it bargains, it has to promise to spend more on public goods, but tax revenue goes up because citizens are now paying voluntarily even without a costly coercive apparatus. The goal of the model below is to take this framework and figure out the conditions under which taxation is more or less likely; when taxation will be coercive; and when taxation will actually lead to more public goods provision and lower rent-seeking by the government. I do this in two phases, corresponding to two types of political regimes: an autocracy in which citizens have no direct leverage over the government, and a democracy where citizens can use elections to remove the government if they are not satisfied with the level of public goods the government is providing. Critically, I assume that when citizens are taxed, their demands on the government will increase, and in a democracy the government must provide more public goods in order to avoid being voted out of office by the citizens.

Taxation without Elections. In the first part of the model, I look at the conditions under which an autocratic government will tax, and when tax bargains will emerge. I consider the most extreme version of an autocracy, in which citizens have no recourse to bad or overly extractive government: an uprising or coup is simply not possible. This is of course extreme, and in almost all cases citizens have at least some power. I consider this more as a more abstract "type" of government to help focus on the different constraints in autocracies and democracies. I find that, provided a tax raises more revenue than it costs to collect, a fully autocratic government will always tax. If the government taxes coercively, it provides no public goods because citizens have no leverage to demand otherwise. However, even the most autocratic government is willing to engage in tax bargaining in some cases. For a tax bargain to be struck—and for it to be sustainable and not break down over time—both the government and citizens must care sufficiently about what happens in the future, and not be too short-sighted. That is, they must be willing to accept slightly less today in order to secure access to a better long-term outcome. Otherwise, the bargain will break down and either citizens will stop paying the tax, or the government will stop providing public goods. The citizens will be more likely to keep the bargain when coercive taxation is especially inefficient (and so government gets little revenue from coercive taxation), and when they highly value money spent on the public good.

Taxation with Elections. The second part of the model considers a similar interaction between the government and citizens, but introduces elections. After the government makes its decision about whether and how to tax, and how much of the budget to spend on public goods vs. its own priorities, citizens can decide whether to keep the incumbent government or elect a challenger instead. This additional dynamic has significant implications for the model. Without elections, the only way citizens could extract any kind of concessions from the government was through tax bargaining. Now, even without a formal tax bargain in place, citizens can remove governments they feel are not providing good policy. Critically, I assume that when the government chooses to tax, citizens will demand more from leaders as theorized in Chapter 3. This means that governments who tax must spend a higher fraction of the budget on public goods if they wish to stay in office, in contrast to governments who do not tax.

The model with elections is much more complicated, and there are more potential outcomes. The most important implications are as follows. First, in a democracy, taxed citizens can extract more accountability from the government even when there is no formal tax bargain and taxation is coercive. This is because taxation increases citizens' electoral demands, and there are at least some cases where governments are willing to meet those demands in order to stay in office. Second, there are cases where an autocracy will tax, but a democracy will not. This occurs when (1) tax bargaining is not possible, and (2) coercive taxation is sufficiently inefficient that the government could spend the whole budget on the public good and still not satisfy citizens' demands. This latter condition is more likely to hold when the citizens do not value the public good, or when the government cannot produce it efficiently.

The next two sections discuss the model in more detail. Section 4.7 then discusses the model's implications and potential limitations.

4.5 Model without Elections

In the model there are two strategic actors: a government and a group of citizens. The government, which could be local or national, has the power to levy taxes on citizens. At the national level in many African countries, the president has broad powers to introduce new taxes in the budget; in electoral authoritarian regimes where executive constraints are more binding, the legislature would also play a role. At the local level, government actors include district legislators and executives. While taxation does often require dialogue and negotiation within governments, this model considers the government as a unitary actor. In doing so, it assumes that any internal debates between legislators and the executive will still be resolved into a single taxation decision; this decision can be understood as considering the factors that drive the preferences of all members. Likewise, even when bureaucrats hold significant power—as Raffler (2022) finds in Ugandan district governments—politicians must ultimately support any effort to increase taxation.

The citizens represent some set of individuals whom the government wishes to tax. In the case of a broad-based income tax or head tax, this could include all citizens. However, it could also indicate a particular subgroup such as agricultural taxes on farmers; school fees paid by parents; or taxes levied on a particular type of business, such as market vendors or taxi drivers. For now I assume that all citizens in the targeted group share the same preferences, and model them as a unitary actor. This means assuming that citizens value the public good to a similar extent, and agree on what public goods should be provided. Later in the chapter I discuss how the model's predictions would be affected if citizens have more heterogeneous preferences.

The model examines when the government will choose to levy a new tax. This takes the form of a two-stage decision in which the government chooses between three subgames representing different tax choices (no taxation, coercive taxation, and tax bargaining), then the citizens and government play an infinitely repeated game of the chosen subgame. In the first stage, the government decides whether to levy a new tax, τ, on the citizens. This proportional tax rate is exogenously determined, and will be levied on citizens' income, y. If the government does choose to tax, it also chooses whether to tax coercively, or whether to try to bargain with citizens. At the time it makes this decision, I assume that the government already has access to some amount of revenue in each period, even if it does not tax. This is denoted F, and represents any foreign aid, resource rents, or other funding the government has access to. This would include revenues raised through any existing taxes levied on other groups.

If the government decides to implement a tax using coercion, all citizens must pay the full tax of $y\tau$. This could be because the government has sufficient monitoring capacity that tax evasion nearly impossible, or because successful evasion is sufficiently difficult that in expectation it costs the same as paying the tax. The former scenario would be likely if the taxed asset is easy to observe, while the latter is consistent with scenarios like the graduated tax in Uganda, where tax avoidance often involved physically leaving home to hide from tax collectors for days on end. However, the measures necessary for coercive taxation to succeed can be very expensive: the government must uncover and prosecute potential evaders, and must gather detailed information about citizens to make evasion less feasible. These costs will have budgetary implications, reducing the percent of tax funds available.

Alternately, the government can choose to engage in tax bargaining, in which the government provides a policy change in return for voluntary tax compliance. There are numerous cases of formal bargains between citizens and leaders, particularly when the citizens have unitary interests. For example, in Chapter 7 I discuss how, in Uganda, some local governments have struck bargains with market vendors to spend a certain fraction of revenues on market upkeep, provided vendors pay their fees voluntarily. At the national level, new taxes may be earmarked for particular sectors such as education or health (Prichard 2015).

In the model, if a bargain is struck, the citizens agree to voluntarily pay taxes and the government in return promises to provide a certain level of the public good in each period; the exact level of the public good is determined through Nash bargaining. A critical element of the bargaining game is that both citizens and government may not be able to credibly commit to their side of the bargain: there are cases where a bargain is struck but almost immediately breaks down. If the long-term costs of breaking the bargain are not sufficiently high, relative to how much each actor values the future, it will be unlikely to hold. For the government the main advantage of tax bargaining is that it will decrease the costs of tax collection; the main cost is that it may have to reduce its own rents in order to provide citizens with their desired level of public goods. Citizens benefit from the bargain in that they receive higher levels of public goods, while the main cost is increased tax payments relative to no taxation.

After the government chooses whether and how to tax, the citizens and government play an infinitely repeated game with the chosen institutions. In this version of the game there are no elections, and citizens cannot remove the existing government: their only form of leverage comes from the ability to withhold taxes in the bargaining subgame. Citizens may want to demand more accountability when they are taxed, but have no mechanism for doing so. Historically, citizens have been able to impose costs on the government even in the absence of taxation, for example through tax riots. In the context of this model, I consider this as part of the costs of collecting a coercive tax: putting down riots is costly to the government, and citizens must pay costs potentially equal to the tax if they protest.

I assume that there is a tension between the government's and citizens' preferences. While citizens care about private income and public goods, the government only cares about the rents it can extract from the budget, and receives no utility from public goods spending. The main results of the model should also hold provided citizens receive more utility from public goods than government rents, and the government receives more utility from rents than public goods. Analyzing the pure case where each actor only values one good simply makes the model more tractable. There are many reasons why governments could be rent-seeking: it could be for private gain, or for policy objectives, such as military power, that are valued by the government but not citizens. What is important for the model is that there is a disconnect between government's spending priorities and those of citizens. The following sections introduce the government's choices in more detail, then discuss how these choices map onto each actor's utility function.

4.5.1 Possible Fiscal Institutions

The government must choose between the three possible fiscal institutions introduced above: no taxation, coercive taxation, and tax bargaining.

No Taxation

If the government chooses No Taxation, its total budget is F, which comes entirely from revenue sources other than the taxes on the citizens. The following infinitely repeated subgame then takes place:

1. The government receives its budget of F.
2. The government chooses a level of public good $G \in [0, F]$ to provide to the citizens, retaining $(F - G)$ as rents.
3. Payoffs accrue—the citizen has no strategic moves in this subgame.

Coercive Taxation

If the government chooses Coercive Taxation, it still receives additional revenues F, but also levies a tax τ on citizens' income y. However, coercive taxation is inefficient—the government must pay potentially high costs to extract revenues, and some revenues may be lost through resistance or evasion.[3] The government therefore receives only fraction $\gamma < 1$ of the tax funds. Here I consider the case where $\gamma > 0$, but if taxes are especially difficult to extract γ may actually be negative. For example, in the late 1990s, some districts in Uganda spent more money collecting the graduated tax than was actually raised in revenues (see Chapter 7). The following infinitely repeated subgame then takes place:

1. Citizens pay a tax of $y\tau$ and the government receives income $F + \gamma y\tau$, where $\gamma \in (0, 1)$.
2. Government chooses a level of public good $G \in [0, F + \gamma y\tau]$ to provide to the citizens, retaining the rest as rents.
3. Payoffs accrue—the citizen has no strategic moves in this subgame.

Tax Bargaining

If the government chooses Tax Bargaining, the subgame is more complicated. At the beginning of the game (time $t = 0$), the government and citizens Nash bargain over the level of public good, G, to be provided in return for quasi-voluntary compliance with taxation.[4] If the bargain holds, the government will provide at least the bargained-upon level of public goods in each period, and all citizens will voluntarily pay their taxes without the need for coercion. For the government bargaining is attractive because it eliminates the revenue losses from coercive taxation, effectively setting $\gamma = 1$.[5] For citizens, the bargain is attractive because it increases the level of public goods they receive. If a bargain is reached, the following stage game is played in each period:

---

[3] I assume all citizens pay a cost of at least $y\tau$ due to coercive taxation; this is due either to the costs of paying the tax, or to the high costs incurred to avoid the tax.

[4] Nash bargaining is a method of bargaining that splits a resource between two parties, each of whom have a "reservation utility" equal to their payoff if the bargain fails. No party will accept a payoff less than their reservation utility, and the bargaining solution is always Pareto efficient.

[5] This could also be modeled as any other increase in γ; here I consider $\gamma = 1$ for simplicity.

1. The government decides whether to keep the bargain or revert to either coercive taxation or no taxation.
2. A simultaneous game is played in which the citizens decide whether to comply with or evade taxation ($\kappa \in \{0, 1\}$), and the government picks $G \in [0, F + y\tau]$.
3. Payoffs accrue.

The no taxation and coercive taxation subgames are absorbing states, meaning that if they are chosen initially they will always continue to be the government's best option in the future. This is not true of the bargaining subgame; in each period the government must choose whether to continue with the bargain or revert to another fiscal institution. This is a simplifying assumption, but a reasonable one: as payoffs from no taxation and coercive taxation are the same in each period, if the government prefers them at time t it must also prefer them at time $t + 1$. It is only in the bargaining subgame that citizens have a strategic choice; if the citizens defect from the bargain, the government may decide to revert to a different subgame, as its payoffs are now altered. In this sense the bargain gives leverage to the government as well as the citizens, especially if the government can credibly threaten a return to coercive taxation and lower public goods provision.

4.5.2 Utility in Each Subgame

Now consider the utility function of each actor. I assume that citizens' utility is linear in income (minus any taxes paid) and the public good. Assuming that each citizen receives income y and faces tax rate τ (where $\tau = 0$ if the government does not levy a tax), the citizen's utility function can be written $y(1 - \tau) + \alpha G$, where α is the utility a citizen receives for each dollar is spent on the public good G. This can also be interpreted as the degree to which citizens value the public good relative to private consumption—if $\alpha < 1$, the citizens prefer no taxation and no public goods to any form of taxation. The parameter α incorporates two aspects of public goods. The first is degree to which citizens value the public good: α is higher when the public good is valued by citizens. For example, if citizens value hospitals more than roads, α will be higher when the public good provided is health care. Citizens with children may likewise have a higher α for the provision of schools. The α parameter also incorporates the production function for G.

As it becomes cheaper to provide each citizen with a unit of the public goods, α will increase. For example, as it is often cheaper to provide public goods to densely populated areas, α may be higher in urban than rural areas. Critically, state capacity also affects α, as higher-capacity states will be able to provide public goods more efficiently.

The citizens' utility in each period of the three subgames can be written as follows, where $\kappa \in \{0, 1\}$ indicates whether the citizens voluntarily comply with the tax under a bargain:

$$U_{Cit}(G|y, \gamma, \tau, \alpha) = \begin{cases} y + \alpha G & \text{Under No Taxation} \\ y(1 - \tau) + \alpha G & \text{Under Coercive Taxation} \\ y(1 - \kappa\tau) + \alpha G & \text{Under Tax Bargaining} \end{cases} \quad (4.1)$$

Next consider the Government's utility. I assume that the Government's per-period payoff is linearly increasing in the rents it extracts after providing some level of public goods. For each subgame, the Government's utility function can therefore be written:

$$U_{Gov}(G|y, \gamma, \tau, \alpha) = \begin{cases} F - G & \text{Under No Taxation} \\ F + \gamma y\tau - G & \text{Under Coercive Taxation} \\ F + \kappa y\tau - G & \text{Under Tax Bargaining} \end{cases} \quad (4.2)$$

Table 4.1 The key variables in the model.

Variable Name	Definition
y	Citizen income
τ	Tax rate, exogenously set
t	Time period
G	Level of the public good (PG)
α	Utility citizen receives for each dollar allocated to G
κ	Citizens' (binary) decision whether to comply with taxation under bargaining
F	Government's available non-earned revenue (aid, oil)
$\gamma y\tau$	Tax revenues raised under coercion, where $\gamma \in (0, 1)$
$y\tau$	Tax revenues raised under tax bargaining
G^B	Level of G agreed upon in bargaining
δ_G	Government's discount rate, where $\delta_G \in (0, 1)$
δ_C	Citizens' discount rate, where $\delta_C \in (0, 1)$

As each subgame is infinitely repeated, all actors make decisions considering not only how it will affect the current period, but also how it will affect their payoffs in the future. The government's discount rate— how much it values the future relative to the present—is $\delta_G \in (0, 1)$, and the citizens' discount rate is $\delta_C \in (0, 1)$. Higher values of δ_i correspond to valuing the future more highly. Table 4.1 summarizes the key variables of the model. I now consider the possible subgame-perfect Nash equilibria of each subgame.

4.5.3 No Taxation and Coercive Taxation

Because in this version of the model there are no elections, the citizens have no way to influence the government in the no taxation and coercive taxation subgames. Citizens have no strategic actions at all: they cannot remove the incumbent, and they cannot refuse to pay taxes if a tax is levied. In either situation, the government therefore has no reason to provide any public goods to citizens. For both subgames, the government's utility is strictly decreasing as spending on the public good, G, increases, and so the unique subgame-perfect Nash equilibrium is for the government to set $G = 0$ in each period.[6]

For the no taxation subgame, the government levies no tax but has access to other revenues F; the citizen pays no tax so has their full pre-tax income y. In equilibrium, in each period of the subgame citizens can therefore expect to receive utility y, and the government receives utility F as it extracts the full budget in the form of rents.

In the coercive taxation subgame, citizen must pay the tax, but because coercion is expensive, the government only receives fraction γ of the taxes citizens pay; the rest is lost. As the government again provides no public goods in this subgame, the government will receive $U_G = F + \gamma y \tau$ in each period. The citizens receive their post-tax income and no public goods: $U_C = y(1 - \tau)$.

Provided $\gamma > 0$, the government will always prefer coercive taxation to no taxation when there are no elections: its budget is strictly higher, and it can extract the entire budget in the form of rents. However, this does not mean

---

[6] In the no taxation game, the government solves $\max_G F - G$, s.t. $G \in [0, F]$. In the coercive taxation game, the government solves $\max_G F + \gamma y \tau - G$, s.t. $G \in [0, F + \gamma y \tau]$, where $\gamma \in (0, 1)$.

that taxation will always be coercive without elections. As we will see next, the government may still have an incentive to bargain with citizens.

4.5.4 Tax Bargaining

Coercive taxation ensures that all citizens pay the tax, but is also costly and inefficient—if citizens can hide their income or otherwise resist taxation, the government may lose a significant fraction of revenues to enforcement. As an alternative, the government can seek to eliminate the inefficiencies of coercive taxation by bargaining with citizens for quasi-voluntary compliance: this eliminates the costs of collection and so increases revenues to $y\tau$—if citizens comply. However, under any bargain the government must guarantee citizens some level of public goods spending in return for compliance. I assume that citizens and government Nash bargain over the level of public good to be provided. Let G^B be the level of public good agreed upon in the bargain. In each subsequent period, both parties must decide whether to comply with the bargain or defect. The government decides whether to set $G = G^B$ or some other level, and citizens decide whether to pay the tax ($\kappa = 1$) or evade it ($\kappa = 0$).[7]

A key element of any Nash bargaining problem is the reservation payoffs—the best each actor can expect if no bargain is struck. In this case, without a bargain the government's next-best option is always to choose coercive taxation and set $G = 0$ in all periods. Thus the per-period reservation utilities are $r_G = F + \gamma y\tau$ for the government (its payoff from coercive taxation, $G = 0$) and $r_C = y(1 - \tau)$ for the citizens. A bargain is only feasible if there is some division of the revenues such that both citizens and the government prefer it to their reservation payoffs. The bargaining problem can now be written as:

$$\max_{G} (F + y\tau - G - (F + \gamma y\tau))^{\frac{1}{2}} * (y(1 - \tau) + \alpha G - (y(1 - \tau))^{\frac{1}{2}}. \quad (4.3)$$

This yields a bargaining solution in which citizens agree to pay the tax if the government provides the following level of G in each period:

---

[7] I assume that the bargain is over the per-period strategy; the solution is identical using the present-discounted expected payoffs of each outcome instead.

$$G^B = \frac{1}{2}(1 - \gamma)y\tau \qquad\qquad (4.4)$$

This has a very natural interpretation. Because voluntary compliance under the bargain reduces the inefficiencies associated with coercion, the government receives an extra $(1 - \gamma)y\tau$ in revenue each period: this is the gain from bargaining. In the bargaining solution, this surplus is split evenly between the citizens and the government. When coercive taxation is more inefficient (i.e. as γ approaches zero), the citizens receive a higher proportion of total tax revenues, but never more than half. In no bargain do citizens receive any portion of the non-tax revenues F; without elections there is a limit on the level of accountability citizens can extract.

When can this bargain can be maintained? In each period of the bargaining subgame, the citizens and government simultaneously select levels of tax compliance and the public good, respectively.[8] In the single-shot version of the stage game, cooperation is not possible and the unique Nash equilibrium is for the government to set $G = 0$, and for citizens to not pay the tax ($\kappa = 0$).[9] In the repeated game, cooperation is possible because each actor has some way to threaten the other: the government can stop providing the public good, and the citizens can stop paying the tax.

While by the folk theorem an infinite number of subgame-perfect Nash equilibria (SPNEs) are possible, I argue that the bargain serves as a coordination mechanism for a particular grim-trigger strategy by both players. Under this strategy, in the first period the citizens comply ($\kappa = 1$) and the government sets $G = G^B$ as promised. In all future periods, both government and citizens comply with the bargain provided both sides have kept it in all previous periods. If either side has ever defected, both players defect in any future tax bargaining period—meaning that the government sets $G = 0$ and the citizens refuse to pay the tax. Once the trigger strategy occurs, the bargaining subgame becomes structurally identical to the no taxation subgame. Because the government strictly prefers coercive taxation to no taxation in this version of the model, the government will then revert to coercive taxation in all periods following a defection, as this is strictly preferred to what is effectively no taxation.

---

[8] I assume that the government can always choose $G \in [0, F + y\tau]$ even if no citizen pays the tax and so actual revenues are only F. This is consistent with most government's access to short-term credit.

[9] This would also be the unique Markov-perfect equilibrium of the infinitely repeated game.

For the grim trigger strategy profile to constitute an equilibrium, neither citizens nor government must wish to defect in any subgame. Because the "punishment" condition consists of always playing the stage game Nash equilibrium ($\kappa = 0$ and $G = 0$), there is no profitable off-path deviation in any of the subgames in which punishment takes place. Therefore profitable deviations are only possible in the on-path subgames. Recall that the discount rate is $\delta_C \in (0, 1)$ for citizens and $\delta_G \in (0, 1)$ for government.

Under the proposed grim-trigger strategies, each player will keep the bargain only when the value of future public goods (for the citizens) or rents (for the government) outweighs the benefits of defection in the current period. For citizens, defection takes the form of non-compliance; for the government, the best possible defection is to set $G = 0$ in some period, then revert to coercion in all future periods, as citizens will cease to pay the tax otherwise.[10] Bargaining will be an equilibrium provided that each actor cares sufficiently about the future. The precise conditions on each actor's discount rate are:

$$\delta_C \geq \frac{2}{2 + \alpha(1 - \gamma)} \quad \text{and} \quad \delta_G \geq \frac{1}{2}. \tag{4.5}$$

Consider first the citizens. As $\gamma > 0$ and $\alpha > 0$, there is always some feasible $\delta_C < 1$ for which the bargain will hold. The citizens will be more likely to keep the bargain when they value the public good or when public goods are cheap to produce (i.e. when α is high), and when coercive taxation is inefficient (γ is small); a low γ improves the level of public goods citizens obtain via bargaining. Note that the government's willingness to keep the bargain does not depend on any of the model's parameters. This is because the short-term benefits of defection are equal to the long-term per-period gains from the bargain.

The conditions on δ_C and δ_G generate two possible equilibria of the tax bargaining subgame. If δ_C and δ_G are sufficiently high, the bargain can be maintained and equilibrium strategies in the bargaining subgame are the grim-trigger strategies described above. If either discount rate is too low, then the equilibrium strategies will be those of the stage game: $G_t = 0$ and

---

[10] For the Citizens the condition for bargaining to be sustained is therefore
$y + \alpha G^B + \frac{\delta_C}{1 - \delta_C}(y(1 - \tau)) \leq \frac{1}{1 - \delta_C}(y(1 - \tau) + \alpha G^B)$; for the Government it is
$F + y\tau + \frac{\delta_G}{1 - \delta_G}(F + \gamma y\tau) \leq \frac{1}{1 - \delta_G}(F + y\tau - G^B)$. In both $G^B = \frac{1 - \gamma}{2}y\tau$.

$\kappa = 0$ in all periods. In this case the government will thus revert to coercive taxation when given the choice at $t = 1$.[11]

4.5.5 Equilibria

Having solved each subgame, we can now examine the equilibria of the full game without elections. Table 4.2 depicts the equilibrium strategies and the government's payoff within each subgame under different segments of the parameter space, and Figure 4.1 graphs the equilibria of the entire game without elections as a function of the citizens' and government's discount rates. If all actors sufficiently value the future ($\delta_G \geq \frac{1}{2}$ and $\delta_C \geq \frac{2}{2+a(1-\gamma)}$), a bargain can be maintained through the grim trigger strategies described above, and the government always prefers tax bargaining to either alternative, setting $G = \frac{1-\gamma}{2}y\tau$ in each period. When bargaining cannot be maintained, the government strictly prefers coercive taxation to either alternative and sets $G = 0$ in each period. Taxation always occurs in equilibrium.

Table 4.2 Subgame strategies in equilibrium, model without elections.

Subgame	Government Strategy	Citizen Strategy	Gov Per-Period Utility
No Taxation	$G_t = 0$	N/A	F
Coercive Tax	$G_t = 0$	N/A	$F + \gamma y \tau$
Bargaining: $\delta_G \geq \frac{1}{2}$ and $\delta_C \geq \frac{2}{2+\alpha(1-\gamma)}$	$G_t = G^B = \frac{1-\gamma}{2}y\tau$ if $(G_j, \kappa_j) = (G^B, 1)$ $\forall j < t$, $G_t = 0$ o.w.	$\kappa_t = 1$ if $(G_j, \kappa_j) = (G^B, 1)$ $\forall j < t$ $\kappa_t = 0$ o.w.	$F + \frac{1+\gamma}{2}y\tau$
Bargaining: $\delta_G < \frac{1}{2}$ or $\delta_C < \frac{2}{2+a(1-\gamma)}$	$G_t = 0$	$\kappa_t = 0$	F

[11] When bargaining is not sustainable, the payoffs from tax bargaining and no taxation are the same.

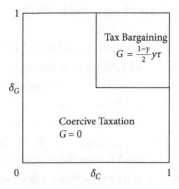

Fig. 4.1 Equilibria of the model without elections, as a function of the discount rates of the citizens (x axis) and government (y axis). Recall that as δ approaches 1, an individual values the future more heavily. In the diagrams the precise boundaries of each equilibrium are not exact, and should not be compared to equilibria in other conditions.

4.5.6 Discussion

In the absence of elections, citizens have limited options for demanding accountability. In the no taxation and coercive taxation subgames, they have no strategic actions and the government never provides public goods. In the tax bargaining subgame the citizens do have limited leverage over the government from threatening tax non-compliance. This allows them to extract some public goods provision, but this leverage is limited; citizens never get more than half of total tax revenue in any bargain. However, bargains are more favorable to citizens when coercion is costly (γ is low). In practice, coercive taxation can take many forms. In Chapter 7, I discuss colonial hut or poll taxes as one such example: in some countries these taxes persisted post-independence, and were highly coercive, with few perceived benefits for citizens. Examples of tax bargaining in autocracies are common, and are often taxes on concentrated occupations or groups with high collective action capacity; Chapter 7 discusses the example of market vendors in Uganda.

Without elections, taxation always occurs in equilibrium. When tax bargaining can be sustained, it is strictly preferred by the government to coercive taxation. Whether the government will keep the bargain does not depend on any of the model parameters; it simply needs to value the lower, constant stream of future revenue it gets from quasi-voluntary tax compliance more than it values stealing the entire budget today. This agrees with earlier models of tax bargaining.

In contrast to earlier tax bargaining models, which focused on explaining when governments would engage in bargaining, this model also has implications for when citizens will wish to bargain. Citizens will also keep the bargain when they sufficiently value the future, but the exact threshold depends on two factors. First, citizens are more likely to keep the bargain when they value public goods spending—i.e. when α is large. Low values of α could occur if the public good is expensive to produce, perhaps because the government lacks the capacity to use funds effectively or because citizens are geographically dispersed. It could also occur if each dollar must be split between multiple public goods that are valued by a heterogeneous group of taxpayers; it may be easier to bargain with homogeneous groups of citizens. Citizens may also care little for the public good if they can access high-quality substitutes in the private market; this is in line with Bodea and LeBas (2016), which finds that compliance norms are lower when private alternatives to government-funded public goods are available.

Second, citizens are more likely to keep the bargain when coercion is costly, i.e. when γ is low; this agrees with earlier models of tax bargaining, but here the focus is on the incentives for citizens rather than the government. Under coercive taxation citizens always pay the same tax, but γ affects how much of that revenue is potentially available to the government. When coercive taxation is inefficient, the government's gains from bargaining are greater, and so the citizens receive a higher fraction of revenues under the bargaining solution. This means that citizens with a wider range of discount rates (δ_C) will wish to keep the bargain.

A key assumption of the model without elections is that citizens' only form of leverage over the government is the ability to withhold taxes in the bargaining subgame: they cannot credibly threaten the survival of the incumbent regime. This means that, even if taxation increases citizens' demands for accountability as proposed in the previous chapter, citizens cannot translate these demands into a higher supply of accountability in the form of public goods provision.

4.6 Adding Elections

Now, consider a similar model in which citizens can decide whether to remove the incumbent government at the end of each period. This could be because the country is a democracy, or because citizens can credibly use protests or other extra-electoral means to remove the government. For simplicity, I refer to this process as "elections." As the focus of the theory presented here is not electoral outcomes per se, but rather equilibrium levels and types of taxation, I use a reduced-form electoral model that still captures the key element of elections: leaders face the possibility of losing office if they stray too far from citizens' preferences.

I model elections as an additional stage in each period. After any taxes are collected and the level of public good chosen, citizens can vote to remove the incumbent government. Doing so incurs a cost to the citizens, but is always successful: the incumbent is removed with certainty. I discuss further below how the model changes if there is uncertainty about whether the citizens can successfully remove the incumbent. If the incumbent is removed, he is replaced with a challenger. I assume that the challenger and incumbent are drawn from the same distribution and, in expectation, the new leader is also rent-seeking. This matches the case in many new African democracies, where changes in who holds power do not always result in changes to the level of corruption; indeed many parties are led by members of the former ruling party even after formal democratic transitions.

In the model, citizens vote retrospectively and so must decide whether they are satisfied with the incumbent, rather than whether voting for the challenger will increase their expected payoff.[12] This is in line with a large literature on retrospective voting (e.g. Fiorina 1981), and with electoral settings, like Uganda, in which very little information is available about the quality of most challengers or what policies they would actually enact if elected. If the incumbent loses the election, they receive a payoff of zero for all future periods, and the victorious challenger takes over and begins to accrue rents. Elections thus grant citizens additional leverage over the government: even when there is no opportunity to tax bargain, the threat of removal can help citizens extract more concessions from the ruling government.

The following sections introduce the voting process in more detail and work through each subgame in turn, discussing how the addition of elections alters the government's decision of when and how to tax. The revised model generates a number of predictions regarding when citizens will be able to use elections to decrease rent-seeking and increase public goods provision. It also has implications for when taxation will be sustainable.

---

[12] As in Chapter 3, the model would also work with at least some versions of prospective voting.

4.6.1 Defining the Citizen's Voting Decision

I assume that citizens vote retrospectively based on the level of public goods provided in the previous period. In particular, I assume that citizens use a threshold strategy similar to that discussed in Chapter 3 to examine how taxation affects citizens' accountability demands. Citizens compare the costs of opposing the incumbent to the benefits of removal, and remove the incumbent from office when the benefits exceed the costs: this occurs when the government provides less than some threshold level of public goods.

The costs of removal could include the collective action costs of organizing against the incumbent, including opportunity costs (such as taking time off work to vote or campaign), but also the possibility of repression or electoral violence by the regime. The benefits could be economic if the challenger is expected to implement better policy. As I assume that the challenger and incumbent have the same preferences, I focus here on the psychological, or *expressive* benefits citizens receive from punishing government wrongdoing.

While the costs of organizing remain constant, the expressive benefits of removing the incumbent increase as the government extracts more and more rents (and therefore provides fewer public goods). At some point the benefits of punishment exceed the costs, and citizens vote the incumbent out of office. Here I define this threshold, not in terms of the dollar amount spent on rents or public goods, but in terms of the *fraction* of the budget that is extracted. Under this model citizens will vote out the incumbent if and only if public goods provision falls below some threshold G^*, which is itself a function of the government's total available budget. This threshold is comparable to the punishment threshold developed in Chapter 3.

Following Chapter 3, I assume that G^* is, in part, a function of the tax rate τ: taxed citizens will demand more public goods from the leader than citizens who are not taxed. The effect of taxation on punishment can be expressed in terms of citizens' cutpoints. If there is no taxation, the citizens' cutpoint is $G_0^*(F) \in [0, F)$—even when they are not taxed, citizens will still demand some public goods from the government. If the government only relies on tax revenue (i.e. $F = 0$ and $\tau > 0$), the cut-point is $G_\tau^*(\tau, y) \in [0, y\tau)$ such that $\frac{G_0^*}{F} < \frac{G_\tau^*}{y\tau}$: if the incumbent wishes to remain in power when citizens are taxed, he must spend a higher *fraction* of the budget on public goods than when there is no taxation. Note that, as $\gamma < 1$, G_τ^* is potentially larger than $\gamma y\tau$, the actual amount of revenue the government receives through coercive taxation. This implies that there will be cases where the government could spend all tax revenue on G and still not satisfy citizens' demands.

If the government receives both tax and unearned revenue ($F > 0$ and $\tau > 0$), the cut-point is $\bar{G}^*(F, y, \tau) = (G_0^* + G_\tau^*) \in [0, F + y\tau)$. The citizens therefore demand a higher fraction of the government's budget when $\tau > 0$: $\frac{\bar{G}^*}{F+y\tau} > \frac{G_0^*}{F}$.[13] Next, consider the equilibria of the three possible subgames with elections.

4.6.2 No Taxation and Coercive Taxation with Elections

If the government chooses no taxation or coercive taxation, the citizens and government engage in an infinitely repeated game where in each period the government chooses G within its budget, then the citizens observe this decision and choose whether to replace the incumbent government (denoted $s \in \{0, 1\}$). If $s = 1$, the incumbent government is replaced: it receives a payoff of zero in all future periods, and a new regime enters and chooses new institutions. As the incumbent and challenger have identical preferences, fiscal institutions are assumed to remain constant: if the incumbent maximizes by choosing the no taxation subgame, so does the challenger. Following the discussion above, the citizens will vote to replace the incumbent government (set $s = 1$) whenever $G < G^*$, with $G^* = G_0^* \in [0, F)$ under no taxation, and $G^* = \bar{G}^* \in [0, F + y\tau]$ under coercive taxation.

Consider first the no taxation subgame. If the government provides at least citizens' threshold level of goods ($G_t \geq G_0^*$), it receives a modest level of rents in each period but stays in power: its expected payoff is $\frac{1}{1-\delta_G}(F - G_t)$. Alternately, if the government sets $G_t < G_0^*$ it receives a larger payout today, but then lose office and receive no rents in any future period: long-run utility is $F - G_t + \frac{\delta_G}{1-\delta_G} * 0$.

As the government's utility is strictly decreasing in G in each section of the parameter space, the government will maximize its utility either by setting $G = G_0^*$ or $G = 0$. When the government cares sufficiently about the future— specifically, when $\delta_G \geq \frac{G_0^*}{F}$—it prefers a smaller long-term stream of rents

---

[13] If $G^* = 0$, it indicates that organizing against the incumbent is so costly that citizens will never do so, even if the government provides no public goods.

and sets $G = G_0^*$. If this condition is not met, the government sets $G = 0$ with the knowledge that it will lose office. As $G_0^* < F$, there is always some feasible $\delta_G < 1$ such that the government will provide a positive level of the public good under no taxation. This is a strict improvement over the case without elections, in which no positive level of the public good is ever provided.

The government's decision is similar under coercive taxation, except that citizens now demand $\bar{G}^*$ instead of G_0^*, and the budget is $F + \gamma y\tau$. The government will now maximize its expected utility at either the citizens' threshold ($G_t = \bar{G}^*$) or at $G = 0$. If $\delta_G \geq \frac{\bar{G}^*}{F+\gamma y\tau}$, the government cares enough about the future to meet citizens' demands and set $G = \bar{G}^*$ in each period. Otherwise, its optimal strategy is $G = 0$ and it loses office at the end of the first period.

In both subgames, the comparative statics on the citizens' punishment cut-point G^* are informative. When G^* is extremely low, the government will provide some low level of G. As G^* increases, the level of public good provided in equilibrium also increases. However, if G^* becomes too high, the government would rather extract the full budget in the short term and be replaced in the future, and G_t^* again drops to zero. Citizens therefore receive the best outcome when they are able to moderate their demands, but may not be able to credibly commit to doing so—especially when they are taxed.

4.6.3 Coercion vs. No Taxation

In the model without elections, the government never provided public goods in equilibrium, and could not be removed from office. Provided $\gamma > 0$, and so the costs of collection do not exceed potential revenues, it therefore always preferred coercive taxation to no taxation. Once elections are introduced this is no longer the case. Whether the government prefers coercive taxation or no taxation—and whether it provides public goods in equilibrium—depends on the government's discount rate δ_G. This shows that there are cases where democracies are actually less likely to tax than autocracies.

There are three possible cases, depending on the relationship between δ_G and the level of public goods citizens demand in each subgame. Recall that the citizens demand a higher fraction of the budget when taxed: $\bar{G}^* = G_0^* + G_\tau^*$, and by assumption $\frac{G_\tau^*}{y\tau} > \frac{G_0^*}{F}$, therefore $\frac{\bar{G}^*}{F+\gamma y\tau} > \frac{G_0^*}{F}$.

Case 1: $\dfrac{\bar{G}^*}{F+\gamma y\tau} > \dfrac{G_0^*}{F} > \delta_G.$

When the government cares little about the future, $\left(\dfrac{G_0^*}{F} > \delta_G\right)$, it sets $G_t = 0$ in both subgames and is removed by the citizens at the end of the period. The government therefore always prefers the higher budget (and rents) it gets from coercive taxation. This resembles a system in which corruption remains high despite frequent electoral turnover, consistent with the incumbency disadvantage that is often found in low-income countries.

Case 2: $\dfrac{G_0^*}{F} < \delta_G < \dfrac{\bar{G}^*}{F+\gamma y\tau}.$

When the government has an intermediate discount rate, the government's equilibrium subgame strategies are to provide citizens' desired level of public goods ($G_t = G_0^*$) under no taxation, but to provide no public goods ($G_t = 0$) under coercive taxation. This occurs because the citizens demand a higher fraction of the budget when taxed, and the government does not care enough about the future to accept this lower share of rents in each period. Here the government prefers coercive taxation to no taxation if and only if $\delta_G < \dfrac{\gamma y\tau + G_0^*}{F+\gamma y\tau}$. If citizens' demands are low relative to the costs of coercion (i.e. if $G_\tau^* < \gamma y\tau$) then the condition always holds and the government always prefers coercive taxation. If $G_\tau^* > \gamma y\tau$, and so citizens' demands cannot be met given actual tax receipts due to the inefficiencies of coercion, coercive taxation will still be preferred if the government does not care sufficiently about the future.

Case 3: $\delta_G > \dfrac{\bar{G}^*}{F+\gamma y\tau} > \dfrac{G_0^*}{F}.$

If the government sufficiently values the future, it will provide the citizens' desired level of public good (G_0^* or G_τ^*) under both no taxation and coercive taxation. Which subgame the government prefers will depend on the efficiency of coercive taxation, relative to citizens' demands. If $\gamma y\tau \geq G_\tau^*$, the government prefers coercive taxation: it can meet citizens' demands and still have excess tax revenue that it can extract as rents. If $\gamma y\tau < G_\tau^*$, coercive taxation is so inefficient that the government could spend 100% of received tax revenues on the public good and still lose the election; the increased revenue from taxation is outweighed by citizens' demands, and the government prefers no taxation. The latter case is made more likely if taxation increases citizens' demands.

Discussion

Depending on the parameters of the model there are five possible equilibria (setting aside for now the bargaining subgame). These are summarized in Table 4.3 along with the government's expected utility from its preferred subgame. While without elections the government always chose coercive taxation and set $G = 0$, there are now three possible outcomes across the five potential equilibria. In several, the government provides a positive level of public goods: there are two in which the government chooses no taxation and provides citizens' threshold level of public goods G_0^*, and one in which the government prefers coercive taxation and provides citizens' threshold level of public goods $\bar{G}^*$. In the remaining two cases, the outcome is similar to that without elections: the government prefers to tax coercively, but provides no public goods ($G_t = 0$). However, in contrast to the game without elections, the government then loses office at the end of the round.

Adding elections changes the dynamics of the game in two key ways. First, in one case (line 3 in Table 4.3), coercive taxation decreases the fraction of the budget that is stolen, relative to either no taxation with elections or the coercive equilibrium without elections. This demonstrates that taxation can increase accountability even in the absence of a tax bargain.[14] In order to stay in office and reap the additional revenues from taxation the government is willing to buy citizens' support and increase the fraction of the budget that is spent on public goods.

Second, Cases 3 and 5 demonstrate that there are areas of the parameter space where the government would rather eliminate taxation than meet citizens' demands for increased accountability under taxation; this is driven by the relationship between the government's revenue under coercive taxation ($\gamma y \tau$) and the fraction of tax revenues citizens demand (G_τ^*). When coercive taxation is efficient, it is more likely that $\gamma y \tau \geq G_\tau^*$ and thus the government prefers coercive taxation and sets $G_t = \bar{G}^*$. When $\gamma y \tau < G_\tau^*$, the government will prefer no taxation, and will set $G_t = G_0^*$. This is a major testable implication of the model, and runs counter to work suggesting that democratization will increase taxation: here I suggest that it may instead lead a rent-seeking government to alter policy in order to decrease citizen

---

[14] If taxation did not decrease tolerance for corruption, i.e. if $\frac{\bar{G}^*}{F + \gamma y \tau} = \frac{G_0^*}{F}$, the absolute level of public good would go up, but not the fraction of the budget that is spent on G.

engagement.[15] The other necessary condition for taxation to be eliminated under elections is that tax bargaining is not sustainable. Section 4.7 discusses these conditions in more detail.

4.6.4 Bargaining under Elections

Now consider the subgame in which the government bargains with citizens over taxation. As before, the reservation utilities for the bargain will be those under the government's next-best alternative should the bargain fail. Without elections this was always to tax coercively and set $G = 0$ in each period. With elections the reservation utilities vary depending on whether the government prefers no taxation or coercive taxation if the bargain fails, as well as the government's choice of G in each. This, in turn, depends on the exact parameter values. Table 4.3 shows that there are three sets of reservation utilities: those for no taxation when $G_t = G_0^*$, coercive taxation when $G_t = G_\tau^*$, and coercive taxation when $G_t = 0$.

Table 4.3 Subgame outcomes under elections. The sections of the parameter space under which the government prefers no taxation or coercive taxation, along with present-discounted future payoffs for each.

Case	Parameters	Preferred Subgame	Subgame Strat	Gov Utility
1	$\dfrac{\bar{G}^*}{F+\gamma y\tau} > \dfrac{G_0^*}{F} > \delta_G$	Coercive Taxation	$G = 0$	$F + \gamma y\tau$
2	$\delta_G > \dfrac{\bar{G}^*}{F+\gamma y\tau} > \dfrac{G_0^*}{F}$ $\gamma y\tau > G_\tau^*$	Coercive Taxation	$G = \bar{G}^*$	$\dfrac{1}{1-\delta_G}(F + \gamma y\tau - \bar{G}^*)$
3	$\delta_G > \dfrac{\bar{G}^*}{F+\gamma y\tau} > \dfrac{G_0^*}{F}$ $\gamma y\tau \leq G_\tau^*$	No Taxation	$G = G_0^*$	$\dfrac{1}{1-\delta_G}(F - G_0^*)$
4	$\dfrac{G_0^*}{F} < \delta_G < \dfrac{\bar{G}^*}{F+\gamma y\tau}$ $\delta_G < \dfrac{G_0^* + \gamma y\tau}{F+\gamma y\tau}$	Coercive Taxation	$G = 0$	$F + \gamma y\tau$
5	$\dfrac{G_0^*}{F} < \delta_G < \dfrac{\bar{G}^*}{F+\gamma y\tau}$ $\delta_G \geq \dfrac{G_0^* + \gamma y\tau}{F+\gamma y\tau}$	No Taxation	$G = G_0^*$	$\dfrac{1}{1-\delta_G}(F - G_0^*)$

[15] This accords with the idea of political business cycles, which argue that governments will reduce tax enforcement around elections times (Cheibub 1998; Ross 2001; McGuirk 2010; Hyde and O'Mahony 2010). It is also in line with arguments in Olson (1993), although the mechanism suggested here is different.

For each case, I consider the conditions under which a specific grim trigger subgame-perfect Nash equilibrium (SPNE), similar to that found in the case without elections, can be upheld: provided all players have abided by the bargain in all previous rounds—meaning that citizens have complied and the government provides $G \geq \bar{G}^*$—then citizens voluntarily pay the tax and re-elect the incumbent, and the government provides $G = \bar{G}^*$. This assumes that the bargain G^B replaces $\bar{G}^*$: the citizens' reference point has been reset by the bargain, and they now only wish to punish the government if they receive less than the promised amount. This is in line with work by Fehr, Hart, and Zehnder (2011), who argue that contracts can serve as reference points, and with work that expectations play a key role in setting reference points (Abeler et al. 2011; Kőszegi and Rabin 2006).

Given these strategies, the government's best potential deviation in any period is, as before, to set $G_t = 0$; if it does this it will then lose office at the end of that round and forfeit all future rents of office. The citizens' best potential deviation is to refuse to pay the tax in some period, after which the government will revert to the next-preferred subgame—either no taxation or coercive taxation—in all future periods. Solutions for each case are presented below.

Case 1: Reservation Payoffs = No Taxation, $G_t = G_0^*$.
Consider first the case in which, absent a successful bargain, the next-best alternative for the government is to choose no taxation, set $G_t = G_0^*$ in each period, and always be re-elected (lines 3 and 5 of Table 4.3).[16] The *per-period* reservation utilities are therefore $r_G = F - G_0^*$ for the government and $r_C = y + \alpha G_0^*$ for the citizens. The Nash bargaining solution is:

$$G^B = G_0^* + y\tau \frac{1 + \alpha}{2\alpha}. \qquad (4.6)$$

In a successful bargain, citizens will receive the level of public good as they would without a bargain (G_0^*), plus fraction $\frac{\alpha+1}{2\alpha}$ of the additional revenues $y\tau$. The citizens' share will be lower when α is high; if citizens care strongly about the public good G, the government can more cheaply compensate them for their tax payments.

---

[16] That is, either ($\delta_G > \frac{\bar{G}^*}{F+\gamma y\tau} > \frac{G_0^*}{F}$ and $\gamma y\tau \leq G_\tau^*$), or ($\frac{G_0^*}{F} < \delta_G < \frac{\bar{G}^*}{F+\gamma y\tau}$ and $\delta_G \geq \frac{G_0^*+\gamma y\tau}{F+\gamma y\tau}$).

If $\alpha \leq 1$, a bargaining solution does not exist, as the government cannot increase its payoff through bargaining. If $\alpha > 1$, the grim trigger strategies described above will support bargaining only when neither player has an incentive to deviate, which holds when:

$$\delta_G \geq \frac{G^B}{F + y\tau} = \frac{G_0^* + y\tau \frac{\alpha+1}{2\alpha}}{F + y\tau} \quad \text{and} \quad \delta_C \geq \frac{2}{\alpha + 1}. \tag{4.7}$$

Note that $\delta_G > \frac{G_0^*}{F}$ is true by assumption for this case. As α increases, it becomes more likely that both citizens and government will keep the bargain; for the government this effect of α is stronger when tax revenues $y\tau$ are large to non-earned revenues F. In this section of the parameter space, if the conditions in Equation 4.7 holds, then the grim trigger strategies are optimal and the government prefers tax bargaining to the alternatives. If either of these conditions does not hold, the bargain cannot be maintained, and the government prefers no taxation with $G_t = G_0^{*}$.[17]

Case 2: Reservation Payoffs = Coercive Taxation, $G_t = 0$.
Next, consider the case, corresponding to lines 1 and 4 in Table 4.3, in which the next-best alternative for the government is to choose coercive taxation, set $G_t = 0$, and be voted out of office at the end of the first period; elections are not sufficient to ensure accountability. The necessary conditions for this case to hold are that the government does not care about the future:

$$\delta_G < \frac{G_0^*}{F} < \frac{\bar{G}^*}{F+\gamma y\tau} \quad \text{or} \quad \left(\frac{G_0^*}{F} < \delta_G < \frac{\bar{G}^*}{F+\gamma y\tau} \quad \text{and} \quad \delta_G \geq \frac{G_0^* + \gamma y\tau}{F+\gamma y\tau} \right).$$

The reservation utilities for the bargain must now be written in terms of the present-discounted expected payout over the entire subgame: $r_G = F + \gamma y\tau$ and $r_C = \frac{1}{1-\delta_C} y(1-\tau)$. Compared to Case 1, the citizens' reservation payoff is strictly lower, while the government's is higher. The bargaining solution in this case is:

$$G^B = \frac{\delta_G}{2}F + \frac{1 - \gamma(1 - \delta_G)}{2} y\tau. \tag{4.8}$$

This solution is more difficult to interpret than many of the previous cases, in part because the exact bargaining solution is affected by the degree to which the government values the future. The level of public good consists of a

---

[17] This is always true if $\alpha < 1$.

fraction of non-earned revenues F, plus a fraction of tax revenue. The bargain is better for the government when coercive taxation is relatively efficient (γ is high), but worse for the government as δ_G increases. In contrast to the first case a bargain is now feasible even if $\alpha < 1$; this is because the outside option is coercion rather than no taxation, and so the Government does not need to compensate the citizens for their entire tax payment in order to generate a feasible bargain. However, citizens are still more likely to keep the bargain when α is high. As G^B increases, the citizens become more likely to keep the bargain, and the Government less so.

If the bargain falls apart, the government will revert to coercive taxation and set $G = 0$ in all future periods. If both of the following conditions are met, the bargain can be sustained, and will always be preferred by the government in equilibrium:

$$\delta_G \geq \frac{G^B}{F + y\tau} \quad \text{and} \quad \delta_C \geq \frac{y\tau}{\alpha G^B + y\tau}. \tag{4.9}$$

If these conditions are not met, the government prefers coercive taxation to tax bargaining.

Case 3: Reservation Payoffs = Coercive Taxation, $G_t = \bar{G}$.

When the government cares sufficiently about the future ($\delta_G > \frac{\bar{G}^*}{F + \gamma y\tau}$ and $\gamma y\tau > G_\tau^*$), it prefers coercive taxation to no taxation, sets $G_t = \bar{G}^*$ in all periods and is re-elected. This corresponds to line 2 of Table 4.3. The reservation payoffs for the bargain are now $r_G = \frac{1}{1-\delta_G}(F + \gamma y\tau - \bar{G}^*)$ and $r_C = \frac{1}{1-\delta_C}(y(1 - \tau) + \alpha \bar{G}^*)$, and the bargaining solution is:

$$G^B = \bar{G}^* + \frac{1 - \gamma}{2}y\tau. \tag{4.10}$$

This case is most similar to the bargain without elections: G^B grants the citizens the level of G they would receive under coercion, plus half of new revenue generated by bargaining. The necessary conditions for this bargain to be sustained are:

$$\delta_G \geq \frac{G^B}{F + y\tau} = \frac{\bar{G}^* + \frac{1-\gamma}{2}y\tau}{F + y\tau} \quad \text{and} \quad \delta_C \geq \frac{2}{3 - \gamma}. \tag{4.11}$$

The government is therefore more likely to keep the bargain when citizens' demands are low in the absence of a bargain ($\bar{G}^*$ is low), and when γ is close to one; this last may not hold if the government has a concave utility function, and so I do not stress it here. However, as γ approaches 1, it becomes less likely that the citizens will keep the bargain, as they receive less of the bargaining surplus.

4.6.5 Equilibria of Model with Elections

Adding elections significantly increases the number of possible equilibrium outcomes. Putting together the previous sections, the parameter space can be divided into six possible equilibria; three in which bargaining cannot be sustained, plus the three corresponding tax bargaining equilibria. In two of the non-bargaining equilibria, the government cares enough about staying in power to provide a positive level of the public good: this is a strict improvement from the case without elections. However, in these cases bargaining is not sustainable given each player's discount rate relative to other parameters. In such a case the government will tax coercively if the inefficiencies of doing so are not too high; otherwise the government will choose no taxation. When the government cares less about the future, it will tax coercively and provide no public goods, unless a bargain can be struck. The six potential equilibria are described in more detail below. Figure 4.2 presents a stylized graph of these equilibria as a function of the discount rates of the citizen (δ_C) and government (δ_G). The graph is split into two sections: the left-hand graph shows the equilibria when coercive taxation is inefficient and raises less revenue than citizens demand ($\gamma y \tau < G_\tau^*$), while the one on the right graphs equilibria where the revenues raised through coercive taxation are sufficient to meet citizens' demands ($\gamma y \tau \geq G_\tau^*$).

Case 1: $\gamma y \tau < G_\tau^*$ and $\delta_G \geq \frac{G_0^* + \gamma y \tau}{F + \gamma y \tau}$.

In this case, the government cares enough about the future to provide some public goods even without a bargain but prefers no taxation to coercive taxation. It does so because the inefficiency of taxation (γ) is such that the government could spend 100% of tax revenues on G and still not meet citizens' demands. It is thus more profitable to simply not tax at all. Within this case two equilibria are possible:

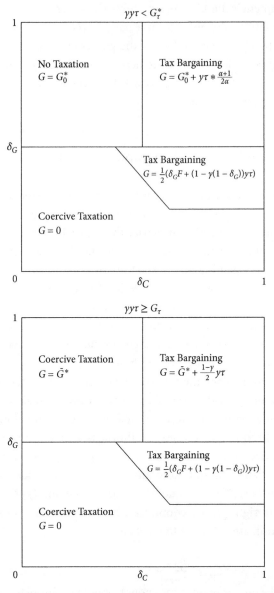

Fig. 4.2 Equilibria of the model with elections, as a function of the discount rates of the citizens (x axis) and government (y axis). Recall that as δ approaches 1, an individual values the future more heavily. The figure on the left depicts equilibria when $\gamma y\tau < G_\tau^*$, i.e. when tax revenue raised under coercion is lower than the level of the public good demanded by citizens. The figure on the right depicts the equilibria when $\gamma y\tau \geq G_\tau^*$. The precise boundaries of each equilibrium are not exact, and should not be compared to equilibria in other conditions.

Outcome 1a: No Taxation, Gov sets $G_t = G_0^*$.
This occurs when bargaining cannot be sustained, i.e. when

$$\delta_G < \frac{G_0^* + y\tau\frac{\alpha+1}{2\alpha}}{F + y\tau} \quad \text{or} \quad \delta_C < \frac{2}{\alpha+1}. \tag{4.12}$$

The government in this case sets $G_t = G_0^*$ in each period and is re-elected by the citizens.

Outcome 1b: Tax Bargaining, $G_t = G^B = G_0^* + y\tau\frac{\alpha+1}{2\alpha}$.
Here bargaining can be sustained, and the reservation utilities should a bargain fail are those of Outcome 1a. The bargain grants citizens the level of G they demand under no taxation (G_0^*), plus a fraction of tax revenues that is decreasing as citizens value the public good more. For this to be an equilibrium it must be that the Case 1 conditions hold, plus

$$\delta_G \geq \frac{G_0^* + y\tau\frac{\alpha+1}{2\alpha}}{F + y\tau} \quad \text{and} \quad \delta_C \geq \frac{2}{\alpha+1}. \tag{4.13}$$

Case 2: $\delta_G > \frac{\bar{G}^*}{F+\gamma y\tau}$ and $\gamma y\tau > G_\tau^*$.
The key difference between Cases 1 and 2 is that here $\gamma y\tau > G_\tau^*$: the government can now satisfy the citizens' accountability demands with the revenues available under coercive taxation, making it the more attractive option in the absence of a successful bargain. The government values the future enough that, it will provide $G_t = \bar{G}^*$ in order to stay in office.

Outcome 2a: Coercive Taxation, $G_t = \bar{G}^*$.
In this equilibrium, bargaining is not sustainable but the government complies with citizens' demands under coercive taxation; the government is thus able to stay in power indefinitely. Because bargaining is not feasible, it must be the case that:

$$\delta_G < \frac{\bar{G}^* + \frac{1-\gamma}{2}y\tau}{F + y\tau} \quad \text{or} \quad \delta_C < \frac{2}{3-\gamma}. \tag{4.14}$$

Outcome 2b: Bargaining, $G_t = \bar{G}^* + \frac{1-\gamma}{2}y\tau$.
The only difference from Outcome 2a is that bargaining can be sustained:

$$\delta_G \geq \frac{\bar{G}^* + \frac{1-\gamma}{2}y\tau}{F + y\tau} \quad \text{and} \quad \delta_C \geq \frac{2}{3 - \gamma}. \tag{4.15}$$

Under these conditions the government will choose to tax bargain and provide the bargaining solution of $G_B = \bar{G}^* + \frac{1-\gamma}{2}y\tau$ in each period and be re-elected.

Case 3: $\delta_G < \min\{\frac{\bar{G}^*}{F+\gamma y\tau}, \frac{G_0^* + \gamma y\tau}{F+\gamma y\tau}\}$.

In the final case, the government no longer cares enough about the future to provide any public goods without a tax bargain. As in the model with no elections, it therefore strictly prefers coercive taxation to no taxation.

Outcome 3a: Coercive Taxation, $G_t = 0$.

The government now prefers to tax coercively, extract the entire budget in the form of rents (set $G = 0$), and then lose office at the end of the period. For this to be an equilibrium, bargaining must be unsustainable:

$$\delta_G < \frac{G^B}{F + y\tau} \quad \text{or} \quad \delta_C < \frac{y\tau}{\alpha G^B + y\tau} \tag{4.16}$$

where $G^B = \frac{\delta_G}{2}F + \frac{1-\gamma(1-\delta_G)}{2}y\tau$.

Outcome 3b: Bargaining, $G_t = G^B = \frac{\delta_G}{2}F + \frac{1-\gamma(1-\delta_G)}{2}y\tau$.

This is the bargain that corresponds to Outcome 3a. To constitute an equilibrium, the "Case 3" condition outlined above must hold, and the discount rates must sustain the bargain:

$$\delta_G \geq \frac{G^B}{F + y\tau} \quad \text{and} \quad \delta_C \geq \frac{y\tau}{\alpha G^B + y\tau}. \tag{4.17}$$

In this case, the incumbent sets $G_t = G^B = \frac{\delta_G}{2}F + \frac{1-\gamma(1-\delta_G)}{2}y\tau$ and is re-elected.

4.6.6 Understanding the Equilibria

The six equilibria can be best understood in terms of their real-world counterparts. In both graphs, governments who insufficiently value the future will simply tax coercively and lose power. This is consistent with Bates (2015), which argues that governments will accept the loss of office, or even a total breakdown in order, if they do not have sufficient incentives to moderate demands and stay in power. It is also consistent with the high electoral turnover in many developing countries; corrupt governments extract for a short while then lose power, and while taxation is present, public goods provision is low.

When the government does highly value the future, but citizens do not, the equilibrium depends on whether coercive taxation generates sufficient revenues to meet citizens' demands while retaining some rents for leaders. If this is not the case, there will be no taxation but still some lower level of public goods provision. This is a common outcome in many developing countries, in which direct taxation is typically low, and key services like health care and education are severely underfunded. Yet, this low level of provision is still enough for leaders to stay in power. In such cases the government may also use limited funds to stay in power via clientelism, rather than programmatic policies. However, when taxation is less inefficient, the same parameter space can support coercive taxation with higher public goods provision. In this case there is no formal tax bargain, and so taxation can still be costly to collect, but citizens do still benefit from it. An attempt at this type of taxation is the Kampala taxi drivers discussed in Chapter 7.

When citizens highly value the future, tax bargaining becomes more likely. It is especially likely when coercive taxation is inefficient, and when citizens receive relatively high utility from public goods spending, either because they value the good or because it is efficiently produced. Chapter 7 uses taxation of market vendors in Uganda to explore how bargaining emerged during a more democratic period, resulting in less coercive taxation and more public goods for vendors.

4.7 Discussion

Starting with a few basic assumptions and a relatively simple model, we now have the full set of possible equilibria with and without elections. Without elections, only two equilibria were possible: coercive taxation or tax bargaining. When citizens and government both cared sufficiently about the future, tax bargaining was sustainable and the government provided some level of public goods; otherwise the government taxed coercively and provided no public goods. Once elections are introduced, a wider range of outcomes are possible, depending on each player's discount rate and the other parameters of the model. In general, tax bargaining is possible when players care sufficiently about the future, but the precise nature of the bargain varies depending on the other parameters. If bargaining is not possible, coercive taxation is the most likely alternative, but if the government cares enough about the future, it may still provide citizens' preferred level of public goods in each period. If, however, citizens' demands are too high relative to the level of revenues raised, the government will choose to not tax at all.

The model produces a number of testable implications. The rest of this chapter focuses on three of these. The first two are tested empirically in Chapter 6. These implications provide insight into why, and when, governments may underinvest in fiscal capacity in order to reduce citizens' demands, and when taxation will lead to lower rent-seeking. The final implication, regarding when governments will tax coercively as opposed to engaging in tax bargaining, is examined using the case studies in Chapter 7.

4.7.1 When Will Governments Support Taxation?

One key contribution of the model is that it sheds new light on when democracy will lead to higher taxation. As discussed in Chapter 2, theories built on the idea of the median voter typically assume that democracies will tax significantly more than autocracies as the income of the median member of the selectorate is significantly poorer under democracy (Meltzer and Richard 1981). In extreme versions of the argument, taxation should be zero under autocracies and 100% under democracy (Meltzer and Richard 1981; Acemoglu and Robinson 2006). Early tax bargaining theories likewise argue that democracy will increase tax bargaining, as elections allow citizens to enact larger punishments on leaders who defect, compared to the case where they can only punish leaders through non-compliance (Bates 1981; North and Weingast 1989). However, other work has suggested that democracy could in fact decrease taxation. Olson (1965) argues that democracy may lead rulers to limit their extraction; this is consistent with Bates (2015)'s argument that rulers with long time horizons will accept lower short-term rents if it increases their duration in office. Supporting these arguments, Kasara (2007) finds that democratic African countries tax agriculture less than autocracies. And Bastiaens and Rudra (2018) argues that democracies will be less able than autocracies to replace tax revenue lost during the process of globalization and trade tax reduction. However, cross-national evidence on whether democracies generally tax more than autocracies is mixed (Easterly and Rebelo 1993; Bird, Martinez-Vazquez, and Torgler 2008; Profeta, Puglisi, and Scabrosetti 2013; Mulligan, Gil, and Sala-i Martin 2004; Boix 2001; Fauvelle-Aymar 1999; Thies 2005).

How can we reconcile these two perspectives? A key contribution of this model is that it provides a framework for understanding how democratization can impact taxation. While democracy can increase both taxation and accountability, it can also lead governments to decrease taxation in order to avoid accountability pressures. By examining when different equilibria of the model are more likely, we can get more traction on when democracies will tax more, or less, than autocracies. Below I discuss the conditions under which democracies will be more or less likely to tax, and how these conditions suggest the model's first implication: that when state capacity is low, and citizens are poor, democracies may be less likely to tax than autocracies. When state capacity is high, democracy will be associated with higher taxation.

Democracy will lead to the elimination of inefficient coercive taxes.
First, the model demonstrates how competitive elections can actually decrease the government's willingness to tax. Without elections, the government always preferred to tax coercively in the absence of a tax bargain. However, once elections are added, there is a segment of the parameter space where the government prefers no taxation to coercive taxation. The no taxation equilibrium requires that $G_\tau^* > \gamma y \tau$: citizens must demand higher public goods provision (G_τ^*) than the government can provide given actual tax revenue $\gamma y \tau$. This in turn could occur because coercive taxation raises little revenue compared to the costs of collection (γ is close to zero), or because citizens' demands are high, perhaps because they care strongly about corruption or place a high value on public goods. It is also more likely to hold if, as argued here, taxation increases citizens' demands on the government: as $\frac{G_\tau^*}{F+y\tau}$ increases relative to $\frac{G_0^*}{F}$, this equilibrium becomes more likely.

Democracy has ambiguous effects on bargaining.
Bargains can only be maintained provided citizens' and leaders' discount rates δ_C and δ_G are sufficiently high. Because elections affect the conditions on δ_G and δ_C, they therefore affect the likelihood that bargaining can be sustained. While it is true that elections can increase the range of discount rates

under which bargaining is feasible (and thus increase the likelihood of tax bargaining), elections can also reduce the area of the parameter space under which bargaining can be maintained. This is contrary to previous work on tax bargaining, which sees institutional concessions in the form of elections as a way to increase the probability of a successful bargain, by increasing the punishments that citizens can enact on leaders who break the bargain.

Consider the condition necessary for citizens to voluntarily pay taxes, and for government to provide the agreed-upon level of public goods, G^B, under a bargain. Without elections, citizens keep the bargain if $\delta_C \geq \dfrac{2}{2+\alpha(1-\gamma)}$; if they break the bargain, they know that the incumbent will revert to coercive taxation and set $G = 0$. Now assume that $G_\tau^* > \gamma y \tau$ and δ_G is sufficiently high. With elections, the citizens will keep the bargain if $\dfrac{2}{\alpha+1}$. If $\alpha > \dfrac{1}{\gamma}$, elections increases the range of δ_C for which citizens keep the bargain. However, if this does not hold, citizens are *less* likely to keep the bargain. Depending on the relation between α and γ, elections could either increase or decrease the ability of citizens to credibly commit to quasi-voluntary compliance under bargaining.

The intuition for this finding is as follows. Elections improve the quality of the bargain citizens receive, and this should make them more likely to keep the bargain. However, elections can also change citizens' outside option should the bargain fall apart: when δ_G is sufficiently high, the government now provides public goods even in the absence of a bargain. In the case described in the previous paragraph, the citizens receive some public goods ($G > 0$) without paying taxes. This makes the consequences of breaking the bargain less severe. Depending on which effect predominates, elections can then make tax bargaining more or less sustainable.

This effect is driven by a key difference between tax bargaining in developing countries today, and the examples found in European state development. In those examples, taxation and democratization occur together, and so the outside option for citizens who break the bargain is not "Democracy and no taxation" but a return to "No democracy"—possibly with coercive taxation. The fact that democratization is largely decoupled from explicit tax bargaining in sub-Saharan African countries creates the possibility that elections could hurt the chances of a successful bargain taking place, unless citizens are sufficiently forward-looking.

The effects of elections on the ability of the government to credibly commit to a tax bargain can likewise go either way. If the citizens have relatively moderate demands (i.e. G_0^* and $\bar{G}^*$ are low as a fraction of government revenues), and if α is high, it is more likely that elections will increase the likelihood that the government will keep the bargain. If, however, taxation drastically increases citizens' demands, it may be the case that bargaining will be difficult to sustain.

Democracy will decrease taxation in low-capacity states.
What this implies is that democratization could lead either to higher or lower overall taxation. It will tend to eliminate inefficient coercive taxes. It may increase tax bargaining if public goods are highly valued and efficiently produced, but decrease it otherwise. This suggests that higher-capacity states may be more likely to increase taxation when they democratize: these are the states in which the government's ability to enforce coercive taxation, and efficiently provide public goods, are likely to be high. In low-capacity states, we should expect smaller gains from democratization, or even a decrease in taxation. Thus, the model derives a new explanation for why modern developing countries fail to tax: doing so will lead to higher accountability demands, and low-capacity states will be unable to satisfy these demands with the revenues raised.

4.7.2 Taxation's Effect on Rent-Seeking

The second implication of the model is that taxation will be, on average, associated with lower government rent-seeking. Both in autocracies and democracies, taxation allows citizens to extract higher public goods provision from governments. In autocracies, this occurs solely through tax bargaining. In democracies, taxation can also improve accountability in the absence of a bargain. This occurs because taxation increases citizens' demands on governments, leading to increased concessions provided governments have (1) sufficiently long time horizons, and thus value staying in office, and (2) taxation produces sufficient revenues to fund citizens' desired public goods provision.

What is less clear is whether taxation should have a larger effect on rent-seeking in autocracies or democracies. In all three bargaining equilibria defined above in the elections model, citizens receive a fraction of the bargaining surplus that is either the same as or larger than that without elections. In the autocratic model, the fraction of revenues citizens extract in the bargain is $\frac{1-\gamma}{2}$. In the democratic model, if the equilibrium without bargaining is no taxation with $G = G_0^*$, citizens get fraction $\frac{\alpha+1}{2\alpha}$ in the bargain. Provided $\alpha > 1$, which is a necessary condition for the bargain to hold, citizens get a strictly higher fraction of tax revenues in the form of public goods under democracy. If the democratic equilibrium without bargaining is coercion with $G = \bar{G}^*$, citizens get the same fraction of additional revenue in the autocratic and democratic bargains. Where the democratic equilibrium without bargaining is coercion with $G = 0$ (which is the case that most closely resembles the autocratic case), citizens are not only able to extract a strictly higher fraction of tax revenues through bargaining, they also are able to extract a positive fraction of additional revenues F. Thus, democracy is likely to have a positive impact on the quality of bargains citizens extract from the government.

However, democracy also generally leads to higher levels of government spending even in the absence of taxation: in the no taxation equilibrium, the government still provides citizens with some level of public goods. In contrast, in autocracies no public goods are ever provided unless a tax bargain exists. Thus, the overall direction of the effect is unclear: democracy decreases rent-seeking in both tax and non-tax equilibria. However, on average, I still expect that the effect of taxation will be stronger in democracies than autocracies.

4.7.3 Bargaining and Coercion

Finally, the model provides insight into when coercive taxation, as opposed to tax bargaining, is likely to emerge. The model shows that bargaining is more likely to hold when citizens receive higher utility from each dollar spent on the public good; this corresponds to a high value of α in the model. This could be because the public good is highly valued, or because production is relatively efficient. Thus, we should expect citizens to support taxation more when it funds valued public goods. If there is declining marginal utility from each good, it may also be that citizens will place more support on increasing goods that are currently under-provided. Likewise, tax bargaining is more attractive to the government when public goods are more efficient to produce. This occurs because it is easier to meet citizens' demands in a tax bargain and still have revenue left over that government can extract as rents.

4.8 Extensions

By necessity, the model makes a number of simplifications. Two of the most serious of these are that the ability of citizens to remove the leader is non-existent in autocracies, and that government capacity is exogenous, unaffected by government behavior. This section discusses how relaxing these assumptions might affect the model's predictions.

First, consider the survival incentives of leaders. The core model considers the two extreme cases of a government that cannot be removed by the citizens, and one in which the citizens are perfectly efficacious and can always remove the leader from office when they so desire. In reality, of course, autocrats can be forced out of power by coups or protests. Even the fairest elections require a strong, united opposition to unseat an incumbent, and in many countries elections are far from free and fair. This suggests an alternative model in which there is an additional parameter, namely the probability that upset citizens can remove the incumbent. Unfortunately, this added complication makes the model intractable. Rather than model it formally, I think about the model as emphasizing the two extreme cases. More nuanced versions of electoral (or non-electoral) accountability would produce results that are somewhere in between the two models, without fundamentally changing the theory's predictions.

Second, consider the role of government capacity. In the model, capacity can best be understood as affecting γ, a government's ability to collect taxes efficiently when compliance is not voluntary. Governments could, in theory, use part of current revenues in a one-time investment that increases γ in all future periods. Governments should only be willing to make this investment if the future anticipated increase in rents pays for the up-front cost. Thus, governments with long time horizons will be most likely to make this investment. The comparative statics of the model suggest that investments in state capacity may lead to an increase in coercive taxation. This occurs for two reasons. First, in both regime types, increased capacity reduces the potential gains from bargaining for both citizens and government, as coercive taxation is now more efficient. In extreme cases, increased capacity could switch from an equilibrium in which public goods are provided under a bargain, to one in which taxation is coercive and no public goods are provided. This is particularly likely in the autocratic case; in the democratic case any government that values the future enough to invest in state capacity will also likely care enough about staying in office long-term to provide citizens with their desired level of public goods spending. In democracies, higher capacity could also lead to more coercive taxation if it increases efficiency enough that a government now gets sufficient revenue from a tax to provide citizens' desired public goods. This could effectively shift government preferences from no taxation to coercive taxation with public goods provision.

In general, then, we should expect an increase in state capacity to lead to more coercive taxation. This could, however, be offset if increasing state capacity also makes public goods provision more efficient, effectively increasing α, the value citizens gets from a dollar spent on public goods. If this is the case, then the gains from tax bargaining will increase (as citizens will be satisfied with a smaller amount of the pie, more rents remain for the government). However, recent studies of state capacity suggest only modest positive spillovers of tax capacity on other areas of the government (Fjeldstad and Moore 2009).

4.9 Conclusion

This chapter introduced a model examining when, and how, a government may decide to tax a particular group of citizens. Governments will only tax when doing so increases their ability to maximize long-term access to rents, conditional on the extent to which they value the future. When additional revenues must instead fund public goods, or threaten leader survival, it becomes more likely that the government will choose not to tax. The model produces several novel findings. It suggests that governments may deliberately under-invest in taxation and public goods provision in order to minimize citizens' demands, and that taxation can improve accountability even in the absence of a formal tax bargain. In contrast to many political economy models, it shows that democratization can actually reduce taxation when states are weak. Finally, it derives a set of conditions for when taxation is likely to improve accountability.

In the next chapter, I test the predictions of Chapter 3, showing that taxed citizens do indeed place higher demands on leaders than non-taxed citizens. This provides support for the microfoundations of the model developed in this chapter. Chapter 6 then tests the two main implications of this chapter's theory using cross-national data. Finally, in Chapter 7 I provide case study evidence on all three of the model's implications, including when bargaining is likely to emerge.

5
Evidence that Taxation Increases Accountability Demands

5.1 Introduction

The previous two chapters detailed a theory of how taxation could affect the accountability demands citizens make of their governments, and how this could affect government decisions of when and how to tax. This chapter is the first of three testing different implications of the theory. In this chapter, I test the most critical micro-level prediction: that taxation will increase the demands citizens make of government officials. If true, this means that leaders who wish to avoid electoral losses or costly protests must either eliminate contentious taxes or provide citizens with their desired policies. I also examine the types of taxes for which this is most likely: as discussed in Chapter 3, there are theoretical reasons to expect taxes to have a larger effect when they are more visible and salient. This suggests that direct taxes should have larger effects on accountability demands than indirect taxes.

However, there is little prior evidence on whether, or why, taxation affects citizen behavior. At the time this project started, Paler (2013) provided the only known test of the loss-aversion hypothesis; while that paper finds that taxation increases citizens' sense of ownership and willingness to monitor, it does not find direct evidence that taxation increases punishment. More recently, Weigel (2020) finds using a field experiment in the Democratic Republic of Congo that enforcing property taxes for the first time leads to higher citizen engagement among all citizens in treatment areas, not only those who pay taxes—this suggests that the experiment is increasing action through multiple or different mechanisms, not the actual payment of taxes. De la Cuesta et al. (2019) finds using survey experiments in Ghana and Uganda that there is no difference in citizen action between taxes, aid, and oil, although those experiments relied on revenue primes rather than having citizens actually pay taxes. De la Cuesta et al. (2022), on which I am an

Strategic Taxation: Fiscal Capacity and Accountability in African States. Lucy E. S. Martin.
Oxford University Press. © Oxford University Press 2023. DOI: 10.1093/oso/9780197672631.003.0005

author, shows that taxation can increase citizens' accountability demands, and uses lab experiments based on the ones presented in this chapter.

This chapter uses lab experiments in Uganda and Ghana to test how taxation affects citizens' willingness to punish leaders, and to provide detailed evidence on the precise mechanism. I show that taxation increases citizens' willingness to punish low transfers from leaders, that loss aversion is a key mechanism behind these findings, and that citizens do receive expressive benefits from punishment. I also show that the main findings are robust across multiple experiments and contexts, including where punishment is uncertain. I then address issues of external validity by using individual-level data from the Afrobarometer to examine correlations between paying taxes and a number of other outcomes, including the likelihood of engaging in political behavior like voting, and satisfaction with government policy. Together, this evidence provides support for the idea that taxation increases political engagement and leads citizens to be less satisfied with a particular level of government performance.

5.2 An Experimental Approach

Testing how taxation affects citizen behavior is not trivial. Taxation is rarely assigned at random, and existing observational data makes it difficult to clearly test mechanisms. The field of behavioral economics suggests one possible answer to this issue: laboratory experiments. Laboratory experiments typically use a controlled environment to isolate specific areas of human behavior. By creating more simplified models of human interaction, we can understand how altering key factors changes behavior.

Many of the assumptions used in formulating the loss-aversion theory of taxation originally came out of laboratory experiments in psychology and behavioral economics. From previous lab experiments, we know that individuals are willing to take costly actions to impose sanctions on fellow players in varied settings and cultures, even when it is costly to do so (Henrich et al. 2006). We also know that individuals punish in part to relieve negative emotions induced by norms violations; Fehr and Gächter (2000) shows that these negative emotions are higher for more serious deviations. Models of reference-dependent utility and loss aversion were introduced in 1979 by Kahneman and Tversky, and numerous studies have confirmed that most individuals do indeed feel losses more keenly than gains, even in riskless choice (Tversky and Kahneman 1991). As discussed in Chapter 3, while recent work suggests loss aversion is not universal, the conditions under which loss aversion is most likely are met for taxation (Gal and Rucker 2018; Yechiam 2019).

More recently, there has been a move towards what are known as "lab-in-the-field" experiments. While many early experiments were conducted on American undergraduates in a university lab setting, scholars of comparative politics are increasingly conducting experiments in the communities being studied. Given existing evidence that there are often cultural differences in how individuals behave in laboratory experiments, using subjects from the societies of interest helps to ensure that we are capturing the relevant attitudes (Henrich et al. 2006). Recent work in political science has also demonstrated that laboratory experiments can be used to measure political preferences (see e.g. Habyarimana et al. 2009; Grossman 2014; Blair and Roessler 2021).

While a lab setting provides a way to randomly vary whether an individual pays taxes, it also helps to isolate the specific reasons individuals act in a certain way. Previous research suggests that a number of psychological mechanisms drive the willingness to punish others. For example, Fehr and Schmidt (1999) shows that punishment is due in part to inequity aversion; individuals often punish if they believe someone is unfairly keeping more than their fair share of a common resource. By holding inequity aversion constant across different versions of the lab experiment, I can ensure that this is not driving any differences between taxed and non-taxed citizens.

While laboratory experiments can help isolate the effects of particular factors, and the mechanisms driving these effects, they are by design relatively abstract in nature. For this reason, in Section 5.8 I test the external validity of the experiments using observational data from 31 African countries.

5.2.1 Experimental Design

To test how taxation affects behavior, I designed a set of experiments to mimic interactions between citizens and leaders. The main experiment consisted of two games, called the "Tax" and "Grant" games. Each is played between two individuals: one "Citizen" and one "Leader." For enumeration, both of these roles were played by ordinary citizens who were randomly assigned to a role. Both games have the same basic structure. The Leader is given a budget, called the "group fund," that he must divide between himself and the Citizen. If the Citizen is not satisfied with this allocation, she can decide to pay a small cost to to punish the Leader. If punishment occurs, the Leader loses a set amount of money; this money is not given to the Citizen, it simply disappears from the game economy. The cost that the Citizen pays represents the fact that political action is typically costly for citizens, while the fine that the Leader pays if punished represents the fact that for a rent-seeking official, losing office or otherwise being sanctioned typically involves the loss of some economic resources.

The only difference between the Tax and Grant games is how the group fund is generated. In the Tax game, the Citizen is given a wage of ten "money units" (10 MU). Half of that money (5 MU) is then taken as a tax; this tax is doubled (to 10 MU), and given to the Leader as the group fund. In the Grant game, the Citizen receives a wage of 5 MU. They do not pay a tax, and 10 MU is then given to the Leader as a non-earned group fund. Thus, in the Grant game, the group fund is similar to foreign aid, oil revenues, central transfers, or any other type of funding that does not rely on taxation. The decision to call the Leader's 10 MU the "group fund" was made in order to eliminate the possibility that, in the Grant game, the Citizen would think that he had no right to the Leader's money. The stages of each game are summarized in Table 5.1.

The Tax and Grant games are designed in such a way that the two games are structurally identical at the time that each player makes a decision. When the Leader makes his allocation decision the Citizen has 5 MU and the Leader has 10 MU. In both games, if the Citizen decides to punish the Leader, he pays 1 MU and 4 MU is removed from the Leader. Any differences in gameplay between the Tax and Grant games must therefore be due to the fact that, in the Tax game, the group fund is derived from a tax on the Citizen.

Table 5.1 Timing of Tax and Grant games.

Stages	Tax Game	Grant Game
1.	Citizen is given a wage of 10 MU.	Citizen is given a wage of 5 MU.
2.	Citizen is taxed 5 MU—this is doubled to 10 MU and given to Leader as the group fund.	Leader is given 10 MU as the group fund.
3.	Leader allocates the 10 MU between himself and Citizen.	
4.	Citizen observes Leader's decision and decides whether to pay 1 MU to have enumerators remove 4 MU from Leader.	

A key feature of the game is that the Citizen and Leader only interact for a single period. If the Citizen decides to punish the Leader, she therefore pays an economic cost but does not receive any immediate monetary benefit in return, nor can she hope for improved economic performance in future periods. This implies that if the Citizen is purely economically rational, she should never punish; in this case the unique subgame-perfect Nash equilibrium of both the Tax and Grant games is for the Leader to offer 0 MU to the Citizen, who never punishes. If we still observe Citizens punishing, it must therefore be that they receive some sort of non-economic, expressive benefit from doing so.[1]

The experiments were also designed to separate the proposed loss-aversion mechanism from other potential effects of taxation. To eliminate the possibility of tax bargaining, the tax rate in the experiments is exogenously set at 50%, and taxation is coercive. This means that citizens cannot use the threat of non-compliance to force leaders to be accountable. To avoid the possibility that taxation conveys information about the size of the budget, the government's budget is held constant across treatments and is observed by citizens; there is no uncertainty. To prevent citizens from using punishment as a signal to leaders in future rounds, the experiments are single-shot interactions. Finally, citizens face no uncertainty about or barriers to punishment; they make an ex ante decision rule regarding punishment which is always enforced.

The 50% tax rate in the game may seem high. However, as this was the first experimental test of taxation's effect on punishment, it was necessary to have a strong treatment that maximized the probability of activating the relevant mechanisms. It is also not too far afield from actual taxes that have existed in Uganda. For example, consumption taxes on some goods approach 40–50%.[2] As described more in Chapter 2, colonial taxes were often equivalent to 50% of cash incomes.

5.2.2 Implementation

I conducted the first Tax and Grant experiments in Uganda in 2012. At the time Uganda collected just under 13% of GDP in taxes, and a substantial

---

[1] Below I provide explicit evidence for expressive benefits.

[2] Cell phones are subject to 18% VAT, plus 25% import tax. Airtime for those same phones includes 18% VAT and a 12% excise tax. Historically, many individuals also paid direct taxes like the graduated tax and property tax.

portion of the national budget came from foreign aid (Government of Uganda (2014)). This makes it a good setting to compare the accountability pressures from different types of funding.[3] In 2021 Uganda ranked 144 of 180 countries on Transparency International's corruption index, and even basic public services are often difficult to obtain. Yet, there is often little concrete outrage about poor governance. This makes it a natural place to study whether taxation affects accountability. Conducting the experiments in Uganda, as opposed to in the United States, also increases the findings' external validity, as cultural differences can have large effects on how individuals behave in such games (Henrich et al. 2006).

Within Uganda, the experiments were conducted in Kampala, Uganda, in three low-income neighborhoods that are primarily composed of the Bagandan ethnic group. Compared to the rest of the country, residents of Kampala are more likely to pay taxes than those in rural areas. Kampala has also seen significant political mobilization in recent years, including around taxation. Both of these factors make Kampala an ideal location. Because taxation is salient for citizens, it is more likely that the experiment would activate respondents' relevant norms and expectations surrounding taxation. It also makes the games less abstract, because respondents can connect the structure of the game to their own experiences.

The experiments were run in sessions of approximately 20 respondents each; there were 18 sessions total, which generated 371 respondents. For each session, mobilizers recruited volunteers from neighborhoods surrounding each enumeration site. To avoid potential respondents learning about the games in advance, a different neighborhood was targeted each day. While respondent selection was not random, mobilizers were instructed to recruit from a range of ages and genders. Respondents in each session played both the Tax and Grant games, but which game was played first was randomly assigned. For the main analysis, I only use the first game played to avoid the influence of ordering effects. Upon arrival at the enumeration site, respondents were randomly assigned an ID number; this was used to randomly assign respondents to be either Citizens or Leaders, and to determine who played against whom in each round of each game.

The final sample was 72% male. While the average age was 22.6 years, a significant portion, 40%, was age 18 or 19. As 70% of Ugandans were

---

[3] Uganda discovered oil in 2006. While extraction has not yet started, the government has received significant revenues from oil concessions.

under the age of 25 at this time, this does not make the sample unrepresentative (*The C.I.A. World Factbook* 2014). About 40% of participants reported zero earnings over the previous four weeks; these individuals were unemployed, students, or homemakers. Among wage-earners, the median monthly income was 110,000 UGX (US$45).[4] Balance tests confirm that the samples for the Tax and Grant games are well balanced on observable characteristics.

At the start of the session, an enumerator introduced the first game (Tax or Grant) to the respondents as a group, explaining the rules verbally and then going through set examples that used pictures to demonstrate the steps of the game. Respondents then met individually with enumerators, who then went over another example that used real coins, asking questions to gauge comprehension.[5] Each respondent was then told whether he was a Citizen or Leader and played the same single-shot game (either Tax or Grant) five times: each interaction is referred to here as a round. For each round, respondents who were Citizens (Leaders) knew that they had been randomly paired with a Leader (Citizen), but did not know which other respondents had which roles, or against whom they were playing. Respondents had a different partner in each round, and enumerators repeatedly stressed the single-shot nature of each round. In rounds 2–5 respondents were told the results and payoffs from their own previous pairing, but not how any other pairings had behaved. This allowed respondents to learn while minimizing their ability to signal their preferences to the entire group.

To increase statistical power, only 20% of the sample was assigned to be Leaders, and each Leader was matched with four Citizens in a given round of the game.[6] For enumeration, 1 MU was set to 100 Ugandan Shillings (UGX). This meant that the group fund was 1,000 UGX, or about US$0.40 at 2012 exchange rates. Respondents were paid 3,000 UGX for their participation, plus their earnings from one randomly selected round of each game.[7]

Above, the game was described in terms of the Leader making an allocation decision, and then the Citizen viewing that decision and deciding whether to punish. To increase statistical power enumerators used an alternative method to get the Citizens' strategy: each Citizen was asked what they

---

[4] All conversions from Ugandan shillings to US dollars are based on contemporaneous exchange rates.

[5] All examples used the same values, altering only the funding source.

[6] To calculate Leader payouts, one of the four matched Citizens was randomly chosen. This meant that all decisions were potentially payoff-relevant.

[7] The average payout was 4,575 UGX (US$1.83); sessions lasted approximately three hours.

would do for every possible decision the Leader could have made.[8] From this the outcome variable was constructed: the threshold below which the Citizen would be willing to pay to punish the Leader. For example, if a Citizen would punish if the Leader passed back 300 UGX or less, the punishment threshold is 400 UGX; this is equivalent to both the punishment threshold described in Chapter 3, and G^* in the model in Chapter 4. The loss-aversion theory developed in Chapter 3 predicts that taxed citizens will have higher thresholds.

5.3 Results: Tax and Grant Games

In both the Tax and Grant games, the key outcome for each round is the Citizens' "punishment threshold," defined as the smallest transfer the Leader can send the Citizen to avoid punishment. Because the group fund was given as ten 100-shilling coins, this threshold could take on any of the eleven 100-UGX increments between 0 and 1,000 UGX. Each Citizen played the same treatment five times, and punishment thresholds typically evolved across the rounds—the average punishment thresholds by treatment, by round are shown in Figure 5.1. While the average punishment threshold in the Tax treatment is consistently higher than in the Grant treatment, punishment thresholds in both treatments change over time.

Qualitative interviews with respondents suggest that in many cases thresholds evolved because respondents were learning their true preferences: some initially decided not to punish low transfers, but after receiving little they regretted not punishing and increased their thresholds. In other cases respondents set high thresholds but then decided that they did not in fact feel better after punishing and lowered them. To allow for changes in strategy, I analyze the five-round average of each Citizen's punishment threshold.

If taxation makes citizens more likely to punish leaders, then the average punishment threshold for citizens should be higher in the Tax game than the Grant game. Here I focus the analysis on Citizens; Leader decisions are discussed further below.

Figure 5.2 shows the distribution of Citizens' punishment thresholds in each treatment, in Ugandan shillings (UGX); the vertical lines show the

---

[8] Enumerators stopped once they reached a sufficiently high allocation such that the Citizen would no longer punish the Leader; this reduced fatigue among respondents.

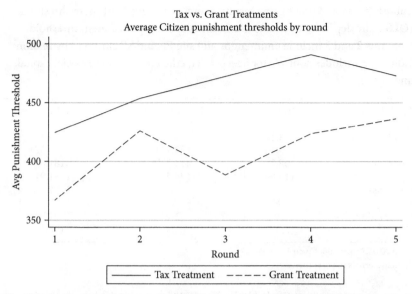

Fig. 5.1 Average punishment thresholds in each round, shown by treatment status.

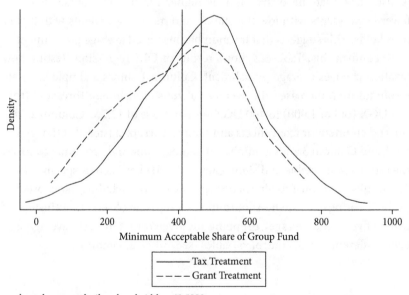

kernel = epanechnikov, bandwidth = 48.5999

Fig. 5.2 Tax vs. Grant treatments: distribution of average Citizen punishment thresholds, with group means.

Table 5.2 Tax and grant game results: average citizen punishment threshold (OLS). The dependent variable is a Citizen's average punishment threshold. Columns 2 and 3 include enumerator and site FE and SE clustered by session; Column 3 includes controls for age, gender, education, income, social capital, and voting.

VARIABLES	Bivariate	Fixed Effects	FE and Controls
Taxation	54.18***	54.25**	56.37**
	(19.10)	(22.44)	(21.52)
Constant	408.3***	413.2***	181.8
	(13.86)	(24.32)	(181.9)
Controls	N	N	Y
FE	N	Y	Y
Observations	296	296	272
R^2	0.027	0.089	0.142

*** $p<0.01$, ** $p<0.05$, * $p<0.1$
Standard errors in parentheses

means for each group. For both the Tax and Grant games, there is significant variation in willingness to punish, consistent with the idea that different individuals have different underlying willingness to punish. However, it is also clear that the distribution is higher for the Tax game: there are fewer respondents with low thresholds, and more respondents with higher thresholds. This suggests that taxation has increased average punishment.

To confirm this, Table 5.2 shows results of OLS regressions testing how taxation changes average punishment. Column 1 shows a simple bivariate result: taxation increased the average Citizen's punishment threshold from 408 UGX (out of 1,000) to 460 UGX—an increase of 12.7%. Column 2 adds site and enumerator fixed effects and standard errors clustered at the session level, and Column 3 adds a number of demographic and economic controls; the estimates are stable and significant at the 5% level across specifications. The results are robust to alternative specifications, including using ordered probit, treating each single-shot round as a separate observation (instead of using a five-round average), dropping any given round from the average, and using different sets of control variables (see online appendix).

5.3.1 Qualitative Evidence

On paper, the lab experiments look very abstract: there are a few short steps, and respondents make decisions that seem far removed from actual taxation. The reality looks quite different. In each enumeration session, respondents first see a group presentation that goes over the game. This helps citizens understand the basic rules of the activity. They then meet one on one with enumerators. All one-on-one enumeration is done using game boards where respondents move around real coins. This helps to make the tasks concrete: Citizens physically hold their wage, and (if taxed) see the enumerator take away the money. They also see the different ways the money could be spent, and (in rounds 2–5), see exactly what happened in previous rounds and get a chance to see how they feel emotionally as a result of the interactions. This all helps make the actual decisions very concrete.

Respondents' own experiences also help to make the game a realistic proxy for government interactions. In Round 6 of Afrobarometer in Uganda, 67% of urban respondents reported attending a community meeting; 50.7% reported they had "joined others in your community to request action from government," and the same percentage had contacted either a government official or the media in the past year. This suggests that many respondents have real-world experiences they can draw on in the lab setting. One way to think about the lab experiments is as a structured focus group: respondents have their own experiences interacting with government officials, and the experimental protocols are designed to simulate these types of activities.

One way to evaluate whether the lab experiments succeeded is therefore to examine whether citizens did in fact draw on these experiences when making their decisions. In a subset of sessions in the Uganda experiments, enumerators asked Citizens to explain their in-game decisions (N = 80). These data were coded, and provide compelling evidence that the treatments activated relevant political experiences. Thirty-six percent of Citizens listed distributive or fairness concerns when justifying their in-game choices, often citing the differing expectations on citizens and leaders in their answers. A number of these respondents also specifically cited the tax as a reason for demanding high transfers. One respondent said that "As a citizen, since my money was taken as a tax, I want to earn more than the leader." Others made similar replies, explaining that "because it's tax money [the leader] has to give back more"; "They took away 500 Sh from him so he at least expects it back"; and "Since it was tax money multiplied, he has to give me some little money."

An additional 24% of respondents cited opinions about real political leaders as justification for their decisions.[9] One respondent in the Tax treatment justified high demands by stating that "[the leader] has to give

---

[9] The remaining respondents justified their actions using economic motivations (16%), or stated other reasons such as "because that is what would solve my problem."

me more because he gets money from different sources." This statement—echoed by several other respondents—was especially interesting as the leaders in this case were actually fellow Ugandan citizens who did not have other ways of getting money. Respondents in the Grant game, in contrast, justified low demands in terms of political leaders' responsibilities. One respondent explained that "Leaders should even take more [than citizens] because they do a lot," and another replied that "I have been asking for little money every time because the leader has many responsibilities to take care of." In fact, these "leaders" had no responsibilities and were simply fellow community members.

Together, these responses strongly suggest that participants seriously considered their responses in the games, structuring their behavior in reference to how they might behave in actual political scenarios and the norms involved in citizen-leader interactions. Below I introduce additional survey and laboratory experiments, as well as observational data, to test the external validity of the lab findings more concretely.

5.4 Testing the Mechanism

The results thus far demonstrate that taxation makes citizens more willing to punish leaders for non-accountable behavior. However, it is also important to pin down the exact mechanism behind this effect. This section uses additional results from the Tax and Grant games, combined with evidence from two other experiments, to rule out alternative mechanisms and provide support for the loss-aversion mechanism. Chapter 3 discussed several alternatives to the proposed loss-aversion mechanism, including the possibility that taxation activates a stricter fairness norm. Note that the loss-aversion mechanism can still hold if citizens punish in part because of fairness, provided fairness does not differ across the two treatment groups. Understanding the precise mechanism is not simply an academic exercise: differentiating between loss aversion and fairness norms has important policy implications. The fairness-norms mechanism suggests that public education might be able to create similar norms surrounding foreign aid or resource rents, potentially alleviating the resource curse and increasing the demand for accountability in affected countries. If the loss-aversion mechanism is correct, however, it suggests that such campaigns are less likely to be successful: citizens must be given a stake in government budgets for accountability demands to increase.

5.4.1 Treatment Heterogeneity

Two additional results from the tax and grant games support the loss-aversion mechanism. First, in each session, respondents played both the Tax and Grant games, randomizing the order of which came first. The analysis above only uses the first game's results, due to strong ordering effects. Among those respondents who played first the Tax and then the Grant game, the average punishment thresholds between the two games were virtually identical; the punishment threshold is only 2 UGX higher in the Tax game (p=.82). However, when moving from the Grant to the Tax game, Citizens' punishment thresholds increased by an average of 31 UGX (p=.03). This suggests that, once taxation pushes citizens into the realm of losses, the effects persisted into subsequent rounds of the Grant game; this kept punishment thresholds high. However, moving from the Grant to the Tax game does change expectations, leading to a strong effect—taxation has again shifted Citizens into the realm of losses, increasing punishment thresholds. This provides suggestive evidence for the theory that the behavioral effect of taxation depends on loss aversion, rather than on more generalized societal fairness norms.

Second, the loss-aversion theory argued that individuals should vary in their underlying willingness to take political action. The theory predicted that the size of taxation's effect on punishment should vary according to this underlying propensity: it should at first increase as the propensity for punishment increases, then decrease over most of the parameter space. This implication is not generated by either the fairness-norms mechanism, or an alternative reference-dependent model in which citizen utility is globally concave; both predict a monotonically decreasing effect of taxation as propensity to punish increases.

To test this prediction, I ran quantile regressions on the Tax and Grant game data. While typical OLS regressions test differences in the *mean* values for a variable across treatments, quantile regressions test for differences at a particular point in the distribution. So, for example, I can test whether the 25th percentile of the Tax and Grant games are different; or the median, or the 95th percentile. This allows me to estimate how taxation affects punishment at different points in the distribution of responses.

There are two necessary assumptions for this analysis to hold. First, the distribution of the propensity to punish must be balanced across Citizens in the Tax and Grant games. This assumption is reasonable due to random assignment of the treatment. Second, if one citizen has a higher propensity for civic engagement than another, that individual's punishment threshold should also be higher. This means that a respondent's average punishment threshold can be used as a proxy for the level of expressive benefits from punishment. As a wide range of covariates fail to predict in-game behavior, this assumption also seems reasonable.

The top half of Figure 5.3 shows a simulation of what the loss aversion theory predicts treatment effect of taxation will be as a function of an individual's propensity to punish. The bottom half plots the estimated coefficients from quantile regressions testing the effect of taxation on punishment, run

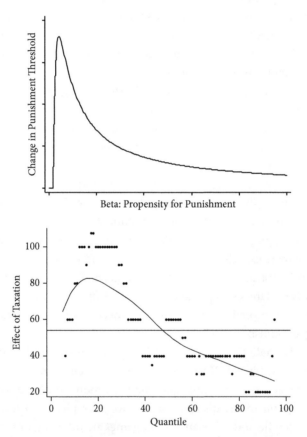

Fig. 5.3 Estimated quantile effects: the treatment effect of taxation on punishment thresholds. Dots depict the estimated regression coefficient of taxation at each quantile from 5 to 95. The solid horizontal line depicts the treatment effect of taxation on the distribution's mean, while the curved line shows the smoothed values for the pattern of the coefficients.

for every quantile between 5 and 95, along with the estimated curve for the coefficients.[10] The effect of taxation is always positive and, as predicted, the coefficient on taxation first rises, then declines as the quantile increases further. This suggests that the taxation treatment has a larger impact on those respondents who are less likely to be politically engaged without taxation. As the highest punishment threshold in the Grant game is 76% of the maximum, ceiling effects are not a concern.

5.4.2 Loss Aversion or Fairness?

To further test the loss-aversion mechanism, I ran additional experiments designed to separate loss aversion from the possibility that there is simply a societal fairness norm that taxes should be used differently than non-earned revenues. Previous research in behavioral economics has used "third-party punishment" games to differentiate between loss aversion and fairness norms in other settings (see e.g. Fehr and Fischbacher 2004). In third-party punishment (hereafter 3PP) games, a neutral respondent watches two other participants interact, and then chooses whether to punish one or both for their behavior. The third-party observer has no personal emotional or financial stake in the interaction between the other two players, and so the assumption is that their behavior is driven by societal norms of what is fair; observers may still be willing to punish if one player sufficiently violates norms. In the standard two-player game, fairness norms may be at stake but so may be more personal dynamics such as loss or risk aversion.

I developed versions of the Tax and Grant games that incorporated this dynamic. In these games respondents were randomly placed into groups of three—a Citizen, a Leader, and an Observer. As before, in both games the Leader had a group fund of 10 MU and had to decide how to allocate it between himself and the Citizen; the Observer could not receive any portion of the group fund. The key difference is that the locus of accountability—the ability to punish—is held by the Observer not the Citizen. In fact, the Citizen is entirely passive in the game. In the 3PP Tax game, the Observer and Citizen were each given wages of 10 MU. The enumerator then taxed the Citizen 5 MU, doubled it, and gave it to the Leader. The Leader allocated this group fund between his own salary and the Citizen, and the Observer

---

[10] All regressions included fixed effects.

Table 5.3 Timing for Tax and Grant games with third-party punishment.

Stages	3PP Tax Game	3PP Grant Game
1	Citizen receives a wage of 10 MU; Observer receives a stake of 10 MU.	Citizen receives a wage of 5 MU; Observer receives a stake of 10 MU.
2	Citizen is taxed 5 MU; this is doubled and passed to Leader as the group fund.	Leader is given 10 MU as the group fund.
3	Leader allocates the 10 MU between himself and Citizen.	
4	Observer sees Leader's decision and decides whether to pay 1 MU to have enumerators remove 4 MU from Leader.	

decided whether to pay 1 MU to reduce the Leader's salary by 4 MU. Note that this game is identical to the original Tax game other than the locus of accountability. The Leader's decision is the same, and the Observer is not directly affected by either taxation or the public good. The 3PP Grant game changes only the funding source; Table 5.3 shows the stages for the 3PP Tax and Grant games.

If stricter fairness norms apply to taxes, then the Observers in the 3PP Tax game should have higher punishment thresholds than Observers in the 3PP Grant game. If, however, the behavioral effect of taxation is primarily due to loss aversion, there should be no difference between punishment thresholds in the two games, as the Observer is not taxed and thus has not suffered a loss. The 3PP games were run in 2013 on a sample of 649 low-income Kampalans; the sample is comparable to that used in the two-player games above.

Table 5.4 presents the OLS regression results for the effect of taxation on an Observer's average punishment threshold. While the point estimate is slightly negative in all specifications, it is small and does not approach statistical significance. This suggests that more general societal fairness norms do not differ by revenue source: Observers are equally likely to punish the Leader regardless of whether the group fund came from taxing the Citizen or from a windfall. This presents a striking contrast to the two-player experiments in which the locus of accountability is with the Citizen, and suggests that the fairness mechanism is not driving the effect of taxation.

Additional evidence sheds light on how notions of fairness may still play some role. As Citizens made no strategic decisions, they were instead asked for each round to select the "most fair" way to divide the group fund between themselves and the Leader—that is, what fraction of the group fund was "fair" for the Citizen to receive. Column 4 of Table 5.4 shows the difference

Table 5.4 Results from 3PP experiment (OLS). Columns 1–3 show the difference between the Observer's punishment thresholds in the 3PP games. Column 4 reports the difference in the allocations Citizens reported as most fair.

VARIABLES	(1) Observer Threshold	(2) Observer Threshold	(3) Observer Threshold	(4) Citizens Fair Dist.
Taxation	−3.018	−5.162	−4.510	54.29
	(14.21)	(16.05)	(15.68)	(37.48)
Constant	392.8***	466.0***	275.9***	476.2***
	(10.16)	(23.10)	(86.92)	(75.33)
FE	N	Y	Y	Y
Clustered SE	N	Y	Y	Y
Controls	N	N	Y	N
Observations	649	649	624	70
R^2	0.000	0.082	0.106	0.086

Standard errors in parentheses
*** p<0.01, ** p<0.05, * p<0.1

in the perceived fair allocation of the group fund by Citizens in the 3PP Tax and 3PP Grant games. While the small number of Citizens makes the analysis underpowered, the point estimate is almost identical to that found in the original experiment: taxed Citizens thought that a "fair" allocation gave them a higher transfer, relative to non-taxed Citizens. This has two implications. First, it supports the claim that the null effect for the Observers is due to a real lack of a treatment effect. If we also saw no differences for Citizens, we might worry that the games were not well run and so did not pick up an effect that does in fact exist. Second, it suggests that citizens may understand their preferences in terms of fairness, even when it is the losses from taxation that have a real impact on their behavior. This makes sense intuitively: few citizens of any country are familiar with the notion of loss aversion or reference-dependence utility, and so use the language of fairness to process their preferences over transfers and punishment.

5.4.3 Measuring Losses and Benefits

A final piece of evidence for the loss-aversion mechanism comes from additional experiments in Uganda. In joint work with Brandon de la Cuesta, Helen Milner, and Daniel Nielson, we ran a set of experiments similar to the original Tax and Grant games, plus some additional treatments that are reported in de la Cuesta et al. (2022). These games, conducted in Kampala in 2017, improved on the original design in several ways. Citizen respondents earned their endowment in each round, making the in-game wage a better proxy for income. The protocols and training materials were also revised to strengthen the link between each aspect of the game and the relevant concept. For example, punishment was explicitly linked to acts like voting or protest, and the amount the leader kept was clearly identified his salary, not money for the community.

Critically, the experiments included an additional measurement tool that was designed to precisely evaluate whether respondents were in the realm of gains or losses at different parts of each lab round. This allows me to test whether taxes send citizens into the realm of losses; whether these losses predict punishment thresholds; and how these losses predict the magnitude of the expressive gains from punishment.

To measure subjective utility, enumerators used a 21-rung ladder that went from 0 (very unhappy or dissatisfied) to 20 (very happy or satisfied). At the start of each round, enumerators placed the respondent at rung 10. The respondent was then asked to update their ladder position at three key points of each round. The first ladder measurement occurs once the Leader is given the group fund. Next, we asked respondents to update their ladder position again once they found out the Leader's allocation decision. We should expect that taxed Citizens will have lower subjective utility for a given level of Leader's transfer. Finally, we asked Citizens to update utility once any punishment took place. Although punishment strictly decreases Citizens' monetary payoff, if respondents receive expressive benefits from punishment, then punishing should on average increase subjective utility.

As an example, consider a Citizen who starts at rung 10. After she pays her tax and the Leader gets the group fund, she updates her ladder position to 7—below her reference point. Say she chooses a punishment threshold of 400 UGX. She then finds out that the Leader has allocated her 300 UGX, and updates her ladder position from rung 7 to rung 6. Finally, she is told that because their punishment threshold was 400 UGX, the punishment takes place. She loses 100 UGX, and the leader loses 400 UGX. She updates the ladder a final time to rung 9, because she is happy the Leader was punished.

The appendix of de la Cuesta et al. (2022) presents the results of the ladder analysis, focusing on the ladder measurements (1) after the leader's decision is revealed, and (2) after any punishment takes place.[11] We find that respondents in the Tax condition had significantly lower subjective utility from a given leader transfer, even controlling for the subject's individual threshold, previous ladder measurements, and the outcomes of previous game rounds. This suggests that taxation does indeed lead to a greater sense of loss from a given leader transfer.

The final ladder measurement, which occurs after any punishment has been enacted, shows that expressive benefits to punishment do exist, and that they are affected by loss. Individuals who punished saw their utility increase by an average of 5.24 points ($p < .01$) from the previous ladder position, even controlling for treatment condition, previous game play, the respondent's punishment threshold, the leader transfer, and previous ladder position. So, even when punishment was economically costly, the average respondent was better off after they punished the leader for a low transfer. This provides strong support for the idea that psychological, expressive benefits to punishment exist. We also find that respondents who were more in the realm of losses prior to punishment received significantly higher expressive benefits from punishment; among those who punish, the size of the utility increase from punishment is on average 0.39 points (on the 21-rung ladder) for each additional point of loss suffered earlier in the game ($p < .01$), even controlling for thresholds and previous transfers.

5.4.4 Ownership and Loss Aversion: Complementary Mechanisms

One potential alternative mechanism not yet considered is that of ownership. If taxation induces a sense of psychological ownership over the government budget among citizens, then this could also lead citizens to demand more from leaders. Initial support for this idea comes from Paler (2013), which shows that respondents have a significantly higher sense of ownership over a budget when they have contributed via taxation. In joint work with Brandon de la Cuesta, Helen Milner, and Daniel Nielson, we show experimentally that taxation does indeed increase citizens' sense of ownership over government

---

[11] The initial ladder measurement, which occurs right after the leader gets the group fund, turned out to be difficult to interpret. In particular, many respondents' subjective utility was essentially prospective, and varied in part to the degree that they anticipated future benefits from the leader. For this reason, this ladder measurement is excluded from the analysis.

revenues, and that ownership can account for a significant fraction of taxation's effect on punishment thresholds (de la Cuesta et al. 2022). We argue that the loss aversion and ownership mechanisms are complementary. After all, individuals are unlikely to feel the loss of something they have no ownership over; owning one's own income is a precondition for loss aversion. Combining the evidence presented here with the evidence in de la Cuesta et al. (2022) suggests that both loss aversion and ownership play a critical role in increasing the demands taxed citizens place on leaders.

5.5 Replications

A growing concern in political science research is that many results hold in a certain sample or context but fail to hold up when someone else attempts to replicate the finding. This concern is driven in part by significant evidence from other social sciences that many key results fail to replicate (Klein et al. 2014, 2018). Perhaps taxation affects citizen behavior in Uganda, but would not hold in a more democratic country, a richer country, or even with a slightly different sample within Uganda. In co-authored work with Brandon de la Cuesta, Helen Milner, and Dan Nielson, we ran a set of studies in Ghana that included a replication of the Uganda experiments, with minor modifications.[12] The data were collected in 2016 in Accra, Ghana's capital. Ghana's GDP per capital is more than twice Uganda's; Ghana is also less aid dependent than Uganda, although it receives a higher fraction of its national income from oil. While Uganda is an electoral authoritarian regime, Ghana has reasonably competitive multi-party elections and has seen several peaceful leadership transitions.

The Ghana experiments consisted of the Tax and Grant games introduced above, but also included two additional treatments: the Aid and Oil games. One concern with the Grant game is that it is not clear how respondents may understand the "group fund," as the source is never explicitly named (the word "grant" is never used in the protocols, the money is simply called the "group fund"). This could lead us to over- or under-estimate the effect of taxation on citizens' willingness to punish. If some respondents think of the Grant group fund as the government's normal budget, including taxes,

---

[12] Other results from this data collection are published in de la Cuesta et al. (2022) and de la Cuesta et al. (2021).

then naming the source as aid or oil could actually *increase* taxation's effect. If citizens think of aid and oil as belonging to the citizens, rather than the government, it could be that explicitly naming the windfall's source could lead to smaller differences between the Tax and Grant conditions.

For the Ghana experiments, we recruited respondents from randomly selected low- and medium-income constituencies in the Greater Accra area. Within those constituencies, we randomly selected polling stations and each session was recruited from a single polling station area. Respondents were bussed to a central location to take part in the experiments. This makes our sample reasonably representative of Accra as a whole, excluding high-income areas due to the difficulty of recruiting volunteers from these areas. For enumeration, 1 MU was set as 0.5 Ghanaian Cedis.

The Ghana results confirm the findings from Uganda: compared to an unnamed grant, citizens have higher punishment thresholds when they are taxed. This effect persists when the grant is explicitly identified as coming from either foreign aid or oil money; we find no significant differences in willingness to punish among the unspecified grant, aid, and oil conditions. The replication in Ghana thus helps assuage several concerns with the initial results. It shows that the Uganda experiments were not a fluke, and that they travel to at least one other African country that is different across a range of measures. They also show that taxation's effect holds for a variety of possible alternative sources of revenue, including not only an unnamed grant but also aid or oil.

5.6 The Role of Tax Modality

In Chapter 3, I discussed the extent to which loss aversion may be activated by different types of taxes. In particular, I introduced ongoing co-authored work in which we argue that taxes must be visible and salient in order to generate accountability dividends (de la Cuesta et al. 2020). A substantial literature argues that, on average, established indirect taxes are typically less visible than established direct taxes, and that this might mute taxation's accountabililty effects (Moore 2004; Bräutigam, Fjeldstad, and Moore 2008). In de la Cuesta et al. (2020), we use lab experiments in Uganda, based on the ones presented above, to show that the exact same tax, when made less visible, has a smaller effect on citizens' punishment thresholds. In those experiments, we simulate an indirect tax by having respondents purchase real items, varying the extent to which an increase in prices is attributable to a tax. When the tax is obscured, taxation still increases punishment thresholds but by a significantly smaller amount. In that paper we also use survey experiments on a nationally representative sample of Ugandans to show that citizens do not feel a loss from paying indirect taxes unless explicitly primed on the tax payment. Combined, the evidence suggests that indirect taxes are indeed less visible in the real world. In the following chapter, I draw on this finding to examine the types of taxes that are most likely to generate lower levels of government rent-seeking.

5.7 External Validity and Scope Conditions

The experimental results show that the taxation treatment increased citizens' willingness to punish. This suggests that taxation does in fact change citizen behavior. However, a skeptic might reply that the games are simply too abstract to accurately model "real-world" political behavior. After all, the main experiments consist of two respondents, both actually citizens, role-playing a nation consisting of a single citizen and a leader. The players' endowments and the group fund are small relative to actual government budgets, and the setting is a lab where citizens face few barriers to punishment and no collective action problems. The rest of this chapter explores the external validity and scope conditions of these results, including how the results might change if there are barriers to punishment.

5.7.1 Subgroup Analysis

One way to look at the experiments' external validity is to look at the treatment effects for different subgroups of respondents. If the games are too abstract and simply pick up generic differences that would exist without the political, taxation-related framing, we should see similar treatment effects regardless of whether respondents have real-world exposure to taxation and political action. If the games are successfully picking up something about actual political behavior, then treatment effects will be strongest for respondents for whom taxation is most salient, as the treatment can better activate the relevant behavior.

In the original 2012 Uganda study, I did not ask about tax payments directly, but can look at heterogeneity according to demographic characteristics. Three potential sources of treatment heterogeneity are gender, age, and income. In Uganda women were historically exempt from the graduated tax, implying that taxation may be less salient for women. Teenagers (those ages 18 or 19) and the unemployed (those reporting no income in the past four weeks) may similarly be less exposed to taxes, and so have smaller treatment effects. Because both groups comprise such a large fraction of the sample, it is also important to check that they are not driving the results. Table 5.5 shows the regression results for each type of heterogeneity. For comparison, Column 1 reports the full-sample results. Columns 2–4 test each potential source of heterogeneity, and Column 5 includes all three interactions.

Age is the strongest source of heterogeneity—the treatment effect of taxation on teenagers is close to zero, while the effect for adults is almost 100 UGX. The results for Female and No Income are weaker; while both interaction terms are negative and substantively large, the effects are imprecisely estimated. The No Income measure may also be imprecise because it

Table 5.5 Treatment heterogeneity in Tax and Grant games (OLS). Column 1 reports the baseline treatment effect of taxation. Columns 2–5 report results for heterogeneity by gender, income, and age, separately and combined. All specifications include controls, enumerator and site FE, and SE clustered by session.

VARIABLES	(1) Baseline	(2) Gender	(3) Income	(4) Age	(5) All
Taxation	56.37**	61.72***	79.54**	95.41***	115.4***
	(21.52)	(19.84)	(28.57)	(32.67)	(28.25)
Female		−24.77			−16.82
		(25.27)			(25.44)
Taxation*Female		−20.46			−47.25
		(53.36)			(46.95)
No Income			43.22		23.03
			(38.86)		(41.95)
Taxation*No Inc			−53.00		−13.08
			(44.60)		(52.70)
Teenager				58.67*	59.17*
				(31.53)	(31.25)
Taxation*Teen				−87.22**	−92.33*
				(39.96)	(43.80)
Constant	216.3	213.2	181.0	115.1	93.41
	(180.4)	(178.6)	(192.5)	(202.3)	(213.3)
Observations	272	272	272	272	272
R^2	0.142	0.142	0.149	0.158	0.164

*** $p<0.01$, ** $p<0.05$, * $p<0.1$
Robust standard errors in parentheses

cannot distinguish between the long-term unemployed, for whom taxation is not salient, and short-term unemployed who still expect to pay taxes in the future. Teens likely lack prior exposure to taxation; they also earn less than adults, are less likely to head households, and are less politically engaged. These factors may mute the effect of taxation.

The treatment effect of taxation is largest among adult, wage-earning men—exactly the group with the most exposure to taxation in Uganda. Running the basic specification on only men, age 20 or older, who reported positive wages shows that the average punishment threshold moves from 362 UGX in the Grant game to 470 UGX in the Tax game, an increase of 29.8%.

In the Ghana experiments, we directly asked respondents whether they paid any direct taxes. The results support the Uganda results. For respondents who did not report paying at least one form of direct tax, the effects of the taxation treatment are close to zero. It is only for the respondents who are able to draw on their real-life experiences paying taxes that we see a significant treatment effect. Again, this suggests that the games are relying on respondents' ability to draw on their own life experiences in how they evaluate government action and their own willingness to punish.

5.7.2 Making Punishment More Difficult

Another potential criticism of the lab experiments is that punishment is too "easy": the Citizen indicates that she wishes to pay a small sum to sanction the Leader, and this always occurs. Perhaps if citizens face barriers to punishment, such as higher costs (from collective action or opportunity costs), or if they face the possibility that sanctions may not succeed, this will overwhelm any effect of taxation. It is certainly likely that if a regime is extraordinarily repressive, or if the costs of action are too high, taxation will have no effect. Indeed, taxation has historically coexisted with repressive, unresponsive governments. We would not expect a totalitarian governments to suddenly change policy after a tax increase. However, in such settings few if any factors would predict political action. What if we focus instead on settings where political action is feasible, but is risky in some way?

One way to test this in a lab setting is by modifying the Tax and Grant games so that punishment is more difficult. One set of treatments in the Ghana experiments (co-authored with Brandon de la Cuesta, Helen Milner, and Dan Nielson) does just this. These "Uncertain Punishment" games were the same as the original games, with one key difference. If the Citizen decided to punish the Leader, they payed a fixed cost of 1 MU. But, the punishment only actually occurred 50% of the time: the rest of the time the Citizen still lost money but the Leader did not lose anything. To make it transparent when punishment was occurring, each enumerator had a bag with ten stones that were identical except that five were red and five were yellow. Punishment was only implemented if a red stone was drawn. In each round respondents first saw all the stones put into the bag (to ensure they believed that the odds were fair) and then drew a stone themselves.

Chapter 3 shows that loss aversion, among its other effects, implies that individuals should be more willing to take risks when they are below their reference point. Meanwhile, untaxed citizens will on average be more likely to be risk-averse. Thus, we should expect not only that taxation still has an effect when punishment is uncertain, but that it is actually larger than when punishment is certain. The uncertain punishment games in Ghana provide some support for this: taxation still significantly affects punishment when there is uncertainty, and the magnitude of the effect is larger than when punishment is certain. While the difference in magnitudes is not statistically significant, it still shows that making punishment more difficult does not decrease the effect of taxation on punishment, and may in fact increase it.

5.7.3 Evidence from Outside the Lab

To provide additional support for the findings outside of a laboratory setting, I conducted a conjoint survey experiment on a sample of citizens in nine Ugandan districts.[13] In the experiment, respondents were shown pairs of hypothetical government officials, each of whom was accused of engaging in some type of corrupt behavior. Each official had five attributes, each of which was independently and randomly assigned from a set of possible levels. One attribute varied whether the official had stolen money from citizens' taxes or donor funds; the other attributes varied additional aspects of the official's identity and financial implications of his crime. Respondents saw four different pairs of corrupt officials; for each pair, they selected which official they would rather see prosecuted and punished for his behavior, then ranked the severity of each official's crime on a five-point scale.

---

[13] The full results of the conjoint experiment are available in Martin (2018).

The results support the lab experiments. Officials who stole donor funds were selected for punishment 42% of the time, while officials who stole citizens' taxes were punished 62% of the time (p=.000). Profiles in which the official stole from citizens' taxes are also ranked much higher on a 5-point severity scale (p=.000). This was one of the strongest results in the conjoint experiment, and suggests that the link between taxation and willingness to punish is not simply an artifact of the lab experiments.

5.8 Observational Data

If taxation affects citizens' propensity for political action, we should observe that taxed citizens participate in various forms of political action in higher numbers. Round 5 of the Afrobarometer survey includes questions that allow an initial test of this. Afrobarometer Round 5 was conducted between 2011 and 2013 in in 34 African countries, with a sample size of either 1,200 or 2,400 per country. The survey included questions on both taxation and political engagement, as well a number of other background characteristics.

Round 5 of the Afrobarometer included a module of questions about respondents' tax burdens. I used these to create binary measures of whether each respondent paid direct taxes, indirect taxes, and local taxes. I separate out the three tax types as there are theoretical reasons to expect differences in how they affect citizen behavior. I anticipate that following de la Cuesta et al. (2020) (and the related discussion above), indirect taxes will have a small or null effect on political engagement, as they are typically much less visible to citizens. Direct taxes, in contrast, most closely match the taxes in the lab experiments, and I expect those to have the largest effect on citizen behavior. I consider local taxes separately because the question phrasing makes it likely they include a mix of direct and indirect local taxes.

An individual is coded as paying direct taxes if they report being required to pay a formal income tax, self-employment tax, or property tax. Individuals who report being required to pay sales tax or VAT are coded as paying indirect taxes.[14] Finally, local tax measures whether respondents report being required to pay a local tax or fee. Note that the questions for all three types of taxes ask about whether paying a tax is *required*, not whether

---

[14] It is likely that almost all respondents in the survey pay at least some indirect taxes. However, if respondents are not aware of their tax payments, taxation is unlikely to affect behavior.

an individual actually paid the tax. While this may introduce a degree of measurement error, these questions should still allow a rough test of the theory.

To measure the relationship between each form of taxation and citizen behavior, I use a module of political engagement from Afrobarometer to create five binary variables for analysis. The first measure is *Vote*, which measures whether a respondent reported voting in the last election. *Collective Action* measures whether respondents reported "joining with others to raise an issue." *Contact Official* measures whether respondents reported contacting a district politician, Member of Parliament, bureaucrat, or party official in the past year. *Campaign* measures whether a respondent reported campaigning in the last election, either on their own or by working for a candidate. Finally, *Protest* measures whether a respondent reported going to a protest in the past year. While all of these are measures of political activity, there is substantial variation in how common each action is. While 73% of respondents reported voting in the last election, fewer than 10% of respondents reported protesting. The rest of the behaviors are in between these two extremes: 53.4% reported attending a meeting, 44.3% reported working with others to raise an issue, 32% reported contacting an official, and 27% reported campaigning or working for a candidate.

Table 5.6 shows the relationship between taxation and each type of political engagement.[15] Because respondents who pay taxes are likely very different from those who do not, I control for gender, age, education, whether the respondent lives in an urban or rural area, and a rough measure of poverty (deprivation).[16]

Because both independent and dependent variables are binary, the coefficients on the three tax variables can be interpreted as the percentage point change in the probability an individual takes each action when they pay a particular type of tax. As predicted, paying direct taxes is positively correlated with several types of political action. Direct tax payers are 1.5 percentage points more likely to have voted, 4.5 percentage points more likely to have campaigned for a candidate, and 4 percentage points more likely to have contacted a government official in the past year. However, taxation is not a strong predictor of whether respondents have engaged in collective

---

[15] All regressions are OLS, and include country fixed effects. Standard errors are clustered by country.

[16] The poverty variable takes a value of 1 if respondents report having gone without at least one basic necessity.

Table 5.6 Effect of taxation on political engagement.

	Dependent variable				
	Vote	Campaign	Contact Official	Collective Action	Protest
	(1)	(2)	(3)	(4)	(5)
Paid Direct Tax	0.015**	0.045***	0.040***	0.010	0.009
	(0.007)	(0.012)	(0.014)	(0.015)	(0.010)
Paid Indirect Tax	−0.012	0.008	−0.002	−0.001	0.010
	(0.009)	(0.011)	(0.013)	(0.016)	(0.009)
Paid Local Tax	0.015	0.002	0.012	0.035***	−0.013*
	(0.009)	(0.012)	(0.015)	(0.012)	(0.008)
Urban	0.004***	0.001**	0.003***	0.003***	0.0001
	(0.0004)	(0.0003)	(0.0003)	(0.0004)	(0.0002)
Age	0.019**	0.104***	0.117***	0.105***	0.015**
	(0.008)	(0.011)	(0.011)	(0.012)	(0.007)
Male	0.001	0.015***	0.021***	0.016***	0.001
	(0.002)	(0.003)	(0.003)	(0.004)	(0.002)
Education	0.004	0.018***	0.026***	0.028***	0.011**
	(0.005)	(0.007)	(0.005)	(0.006)	(0.004)
Deprivation	0.045***	0.044***	0.073***	0.101***	−0.011
	(0.009)	(0.009)	(0.012)	(0.014)	(0.007)
Constant	0.754***	0.202***	−0.031*	0.249***	0.079***
	(0.021)	(0.017)	(0.017)	(0.026)	(0.010)
Observations	20,806	21,633	21,675	21,602	21,124
R^2	0.058	0.061	0.099	0.140	0.044

$^*p < 0.1;^{**}p < 0.05;^{***}p < 0.01$

action in the past year, or gone to a protest. The coefficients are still positive, but are smaller and not statistically significant. One reason for this might be that the types of collective action asked about in the survey are typically local, and if taxes are seen as the purview of the national government, tax payment will not affect local action. Protest may likewise be more local in nature.

In contrast, paying indirect taxes consistently has no effect on political action. This is in line with the discussion above, which shows that less visible indirect taxes will have smaller accountability dividends. Finally, the effect of local taxes on action is more mixed. While there is no effect on voting, campaigning, or contacting an official, paying a local tax does increase the likelihood of engaging in community-level collective action; this would be in line with a world in which local taxes generate local action, while national taxes do not. Interestingly, local tax payment is negatively correlated with protest. This could occur if, for example, local taxpayers are able to get concessions from government without the necessity of protesting; taxation makes protest an "off-path" outcome.

Together, the Afrobarometer data therefore suggests that, across a larger number of countries in sub-Saharan Africa, paying direct taxes is strongly correlated with a number of forms of political engagement, while indirect tax payments are not. However, there are limits to what we can learn through these data, and all results should be taken as identifying correlations, not causal relationships. First, the measures of political engagement are self-reported. We know that survey respondents often over-report voting (due to social norms that voting is a civic duty), and may also over-report other forms of behavior. There may also be systematic under-reporting of contentious behaviors like protesting. It is also possible that some types of tax payments are underreported: virtually all citizens pay at least some indirect taxes in most countries, suggesting that the nulls for indirect taxation may result from measurement error. Second, while the analysis controls for a number of demographic and economic variables, it may still be that taxed and non-taxed citizens vary along a number of other dimensions, and these dimensions may also affect political engagement. Thus, while these results are suggestive, they cannot give us strong causal evidence of taxation's effect on behavior. This is where the lab experiments from above provide more causal leverage. Finally, this analysis cannot provide insight into the exact mechanisms behind the various effects.

5.9 Conclusion

The evidence introduced in this chapter supports one of the key claims of this book: that taxation increases citizens' political engagement, making them more willing to punish poor government performance, even when doing so is costly and the payoff is uncertain. However, taxation's effect is not uniform. It will have a larger impact when taxes are visible and salient to citizens. Of course, citizen demands for improved accountability are only part of the story. It may also be necessary that politicians and other government officials *recognize* that taxation changes citizens' behavior. While this has not been studied extensively in developing countries, there is recent work by myself and Adam Dynes on this issues in the United States (Dynes and Martin 2019). We embedded a series of questions on taxation and electoral accountability into two large surveys of American municipal officials, including both city councilors and mayors. We find that these officials do in fact believe that they face stronger accountability pressures for how they spend local taxes, relative to outside grants and federal transfers, and that they are more likely to lose office if a scandal involves local taxes. While this result has not yet been replicated in other parts of the world, or with other forms of revenue than taxes and intergovernmental transfers, it is encouraging.

Finally, even if governments recognize that taxation increases citizens' demands, it does not mean that they will respond by improving performance. The model developed in Chapter 4 suggests that there are multiple possible equilibria, only some of which will lead to high taxation and high accountability. The next chapter provides evidence on how governments respond to the accountability pressures that taxation creates.

6

Taxation, Democracy, and Accountability

The previous chapter provided extensive empirical support for one major claim of this book: that when citizens are taxed, they will increase their demands on government. This chapter tests this book's second claim, that these citizen pressures will lead governments to be strategic about how and when they tax citizens. In particular, Chapter 4 developed a theory to examine how and when governments will react to such pressures. I showed that multiple equilibria were possible, including not only a high-tax, high-accountability equilibrium but also outcomes where governments simply extort taxes and provide little in return, and equilibria in which taxation is low but so is accountability. Critically, the model shows that if governments realize that taxation can increase citizen demands, they may respond by systematically under-investing in fiscal capacity and reducing taxation, rather than by decreasing rent-seeking and increasing public goods or other transfers to citizens. The model suggests two concrete sets of testable implications: that democratization can lead to lower taxation, not higher, and that taxation should on average lead to lower rent-seeking, but the strength of this relationship will vary based on both regime type and tax type.

First, the model shows that in some cases, an increase in the level of democracy can actually lead the state to eliminate some forms of taxation. This occurs when it is too costly to produce the public goods citizens demand relative to the level of taxes collected. The cost of producing public goods will depend heavily on state capacity, while the level of taxes collected will depend on both the tax base and and collection capacity. I therefore expect that in poor, low-capacity states, an increase in democracy will be associated with a decrease in taxation, while in higher-capacity states, democracy will lead to an increase in taxation, as governments are able to produce citizens' desired public goods efficiently.

The first half of this chapter draws on cross-national data to test this prediction. A central challenge of these tests is how best to proxy for states' ability to efficiently provide public goods. While standard measures of state capacity are appealing, they are often based, at least in part, on states'

Strategic Taxation: Fiscal Capacity and Accountability in African States. Lucy E. S. Martin.
Oxford University Press. © Oxford University Press 2023. DOI: 10.1093/oso/9780197672631.003.0006

ability to collect taxes efficiently. For example, ICRG's Quality of Governance measure explicitly considers the presence of corruption in tax collection, while VDEM's measure for effective public administration considers the whole bureaucracy, including the performance of the tax unit. This is a problem because the key outcome of interest is tax take, which we should expect to be highly correlated with states' ability to collect taxes. Ideally, we need a measure of state capacity that is completely detached from states' decisions regarding tax collection. As this does not exist, I instead use GDP per capita as my primary proxy for states' ability to produce public goods cheaply and effectively. I expect that modern low-income states will typically have lower capacity to efficiently build infrastructure or fund other desired public goods. I also expect this measure to be less closely related to taxation, and thus a better independent measure. This measure is also in line with other theoretical work: Kiser and Karceski (2017) argues that "economic development is the main determinant of administrative effectiveness" (86). However, in Section 6.1.5 I examine how robust the results are to the use of alternative state capacity measures.

Section 6.1 uses a panel dataset of 143 countries across 38 years to test the hypothesis that democracy will not always lead to higher taxation. I start by considering average tax take across democracies and autocracies, both overall and at different levels of development, as proxied by GDP per capita as discussed above. While democracy is associated with higher taxation overall, this pattern is much more pronounced in high-income countries, even without controlling for many potential confounding factors. I then turn to regression analysis, showing that higher levels of democracy are primarily associated with higher taxation in high-income countries. In medium- and low-income countries, the effect is muted and close to zero. When I run regressions interacting the level of democracy with the level of development, I find that for low-income countries, the predicted level of taxation actually decreases as democracy increases. Only for higher-income countries does democracy produce a strong, positive effect on tax revenues. Testing whether political liberalization and democratization lead to higher or lower taxation, I find that democratization is associated with significantly lower taxation in subsequent years. I finish by discussing how robust the results are to alternative specifications and variable choices.

As an alternative test of the first prediction, I then examine the correlation between regime type and the size of the tax net. If low-capacity democracies tax less than low-capacity autocracies, then one implication is that the size of the tax net should be smaller in such democracies. While global tax net size data were not available, Section 6.2 uses data from Afrobarometer to test this prediction in a cross-section of 29 African countries. I find that, on average, the tax net is smaller in democracies, and that this difference in accentuated in high-corruption states where providing public goods is more difficult.

The model's second testable prediction is that taxation should be associated with better governance, but that the strength of this relationship should vary based on regime type and tax type. Specifically, the model predicts that, when governments meet citizens' demands, they will reduce rent-seeking. The second half of this chapter examines the relationship between taxation and one type of rent-seeking: corruption. I expect that while taxation will be correlated with lower corruption overall, the effect will be strongest under two conditions. First, following the evidence on tax modality in Chapter 5, I expect that taxes will have a stronger relationship with corruption when when taxes are visible and highly salient—that is, for direct taxes. Second, the model predicts that taxation is more likely to lead to accountability in democracies, as citizens can extract concessions from government even in the absence of tax bargaining. Thus, I expect that while taxation might decrease corruption in both regime types, the effect will be strongest in democracies.

While a full discussion of causal identification issues is contained below, here I will simply state that all of these results should be viewed as suggestive correlations. In all cases I find evidence that is *consistent with* my theory, but it is difficult to fully rule out issues of endogeneity or reverse causation. To better address these issues, the next chapter provides additional tests of the theory through case studies in Uganda. Combined, these different pieces of evidence increase confidence in the results.

6.1 Democracy and Tax Revenues

To test the conditions under which democracy will lead to higher or lower taxation, I compiled a global panel dataset on taxation, democracy, and state development. The dataset covers 143 countries from 1987 to 2018. For this analysis, the main dependent variables are measures of tax-to-GDP ratios from the International Centre on Taxation and Development (ICTD)'s Government Revenue Database (GRD). I use three measures of taxation: one that includes all non-resource taxes (excluding social contributions), and two that report similar measures for direct and indirect tax-to-GDP ratios separately. These variables are scaled from 0-100. For all analysis I exclude country-years that ICTD marks with "caution notes"; these mark observations where the authors suspect issues with reporting accuracy, or where they cannot separate out resource revenues.[1] The main independent variable is Polity's 21-point democracy scale, although I consider alternative measures below.

The rest of this section examines the extent to which democracy appears to increase different types of taxation, and under what conditions. I start by considering descriptive data on taxation and democracy. I then turn to regression analysis, examining how democracy appears to affect taxation in different types of countries, and the interaction of democracy with state development.

6.1.1 Summary Statistics

Before turning to formal regression analysis, it is helpful to look at raw average tax-to-GDP ratios for different levels of democracy and state development. To do this, I take the five-year average tax-to-GDP ratio (for total taxes, direct taxes, and indirect taxes) for each country from 2013 to 2017. The top panel of Table 6.1 shows average taxation broken down by whether a country was a democracy, defined as a 5 or higher on the 21-point Polity scale.[2] In the raw data, democracies do appear to generate higher tax revenue than autocracies, and most of this increase appears to come from direct taxes.

The middle panel then breaks down tax revenue by the World Bank's income classifications, which are available starting in 1987. The World Bank codes countries as low, lower-middle, upper-middle, or high-income in each year, based on a country's GNI and that year's cutoffs, which are adjusted annually for inflation. Both here and in the regression analysis below, I pool together lower-middle and upper-middle income countries into a single "middle income" category. As one might expect, low-income countries tax the least, while high-income countries tax the most. However, the patterns for direct and indirect taxes are slightly different. When we look at direct

---

[1] This excludes 942 country-years out of 7,448, leaving a sample size of 6,506 observations. This does not affect the substantive interpretation of the results.

[2] The number of countries differs across sections of the table because there are cases where a single country falls into two categories in the five-year interval.

Table 6.1 Average tax-to-GDP ratios, 2013–17. Countries may appear in multiple categories if they change income or regime status over time.

Regime Type	Income Type	Total	Direct	Indirect	Countries
Autocracy	All	15.86	5.07	10.79	31
Democracy	All	20.71	9.13	11.55	81
All	Low	12.81	4.05	8.76	18
All	Medium	18.71	5.99	12.74	67
All	High	23.46	11.47	11.86	49
Autocracy	Low	12.06	3.58	8.48	10
Democracy	Low	13.39	4.41	8.98	12
Autocracy	Medium	17.42	5.50	11.91	22
Democracy	Medium	18.54	6.39	12.21	37
Autocracy	High	13.95	6.64	7.31	2
Democracy	High	24.21	12.52	11.56	35

taxation, low- and medium-income states both raise relatively little, while a large jump is seen for high-income states. For indirect taxation, there is a big jump between low- and middle-income countries, then if anything a small decrease for high-income countries.

Finally, the bottom panel breaks the data down by both regime type and income category. Here we see a more complicated relationship between regime type and taxation. While for high-income countries democracies tax much more than autocracies across all three tax measures, the differences are much more subdued for low- and middle-income countries. It appears that democracies might tax more, but only by a very small amount. However, the summary data cannot control for the myriad of factors that may influence regime type and taxation. For this reason, I turn next to regression analysis.

6.1.2 Initial Regression Analysis

Table 6.1 only examines cross-sectional variation in taxation across countries. To further test the relationship between democracy, taxation, and income, I ran regression analysis on the full panel dataset, from 1987 to 2018. All regressions are OLS. Following Plümper, Troeger, and Manow (2005), I do not use country and time fixed effects in the main analysis, as this can cause bias when variables have level effects. Instead, I include a cubic time trend and cluster robust standard errors by country and year. As discussed further below, the results are robust to alternative modeling choices, including the use of fixed effects.

Because a number of factors may be endogenous to both taxation and regime type, all regressions include a vector of controls. As richer countries are more likely to be democracies, and may be more likely to tax, I control for logged GDP per capita and GDP growth (both from the World Bank (2020)). I also control for trade levels, as this is related to economic development but also affects the tax bases available to governments. To measure trade, I use a WDI measure that calculates the sum of imports and exports of goods and services as a fraction of GDP. Second, the resource curse literature argues that windfalls may lead to poor governance or autocracy; they may also reduce the incentives for governments to tax. I therefore control for logged resource rents as a percent of GDP (World Bank 2020). Because foreign investment may be correlated with both tax receipts and democracy (perhaps because of stronger property rights), I control for inward FDI, using a measure from the World Bank (2020). Because conflict may impact a country's ability to tax, I also control for whether the country is engaged in a civil or interstate conflict in a given year, as measured by PRIO (Gleditsch et al 2002). Finally, I control for a country's logged population and its percent urbanization, both from WDI.

If democracy does affect overall levels of taxation, it seems reasonable that the effect will not be immediate: it may take several years for political institutions to affect tax outcomes, as elections take effect and legislatures pay and implement new policy. For this reason I lag both Polity and all controls by one year; results are very similar if I use a three- or five-year lag instead. Finally, I run the analysis both for the full sample, and broken down by a country's level of income. My theory predicts that democracy will only lead to higher taxation when government is willing and able to efficiently use tax revenues on public goods valued by citizens; otherwise democracy can lead to lower taxation. I anticipate that democracy will therefore tend to have a more positive effect on taxation in high-income countries where state capacity is higher, and a smaller or even negative effect on taxation in low-income countries.

Table 6.2 shows the main regression analysis. Panel A shows the results for total taxes as a percent of GDP, while Panels B and C show the results for direct and indirect taxes as a percent of GDP. The coefficients for the included control variables are available in the online appendix. The first column, "Pooled Income," shows the predicted change in the relevant tax-to-GDP ratio when Polity increases by one point. These initial results suggest that across all income groups democracies do tax more: a one-point

Table 6.2 Relationship between democracy and taxation.

	Pooled Income	Low Income	Medium Income	High Income
	Panel A: Total Tax Revenue			
Polity	0.319***	0.074	0.159	1.451***
	(0.089)	(0.065)	(0.101)	(0.181)
Countries	143	58	94	44
Observations	3,273	943	1,471	859
Controls	✓	✓	✓	✓
R^2	0.460	0.227	0.165	0.645
	Panel B: Direct Tax Revenue			
Polity	0.132***	−0.009	0.093**	0.889***
	(0.040)	(0.030)	(0.040)	(0.144)
Countries	138	55	88	42
Observations	3,029	832	1,362	835
Controls	✓	✓	✓	✓
R^2	0.572	0.270	0.182	0.631
	Panel C: Indirect Tax Revenue			
Polity	0.162***	0.074	0.035	0.607***
	(0.061)	(0.052)	(0.076)	(0.071)
Countries	138	55	89	42
Observations	3,037	867	1,336	834
Controls	✓	✓	✓	✓
R^2	0.212	0.223	0.209	0.584

$^*p<0.1$; $^{**}p<0.05$; $^{***}p<0.01$

increase in Polity is associated with an increase of 0.3 percentage points in the tax-to-GDP ratio; a country that increased its polity score by one standard deviation (6.4 points) would increase total taxes by 2 percentage points, or one-fourth of a standard deviation. This is driven almost equally by direct and indirect taxes.

However, the results by income group suggest a different story. In high-income countries, democracy is consistently associated with higher taxation. However, in low-income countries there is no significant relationship, and the coefficient on Polity for direct taxes is actually negative. Middle-income countries show mixed patterns; higher polity scores are associated with higher direct taxation, but not indirect. Even when the coefficients on Polity are positive for low- and middle-income countries, the magnitude of the predicted effect is small, 10% or less of the effect for high-income countries. If we look at the results for total taxes, a one standard deviation (SD) increase in Polity would predict a 9.4 percentage point increase in the tax-GDP ratio, or 1.2 SD. For low-income countries, the same increase in polity would predict taxes to increase by only 0.4773 percentage points, or 0.06 SD.

6.1.3 Interaction Effects

Combined, the results of the panel data so far show that while democracy overall is associated with higher taxation, this conceals a more complicated relationship. Democracy is associated with either small or null effects on taxation for low-income countries, while high-income countries show the more typically positive effect that previous literature has shown. To further test this finding, I ran additional OLS specifications on the full panel dataset in which the main independent variables are the 21-point Polity scale; logged GDP per capita; and the interaction of the two. All specifications include the full set of controls described above, along with a cubic time trend and clustered, panel-corrected standard errors. The results of this analysis are shown in Table 6.3.

The interaction analysis supports the core hypothesis: at low levels of GDP per capita, an increase in Polity is associated with a significant *decrease* in total tax revenue, driven entirely by a drop in direct tax revenue. Also as predicted, the coefficient on the interaction of polity and country income is positive and significant. At high levels of country income, higher levels

Table 6.3 Effect of full Polity score interacted with GDP per capita.

	Total Tax Revenue (1)	Direct Tax Revenue (2)	Indirect Tax Revenue (3)
Full Polity	−1.598***	−1.502***	0.075
	(0.317)	(0.189)	(0.226)
GDP Per Capita (logged)	1.026*	1.220***	−0.026
	(0.581)	(0.261)	(0.461)
Full Polity X GDP (logged)	0.239***	0.204***	0.011
	(0.041)	(0.024)	(0.030)
Countries	143	138	138
Observations	3,273	3,029	3,037
Controls	✓	✓	✓
R^2	0.516	0.656	0.212

$^*p<0.1; ^{**}p<0.05; ^{***}p<0.01$

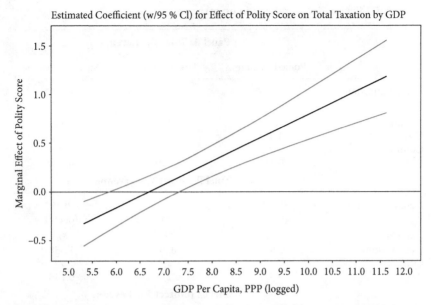

Fig. 6.1 Predicted marginal effect of an increase in Polity on taxation, by logged GDP.

of democracy are associated with increases in taxation. Figure 6.1 plots the predicted effect of Polity on overall tax-to-GDP ratios for each level of GDP per capita. The effect of Polity is negative until a GDP per capita of about US$735; it does not become positive and significantly different from zero until US$1480. In 2020, World Bank data shows that seven countries, all in Africa, had GDP per capita below US$1500. However, in 1995, 38 countries had GDP per capita under US$1500. This means that, during the wave of political liberalizations in the 1990s, many states were sufficiently low-income that we would expect taxation to decrease or stay flat.

6.1.4 Democratization

So far, the analysis has considered the equilibrium association between a certain level of the Polity variable on taxation. This is in line with Chapter 4, which likewise considers equilibrium outcomes. However, an alternative way to view the theory is that a *shift* in the level of democracy should induce changes in taxation. To examine this further, Table 6.4 shows similar analysis

Table 6.4 Effect of democratization on taxation.

	Panel A: Total Tax Revenue		
	Pooled Income	Low Income	Medium Income
Democratization	−1.483**	−0.545	−1.172
	(0.605)	(0.510)	(1.068)
Countries	143	58	94
Observations	3,267	941	1,467
Controls	✓	✓	✓
R^2	0.418	0.219	0.148
	Panel B: Direct Tax Revenue		
Democratization	−0.967***	−0.324	−0.482
	(0.353)	(0.247)	(0.437)
Countries	138	55	88
Observations	3,023	830	1,358
Controls	✓	✓	✓
R^2	0.557	0.271	0.148
	Panel C: Indirect Tax Revenue		
Democratization	−0.244	0.074	−0.111
	(0.538)	(0.499)	(0.832)
Countries	138	55	89
Observations	3,031	865	1,332
Controls	✓	✓	✓
R^2	0.173	0.205	0.210

*$p<0.1$; **$p<0.05$; ***$p<0.01$

to the previous section, but instead of looking at the effects of the full polity scale, I created a binary indicator called *Democratization*. This was coded as a 1 for any country-year where the Polity score is five or more points higher than the previous year. I use this coding to capture significant jumps in the citizens' ability to hold governments accountable, which according to the model should trigger low-capacity states to reduce taxation. This variable should capture a wide range of political liberalizations, not only those in which a country formally moves from autocracy to democracy. In the sample, there were 111 democratizations in 74 unique countries. Because no high-income countries democratized during this period, I only show the by-income results for low- and medium-income countries.

The results are striking: in the pooled sample, democratization is associated with a significant *decrease* in total tax revenue. This predicted decrease of 1.48 percentage points is substantively large, representing a much larger percentage of the average government budget. For example, in Uganda a drop in taxation of 1.48 percentage points of GDP would necessitate a 6% cut in total government spending unless alternative revenues were found (Government of Uganda 2022). This decrease is driven primarily by the drop in direct tax revenue; the drop in indirect tax revenue is smaller and not statistically significant. When we only look at low-income countries, higher Polity scores are associated with lower overall and direct taxes, but the differences are imprecisely estimated. For indirect taxes the coefficient is positive but very close to zero. For medium-income countries, an increase in polity is associated with lower overall, direct, and indirect taxes, although the differences are not statistically significant from zero.

6.1.5 Robustness

So far, the results paint a clear picture: at low levels of GDP, an increase in the level of democracy is correlated with a decrease in overall tax-to-GDP ratios, and this is driven by the effect on direct taxes, which are exactly the taxes that are most likely to generate accountability demands from citizens. However, the results are also from a single set of specifications. This makes it important to consider alternative ways of measuring the key variables and specifying the regression, to ensure that the results are stable across multiple possible measurements and assumptions. I therefore conducted additional tests in which I varied the use of fixed effects; the lag structure; and the measures used for democracy and state development. All of these alternative specifications are available in the online appendix.

Table 6.2 showed the effect of Polity on taxation broken down by World Bank income classifications, and found that while higher Polity scores were strongly correlated with more taxation overall, this was driven almost entirely by high-income countries; for low-income countries the result was close to zero and not significant. This pattern of results is extremely robust to additional specifications. First, using an alternative, binary measure of democracy created by Boix, I get the same results as the main analysis: democracy is only associated with higher taxation for high-income coun-tries. Second, when I turn Polity into a binary measure in which country-years of 5 or higher are considered democracies, all income levels are associated with more overall taxation, but the effects for low-income coun-tries are extremely small, with coefficients only 5–10% of their high-income counterparts. Even in this specification, however, low-income countries do not see significantly higher direct taxes as Polity increases. Finally, I reran the main specification (using the 21-point Polity scale as the main independent variable) with country and year fixed effects but no time trend; year fixed effects without a time trend; and lagging the independent variables by zero, three, and five years instead of one year. I also ran models dropping GDP and GDP growth from the set of controls, and models that include the observations that the ICTD tax dataset recommends removing due to data quality issues. I consistently find that while the pooled data show a positive effect of Polity on taxation, this is driven primarily by high-income countries. In some of the specifications the increases are significant for middle- and/or low-income countries, but the coefficients are always 5–10% of their high-income counterparts. In no specification is higher Polity associated with higher direct taxation in low-income countries. Thus, the results are remarkably robust.

Table 6.3 reported the results when regime type is interacted with GDP per capita as a proxy for state development. To test the robustness of this result, I first ran versions of the analysis with three- and five-year lags, instead of the one-year lag in the main specification. The results are unchanged. Next I ran the main specification using year fixed effects instead of the cubic time trend, and using country fixed effects. Again, the results are unchanged. Finally, I ran a version of the analysis using the binary "democratization" variable instead of the full Polity scale, and the World Bank income classifications instead of GDP per capita. I find similar results, although statistical significance is weaker, likely because the measures used are simply more blunt and thus losing much of the identifying variation.

To further test the results, I considered potential alternative measures for the independent variables. In the main analysis, I use GDP per capita as a proxy for state development because many existing measures of state capacity are too closely related to the government's taxation decisions: a country that taxes more almost by definition needs higher state capacity and a better bureaucracy. This creates the worry that, rather than measuring a true independent variable, state capacity is simply another way of measuring taxation. Still, to explore the robustness of the main findings, I reran the interaction analysis, replacing GDP per capita with two different measures of state capacity. First, I use the VDEM measure for "rigorous and impartial public administration," as a measure that might affect state capacity. Second, I use the International Country Risk Guide (ICRG)'s "Quality of Governance" measure, which combines measures of corruption, law and order, and bureaucratic quality. In both specifications I keep the full Polity scale as the measure of democracy.[3]

The results using the alternative measures of state capacity are more mixed, but still provide some support for the theory. For the ICRG Quality of Governance measure, the results are similar to the main specification for direct taxes: the Polity variable has a significant, negative effect on taxation while the interaction with state capacity is positive and significant. However, for indirect taxation Polity has a positive effect, and the interaction is not significant. When we look at overall tax revenues, Polity has a negative (but not significant) effect at low levels of state capacity, and the interaction with state capacity is positive. Thus, the results mainly replicate, although the ICRG measure suggests that democracy's negative effect on direct taxes for low-capacity states may partially be offset by higher indirect taxation. For the VDEM state capacity measure, Polity has a small but positive effect on all types of taxes even at low levels of state capacity. However, the interaction term for direct taxation is also positive and significant, suggesting that even here, democracy's effect on taxation is much stronger when state capacity is high.

Finally, I ran additional versions of the analysis in Table 6.4. All results are robust to using a three- or five-year lag in the independent variables, instead of the one-year lag in the main model. In the main specification, I coded democratization as an increase of 5 or more points in Polity. When I change the coding to be a 4-point change, the results all hold. When I change the coding to be a 6-point change, all coefficients are in the same direction, but the results are weaker. This is likely because, by requiring larger Polity changes for a country to count as liberalizing, I am excluding a number of significant political changes from the coding. I also ran versions of the model in which I include country fixed effects with a time trend, and in which I include both country and time fixed effects. In these specifications, the coefficients are similar and all in the same direction, but the coefficient on democratization is no longer statistically significant. Note that, because democratization is a rare event and does not occur across all countries, fixed effects are absorbing a large amount of the variation for the key variables, making this a very difficult test. Still, even in when democratization is not

---

[3] While VDEM has a measure of democracy, it is correlated with the VDEM state capacity measure at 0.74, suggesting significant overlap in the measures. I thus do not use it here.

significant, we still see negative coefficients: democratization does not have a positive effect on taxation.

6.2 Democracy and the Tax Net

Even wealthier countries in sub-Saharan Africa still struggle with relatively low levels of state capacity. Based on the results so far, we should therefore expect that African countries in general will have lower levels of taxation when they are democracies. While this could manifest in lower tax-to-GDP ratios, there are also ways government could significantly reduce taxation on most citizens while tax-to-GDP ratios stay constant or even increase. For example, governments could eliminate relatively low-revenue taxes on poor citizens while increasing taxes on wealthy citizens. If this was the case, we would need to have data on the actual size of the tax net. While cross-national measures of the tax net are not readily available, Round 5 of the Afrobarometer included a module asking respondents about whether they are required to pay several forms of taxes, including income, property, and VAT or sales tax. I used these questions to construct country-level measures of the share of respondents in each country who report paying direct and indirect taxes.[4] Respondents who replied that they are required to pay income tax; self-employment tax; or property tax are coded as paying a direct tax. Those who replied that they are required to pay VAT or sales tax are coded as paying an indirect tax. These are the main outcomes variables for this analysis.

Because this results in a very small sample size of 29 country-level observations (one per sub-Saharan country in Afrobarometer), traditional regression analysis would be severely under-powered. Instead, I simply look at summary statistics for the average proportion of respondents who report paying each tax type in democracies and autocracies. Following standard practice, I code a country as a democracy if it has a score of 5 or higher on the Polity scale. I also consider the effect of democracy separately by whether a country is above or below the median on the corruption measure from the Varieties of Democracy (V-DEM) dataset. As corruption limits the extent to which public goods can be provided by taxation, the model

---

[4] Country-level measures were constructed using the within-country survey weights provided by Afrobarometer.

Table 6.5 Fraction of each country required to pay each tax, by democracy. Full sample includes 18 democracies and 16 non-democracies.

	Full Sample	Low Corruption	High Corruption
Panel A: Direct Tax Net Size			
Non-democracy	0.751	0.736	0.766
Democracy	0.711	0.723	0.699
Panel B: Indirect Tax Net Size			
Non-democracy	0.622	0.660	0.584
Democracy	0.577	0.649	0.505

predicts that the drop in taxation in democracies will be most pronounced by high-corruption countries. This is because high corruption will make it more challenging for leaders to meet citizens' demands for public goods, increasing the incentives to reduce taxation in order to reduce citizens' demands.

Table 6.5 reports average tax net size, by category, for the Afrobarometer countries. The top panel reports direct tax results, the bottom panel indirect tax results. As predicted, democracies have smaller tax nets than autocracies. In the full direct tax sample, 75% of respondents in non-democracies report paying direct taxes, compared to 71% of respondents in democracies. This difference is driven primarily by high-corruption countries. While in low-corruption countries the difference in tax net size is only 1.3 percentage points, the gap is 6.7 percentage points in high-corruption countries. Indeed, the category with the smallest tax net is high-corruption democracies. This is consistent with the idea that, when corruption hinders the efficient provision of public goods, governments are less likely to tax in democracy.

The results for indirect tax net size, presented in Panel B, are very similar. Democracies have indirect tax nets that are about 4.5 percentage points smaller, on average, and this gap almost doubles in high-corruption countries. However, the indirect tax results should be interpreted with caution. Common indirect taxes, such as VAT and excise taxes, are paid by almost all citizens. Thus, the indirect tax results could result from lower indirect taxation in democracies, or simply from lower *awareness* of such taxes in democracies. However, direct taxes are not subject to the same issue: direct taxes are typically highly visible, and it is unlikely that a respondent is unaware that she pays income tax, for example (de la Cuesta et al. 2020).

6.2.1 Discussion

The results from this section provide new insights into the relationship between democratization, corruption, and taxation. I find that while democracy follows the standard, "democracies tax more" prediction for high-income countries, democracy has either a null or even a negative effect on taxation for low-income countries. Critically, democratization itself is associated with lower taxation in subsequent years. A secondary test, using data from the Afrobarometer surveys, suggests that when governance is poor, democracies will tend to tax fewer citizens than non-democracies. When corruption is low, democracies do not appear to suffer a reduction in taxation.

A country's tax net does not necessarily predict its tax take as a fraction of GDP. For the countries in the Afrobarometer sample, there is in fact a negative correlation between the two measures. This can occur in several ways. For example, if a country taxes almost all citizens, but obtains only small amounts of revenue from each, then the tax net is large but tax/GDP will be low. In contrast, a country that only taxes the wealthy, but levies higher tax rates, might see much higher tax/GDP ratios despite the small tax net. In both cases, however, I find that low-income democracies do not necessarily tax more than low-income autocracies, as my theory predicts.

Of course, one must be careful in interpreting these results. Taxation is not randomly assigned, and the relationship between taxation and democracy should be taken as correlational only. While these data cannot show that democracy *causes* lower taxation, it does provide observational evidence that is *consistent* with the theory.

6.3 Taxation, Accountability, and Rent-Seeking

In low-income countries, an increase in citizens' *ability* to hold governments accountable through democracy may not lead to higher taxation in the way standard models predict. However, this does not imply that the link between taxation and accountability will break down.

In the model developed in Chapter 4, when governments are willing to tax, there are two possibilities. In many cases they will limit rent-seeking and provide citizens with their desired public goods. This is the standard "high taxation, high accountability" story. Yet, this is not universal: leaders who do not sufficiently value the future may prefer to keep rent-seeking high and accept loss of office. Likewise, non-democratic leaders may be able to tax, keep rent-seeking high, and still hold on to office due to limited political competition. On average, however, we should see that governments who tax will have lower levels of rent-seeking that governments who avoid taxation. This prediction is consistent with existing empirical work suggests that taxation does have a positive effect on different measures of accountability. For example, Prichard (2015) shows that higher tax reliance is associated with higher levels of democracy. Baskaran and Bigsten (2013) use data from sub-Saharan Africa to show that higher levels of taxation are associated with lower levels of corruption.

Beyond this overall relationship, I expect that there will be variation in the strength of the relationship between rent-seeking and taxation. First, I expect that the relationship will be stronger for direct taxes, compared to indirect, as these are more likely to generate citizen accountability demands. This follows joint work presented in de la Cuesta et al. (2020). Second, I expect that the relationship will be stronger in democracies. While citizens in autocracies and democracies may both want to demand public goods and limited rent-seeking, citizens in democracies will be better able to use protests and elections to effectively threaten governments who do not meet these demands. However, as few autocracies are absolute, I still expect that taxation will be associated with lower rent-seeking in autocracies. Finally, I expect that this relationship will be strongest in lower-income countries. In high-income countries, stronger state capacity means that the ability of governments to rent seek is relatively lower overall, compared to poorer, low-capacity states. There is therefore more room for taxation to have a stronger effect on citizens' capacity to hold governments accountable in low-income states.

In Chapter 4, and in the analysis in the previous chapter, I examine how taxation affects predicted levels of *rent-seeking*, the extent to which governments divert state resources for their own ends. When rent-seeking is high, one observable implication is high levels of corruption. Corruption has significant deleterious effects on the ability of governments to carry out policy, and on the efficiency of public goods provision. For analysis, I represent this with the combined corruption measure from the Varieties of Democracy (V-Dem) dataset. This variable measures "How pervasive is political corruption?", and draws on measures of executive, legislative, public sector, and judicial rent-seeking through bribes and embezzlement. I use this combined measure, rather than more specific measures of embezzlement, because it captures the overall extent to which the state apparatus is focused on rent-seeking.

For analysis, the main independent variable is tax revenues as a percent of GDP. As before, I run the analysis using total tax, direct tax, and indirect tax revenues. All regressions are OLS, and include a cubic time trend as well as a vector of controls that includes the same measures used in the previous sections.[5] Robust, panel-corrected standard errors are clustered by country and year. Below I discuss the robustness of the results to alternative specifications.

I treat all analysis here as correlational, not causal. Both tax revenues and corruption will likely be affected by a number of factors, including overall levels of state capacity and development. While I control for a number of such potential confounders, I cannot rule them out entirely. In short, even if higher levels of taxation are strongly correlated with lower subsequent levels of corruption, we cannot know if this is because taxation is causing the change. The experimental evidence in Chapter 5 shows that citizens will certainly demand more when taxed, but we cannot rule out that the correlation arises for other reasons. Additionally, the relationship between taxation and accountability is very difficult to sequence temporally. A government who needs additional tax revenue may decrease rent-seeking before the new tax, in order to increase support for the new tax, or may only decrease rent-seeking once the tax is in place and citizen demands increase.

With those caveats in mind, Table 6.6 shows the basic results of the analysis. Each column represents the results from a different regression, and each panel uses a different type of tax as the main independent variable. The first column shows the results for all countries pooled together. Both indirect and direct taxes are associated with lower corruption in the following year, as is taxation overall. However, as predicted, the magnitude of the effect is much larger for direct taxes. For each additional percentage point of GDP a government collects in taxes, the model predicts a drop of 0.011 on the corruption scale; this implies that if total taxes increased by one standard deviation (7.878 percentage points of GDP), we would expect corruption to

---

[5] The controls are: log GDP per capita, log percent GDP growth, trade as a percent of GDP, log resource revenue, net FDI as a percent of GDP, log population, urbanization, civil war, and interstate war.

Table 6.6 Effect of tax revenue on political corruption (Vdem).

	Dependent Variable: Corruption				
	Pooled	Autocracies	Democracies	OECD	Non-OECD
Panel A: Total Tax Revenue					
Total Tax Revenue	−0.011***	−0.004	−0.009***	−0.0003	−0.010***
	(0.002)	(0.003)	(0.003)	(0.003)	(0.002)
Countries	143	83	102	36	107
Observations	3,272	1,199	2,071	965	2,307
Controls	✓	✓	✓	✓	✓
R^2	0.666	0.388	0.679	0.644	0.352
Panel B: Direct Tax Revenue					
Direct Tax Revenue	−0.021***	−0.016**	−0.016***	−0.002	−0.027***
	(0.004)	(0.007)	(0.004)	(0.004)	(0.006)
Countries	138	78	98	35	103
Observations	3,028	1,042	1,984	949	2,079
Controls	✓	✓	✓	✓	✓
R^2	0.680	0.410	0.680	0.625	0.364
Panel C: Indirect Tax Revenue					
Indirect Tax Revenue	−0.010***	−0.004	−0.008**	−0.001	−0.012***
	(0.003)	(0.004)	(0.004)	(0.005)	(0.003)
Countries	138	79	99	35	103
Observations	3,036	1,049	1,985	947	2,089
Controls	✓	✓	✓	✓	✓
R^2	0.652	0.400	0.673	0.624	0.343

*$p<0.1$; **$p<0.05$; ***$p<0.01$

be lower by 0.087 points, or 0.27 SD. For direct taxes this effect size is even larger: a one standard deviation increase in direct taxes would predict a 0.35 standard deviation drop in corruption. These results are robust to a number of alternative econometric choices, including lagging independent variables by three or five years instead of one year; including country fixed effects along with the time trend; and including country and year fixed effects.

Columns 2 and 3 of Table 6.6 show the same results, but broken down by whether each observation has a Polity score of 5 or higher. As one might expect, the results for overall levels of taxation are strongest for democracies: when citizens have more favorable political institutions, they are better able to translate higher demands into better governance. However, when we look at direct taxes, the effect is actually identical for autocracies and democracies:

in both cases, higher levels of direct taxation are associated with lower levels of corruption. This is consistent with the model, which showed that even in autocracies, citizens may still be able to use taxation, and tax bargaining, to extract concessions from the government. Robustness checks that use the binary Boix measure of democracy, rather than the binary Polity measure, actually show much stronger results for autocracies, with both direct and indirect taxes associated with lower corruption.

Finally, columns 4 and 5 of Table 6.6 show the results broken down by whether a country is a member of the OECD. OECD countries, as high-income democracies, have limited variation in the degree of corruption; the standard deviation of the corruption measure is 42% that of the non-OECD sample. Thus, is it important to ensure they are not driving the results, and that taxation is still associated with lower corruption in non-OECD states. This is exactly what the results show. While the coefficients are negative across the board, they are only statistically significant for non-OECD countries; the coefficients are also much smaller for the OECD specification. Critically, when we just look at non-OECD countries, we still see that direct taxes have a much larger effect on corruption than indirect taxes do. The online appendix for this chapter presents additional results, including the analysis broken down the the same World Bank income classifications (low-, medium-, and high-income) used in the previous sections. I find that while higher levels of direct taxation are associated with lower corruption in all three income groups, indirect taxation consistently has a smaller coefficient that is only significant for low- and medium-income countries.

6.3.1 Robustness and Additional Work

The results thus far show correlations that are consistent with the model's theoretical predictions. However, previous work on taxation and accountability suggests that many results are fragile, and only hold under particular variable choices, sets of controls, or other statistical modeling decisions. In joint work with Brandon de la Cuesta, Helen Milner, and Daniel Nielson, we provide more extensive analysis of the relationship between taxation and accountability (de la Cuesta et al. 2020). To do so, we use a panel dataset of 194 countries from 1980 to 2018. As our independent variables, we use the one-year lag of the tax-to-GDP ratio of a country in a given year for either direct or indirect taxes, as measured by the same ICTD dataset used above. We considered two dependent variables, both from V-Dem: the same combined corruption measure used in Table 6.6, and an index measuring vertical accountability. This second measure is based on a number of indicators, including the presence of free and fair elections, and is designed to capture "the extent to which citizens have the power to hold the government accountable."

Rather than picking a single specification for this analysis, we used a modified extreme bound analysis as described in Sala-i-Martin (1997). The resulting analysis, which is described more fully in de la Cuesta et al. (2020), resulted in almost 5,000 regressions, which differed in the set of controls included; all of our results are robust to allowing variation in additional modeling assumptions, such as the type of fixed effects used and the way that time trends are modeled. All models cluster standard errors by year, include country fixed effects, and include a set of 11 core control variables that were the most likely confounders. Critically, we ran this analysis separately for direct and indirect taxes.

Our results show clear patterns, and clear differences across the tax modalities. Direct taxes are consistently associated with lower corruption; the coefficient is almost always positive, and is statistically significant across a wide range of specifications. In contrast, indirect taxation has little effect on corruption. The distribution of coefficients is centered around zero, and rarely approaches statistical significance. This suggests that, on average, higher direct taxation of citizens is associated with lower rates of corruption at the country level. However, increases in indirect taxation may not have the same benefits.

We see similar patterns in our accountability index analysis. Here indirect taxation if anything is associated with a *negative* effect on accountability, while direct taxation has an ambiguous effect. As the accountability measure includes institutional indicators that are difficult to move—in contrast to the corruption indicator that is more reflective of (comparatively) easy-to-change behavior—it is perhaps not surprising that we are unable to pick up positive effects of direct taxation. Combined, this analysis suggests that, as predicted by the model, taxation will may be able to improve accountability. However, it is most likely to do so for forms of taxation that are visible and salient to citizens, such as direct taxes.

6.4 Conclusion

In this chapter, I presented new evidence how governments will respond if taxation increases citizens' demands. I showed that in a cross-national panel dataset, an increase in the level of democracy is only associated with higher taxation in higher-capacity states. In low-capacity states, governments may decrease taxation, and with it citizen pressures, rather than meet citizens' demands. As predicted, this pattern is strongest for direct taxes, which are exactly those most likely to generate higher citizen demands. This finding is supported by data on the tax net: in African states, the tax net is lower in democracies, especially in high-corruption states. I also demonstrated that, while higher levels of taxation are correlated with lower levels of corruption overall, this pattern is stronger for direct taxes, for democracies, and in low-income states.

Put together, these results suggest the need for a more nuanced understanding of the connections between taxation, democracy, and good governance. While democracies do tend to tax more than autocracies, this relationship is driven almost entirely by high-income countries. In low-income countries, we should not expect that a simple transition to multi-party elections is going to lead to strong, stable states—something that has become increasingly apparent to observers since the wave of democratizations in the 1990s, combined with recent democratic backsliding in some states. Similarly, while taxation can lead to higher accountability, this is most likely for direct taxes: exactly those that are hardest to implement in low-capacity states.

However, the analysis also has several weaknesses. Some of the results, particularly the result that higher levels of democracy are associated with significantly lower taxation in low-income states, only held in a subset of the specifications tested. One reason for this may be that eliminating taxes on some groups of citizens may have little impact on a government's tax-to-GDP ratio, while having a large impact on the average citizens' willingness to hold leaders accountable. As discussed above, for the countries in the Afrobarometer sample, there is in fact a negative correlation between the estimated size of the tax net and taxes as a fraction of GDP.

Another weakness of the analysis is that, as discussed above, the temporal sequencing of decisions about taxation, corruption, and political openness is not clear, making it difficult to interpret the results and make causal claims. While this chapter was able to test multiple implications of my theory, it could not tease out the actual political calculus of leaders as they decide whether and how to tax. To get a better sense for these dynamics, and to further test my argument that governments will avoid taxing when doing so will increase accountability demands, the next chapter draws on a history of taxation in Uganda.

7

Understanding Taxation in Uganda

When taxes are paid by the public, they are inclined to hold politicians to account for their conduct.

Ministry of Local Government (2014)

7.1 Introduction

The previous chapter used cross-national data to show that, as predicted,
democracy can reduce rather than increase taxation in low-capacity states.
However, the large-N data is not able to test the mechanisms behind this
effect, or to show more directly that the accountability pressures that taxation
creates are the impetus for governments to avoid investing in fiscal capacity.
To gain a better sense for these dynamics, this chapter uses a series of case
studies of taxation in Uganda to test the model's predictions at a more
disaggregated level. I trace the evolution of different forms of taxation over
the past 25 years, arguing that the model's predictions map closely onto
which types of taxation have been successful in Uganda. I explain why the
move to multi-party politics led to the elimination of some forms of taxation
but not others, and how the recent return to more authoritarian rule is
already leading to higher taxation in some cases. Facing more electoral competition, the Ugandan government reshaped taxation to minimize accountability pressures, only taxing when accountability demands were easily met,
or when taxation was invisible to citizens and thus unlikely to generate
accountability pressures at all. More contentious taxes have only recently
started to increase as Museveni further consolidates his hold on power.

The chapter proceeds as follows. I first discuss why taxation in Uganda
makes a particularly good case study, focusing on the national and subnational shifts in regime type and the degree to which taxation has changed
since 2000. I then examine three distinct direct taxes: the graduated tax,
market fees, and a tax on motorcycle taxi drivers. Finally, I discuss other

Strategic Taxation: Fiscal Capacity and Accountability in African States. Lucy E. S. Martin.
Oxford University Press. © Oxford University Press 2023. DOI: 10.1093/oso/9780197672631.003.0007

recent changes to the structure of taxation in Uganda, focusing on a number of indirect taxes as well as the contentious attempt to tax social media usage.

7.2 Why Uganda?

Uganda has several attributes that make it a good place to test this book's predictions regarding taxation. First, it is a relatively representative country within sub-Saharan Africa. It is near the continent's mean on several key economic indicators. GDP per capita is currently US$817 in raw terms, and US$2297 once adjusting for purchasing power (World Bank 2020). Between 2000 and 2020, GDP per capita grew at an average rate of 2.9%, making it a relative success story. However, the economic condition is also tentative, reflecting the effects of the COVID-19 pandemic on growth across the African continent. Due in part to COVID-19, Uganda's debt-to-GDP ratio by December 2021 was 47% of GDP, and the projected budget deficit for the 2021/2 fiscal year was 7.3% of GDP (Ministry of Finance, Uganda 2022). This raises concerns about the long-run fiscal stability of the country, and makes it critical to understand whether, and how, the government will use taxation to restore fiscal balance.

Uganda's historical legacies are likewise characteristic of sub-Saharan Africa. In the colonial period, taxation fell disproportionately on Black Ugandans, who received few benefits in return (Jamal 1978).[1] While taxpayers did attempt to demand some accountability, often through tax protests, the authoritarian nature of the colonial government made success impossible. In 1962 the newly independent government inherited the colonial tax structure largely intact, and other than removing some of the worst inequities of the previous system, significant changes do not appear to have been made until the 1980s. Like many African countries, commodity price shocks in that period decimated Uganda's export tax revenues, which until that point had formed a large percentage of the government's budget (Gloppen and Rakner 2002). Subsequent IMF agreements led to the complete elimination of export taxes, leading to a broad push to improve the collection of existing taxes. These measures were less successful in bringing new groups

---

[1] In addition to Poll and Hut taxes that were paid only by Africans, export taxes were substantially higher on African-grown crops, and import taxes were higher on goods consumed by the African population than on goods consumed by white colonialists Jamal (1978).

into the tax net (Gloppen and Rakner 2002). When Yoweri Museveni and the National Resistance Movement (NRM) assumed power in 1986, new revenues need to be raised, and the tax system finally began to undergo more significant changes.

Uganda's political structure is also characteristic in many ways. It is formally a decentralized system, with local governments at the district (Local Council 5, or LC5), subcounty (LC3), and village (LC1) levels. The district and subcounty levels are staffed and funded, and can pass ordinances and levy taxes. The village level is more informal, with an elected head but no funding and a more limited mandate. The subcounty and district governments have extremely limited local revenue generation, and rely almost entirely on transfers from the central government. Still, elections for local government elections have remained relatively competitive compared to the national level.

Uganda's political trajectory involves several expansions and contractions of democracy, making it a good case to study how regime type affects taxation. Yoweri Museveni and his National Resistance Movement (NRM) initially took power in 1986 following a protracted bush war, ushering in a period of relative peace and stability. Over the next decade the country became a favorite of donors, and economic performance saw significant improvements. Political development took longer, with no elections held until 1996. This ushered in a period of "no-party" politics, essentially a one-party state under the NRM. Like many other African countries, multi-party elections did follow, although not until 2006. The switch occurred following a referendum held in 2005. A similar referendum had been held five years prior, but had failed; in 2005 it passed with over 90% of the vote. While multi-party elections did introduce more formal opposition in Parliament and local government, President Museveni managed to stay in power during the electoral transitions. In recent years, however, the political landscape has again become more closed. While regular elections are still held, the NRM has instituted a number of restrictions on political discourse, and opposition members are frequently arrested or harassed. In the most recent elections, held in early 2021, the main opposition candidates were repeatedly arrested and abused, their supporters attacked, and the vote heavily guarded and influenced. Uganda is now best characterized as an electoral autocracy.

President Museveni's hold on power throughout changes to electoral institutions makes Uganda an excellent case to study the effect of institutions on taxation. The case studies presented here draw on the evolution of taxation under a single leader when facing varying degrees of electoral competition. There are clear patterns visible as electoral survival incentives became more, or less, pertinent, with some taxes being introduced, and others being abolished. The special case of Uganda's capital, Kampala, is also instructive: in 2011 Parliament wrested control of the city away from the opposition-led Kampala City Council, vesting power in an appointed agency, the Kampala Capital City Authority, instead. This essentially created a subnational autocracy in the midst of a national democracy, with intriguing results.

Like many other African countries, Uganda relies on a mix of foreign aid, resource rents, and taxes for its budget. In 2019, Uganda received US$2.1 billion in official development assistance (WDI), equal to approximately 43% of central government expenditures.[2] Still, Uganda's aid dependence is lower than it was 20 years ago. In the 2000s, official ODA was equal to 12–16% of GNI. This dropped precipitously in 2009 following a corruption scandal in which millions of aid dollars went missing from the office of prime minister. Numerous donors cut off or reduced aid in return, and since 2009 aid has dropped to 5–7% of GNI (World Bank 2020).

Uganda is also a relative newcomer to oil extraction. Significant oil reserves were discovered in Uganda's western region in 2006, and after years of delays and negotiations a final agreement to extract the oil and build a pipeline was finalized in early 2022; oil production is expected in 2025 (Ojambo, Fred, and Burkhardt, Paul 2022). While oil has yet to flow, the central government had already been able to reap benefits: by 2018 it had received 2.7 trillion UGX (about US$771 million at current exchange rates, but more at the time paid). There has been intense public debate about the use of oil-based revenues, and many citizens already believe that the government is consistently receiving money from oil. Data collected in Kampala on citizens' beliefs about the budget show that citizens believe oil comprises 20% of the government's budget, on average (de la Cuesta et al. 2022).

This chapter outlines the evolution of taxation in Uganda between 1996 and 2021. I focus first on the period between 1996 and 2006; this covers Uganda's democratic expansion from the time non-competitive elections were introduced to the time of the first multi-party elections in 2006. Over this period citizen pressure, combined with the advent of elections, led to the elimination of several forms of mass taxation, including the Graduated Tax, school fees, health center fees, and many property taxes. In other cases

---

[2] This amount includes aid funds that went to NGOs or IGOs, as well as on-budget aid.

taxes were kept but tax bargains served as a basis for increased accountability; market fees are the primary example of this dynamic.

I then consider the recent period, from about 2011 to 2021, in which Museveni began to crack down on political competition and Uganda became less democratic. During this period a number of new taxes were introduced, notably a highly coercive tax on motorcycle taxi drivers, a tax on social media, and a number of indirect taxes. The remainder of this chapter discusses the evolution of taxation in Uganda in more detail, focusing on how variation in the groups being taxed, along with the changing level of political competition, determined the equilibrium outcomes.

7.3 The Graduated Tax

When the NRM came to power in 1986, Ugandan citizens paid a number of direct taxes. These included health center fees, school fees, property taxes, and, most prominently, the Graduated Personal Tax (GPT). The GPT has its roots in the head and hut taxes of the colonial period, and similar taxes are or were found in Kenya, Tanzania, and other colonies. British colonies were under substantial pressure to be self-financing, and taxing the African population was one way to achieve this (Gardner 2012). The colonial government introduced a hut tax in 1900, and a poll tax in 1904 (Therkildsen 2006); both levied a fixed amount on each adult male or each hut, rather than a proportion of income. These taxes provided necessary revenues for the colonial government but had the added effect of pushing Ugandans out of subsistence farming and into the cash economy, as those who were unwilling to work for wages or to plant cash crops such as cotton would have a hard time obtaining the funds necessary to pay the tax (Therkildsen 2006). While more traditional income taxes were introduced by the 1940s, these applied primarily to white and Asian residents, affecting only a small number of higher-income Ugandans.[3]

---

[3] Black Ugandans also paid a number of other taxes, including excise taxes and those imposed by marketing boards; in 1936 the colonial Government Treasurer acknowledged the high tax burden but also argued for its central role in providing a low-wage workforce, explaining that "In Uganda the bulk of the taxation is paid by large numbers in rural areas and the amount paid by each individual represents a very large proportion of his money income. In many cases the proportion approaches 100%. In Uganda taxation is the principal incentive to labor and production" (quoted in Jamal (1978), 428). Thus, taxation was used to effectively coerce Black Ugandans into working for white-owned farms and factories.

7.3.1 Low Electoral Accountability

By the time Uganda became independent in 1962, the Hut and Poll Taxes had been transformed into the Graduated Personal Tax (GPT), a fixed fee levied on all adult men and some wage-earning women. In theory the tax was progressive, as those with higher wealth or income paid a slightly higher fixed amount; in practice the system for establishing an individual's rate was complex and often implemented arbitrarily. While the national government received revenues from the income tax, which only affected more prosperous Ugandans, funds from the GPT went to subnational District governments. The GPT was one of the largest sources of funding available for these local governments; by 1993 it accounted for between 57.6% and 88.9% of own revenues for each District and 18.3% to 40.7% of revenue for each Municipality (Livingstone and Charlton 1998). As central transfers during that period were substantially lower than they are now, the GPT was critical to funding local public goods provision.

However, the GPT has never been popular among Uganda's citizens. This discontent stemmed from how tax obligations were decided, how taxes were collected, and how taxes were used. In a rural economy like Uganda's, where subsistence farming forms a large part of the economy, evaluating wealth and income for tax purposes is cumbersome. While official rules for evaluating an individual's tax rate existed, even an honest and hard-working official would have found it difficult to implement the rules fairly. Given the low capacity of local governments to implement the tax, it is not surprising that tax evaluations were perceived as biased and inconsistent. Livingstone and Charlton (1998) argues that "assessments of income and therefore actual payments of tax are revealed by available data to be extremely arbitrary" (507), adding that there was little correlation between the average income in a district and the average tax band that residents fell into. In practice many individuals paid the same level despite differing incomes. Yet, even collecting this simplified tax was very costly: "Enumeration of taxpayers and assessment and collection of GPT are each major administrative exercises which occupy an 'army' of people annually in each district over a period of some three to four months" (507).

Collection of the GPT was also extremely coercive. In contrast to the income tax, where the penalty for tax evasion was usually a fine, and the burden of proof was on the government, evading the GPT carried a one-month jail term, and the burden of proof was on the accused (Therkildsen

2006). In 2000, a survey of Ugandan prisoners revealed that a full 2% were in jail for evading the GPT (Therkildsen 2006). Livingstone and Charlton (1998) document numerous incidences of extreme coercion. In 1996 and 1997 alone, this included the "beating to death" of a tax defaulter; an armed raid by tax collectors on a wedding in Hoima District in which 18 people were "critically injured"; and a case in which a local bureaucrat in Rukingiri District ordered armed forces to "shoot to kill" any tax defaulter who attempted to escape (510). Perhaps unsurprisingly, the dominant image used by those describing the situation is of a man hiding "in the bush" (i.e. the wild areas surrounding a village or town) until the tax collector goes away again.[4]

Why was such coercion necessary? Local governments relied heavily on GPT revenues, so why were they not able to find a way to either bargain for quasi-voluntary compliance or pacify the population through public goods provision? The costs of such a coercive system were high: an independent report by PriceWaterhouseCooper in 2000 found that collecting the GPT cost on average 40% of revenues collected in a given district, although in some especially recalcitrant subcounties it could reach 150% of revenues (Local Government Finance Commission 2001). Coercion was also costly in terms of civil unrest—tax riots in Uganda have been relatively common, both in the colonial period and in the 1980s and 1990s; riots in Iganga District led to an independent inquiry report, which said that "taxpayer resentment of GPT was increasing and spreading" (quoted in Livingstone and Charlton (1998), 502). Livingstone and Charlton (1998) link tax resistance to the "perceived failure by local authorities to deliver the corresponding level or quality of services in return" (513); GPT revenues were seen as covering primarily administrative costs and officials' wages, rather than providing public goods to citizens.

Despite the fact that the GPT was a local tax collected by local governments, it was still seen as a national issue. Even under decentralization, local taxes required approval from the national government, and power was for so long centralized in the office of the presidency that citizens viewed Museveni as the one with real power to change policy. Thus, this local tax was ripe to become a national political issue.

Prior to 2001, electoral accountability in Uganda was weak to non-existent. President Museveni took power in 1986, but the first elections

---

[4] Or, as a government report euphemistically called it, "hid[ing] in socially undesirable conditions to avoid arrests" (Local Government Finance Commission (2001), 5).

were not held until 1996. While multiple candidates were allowed to run in these elections, political parties were banned, making it difficult for the opposition to gather strength. President Museveni was re-elected with 75% of the vote in 1996, and opposition candidates largely boycotted the subsequent Parliamentary elections (Inter-Parliamentary Union 2015). In this climate citizens could and did launch informal protests about how tax funds were used, but could not effectively hope to hold officials accountable: the costs they could force governments to endure were simply too low relative to the gains from taxation.

How does this situation map onto the predictions of the model developed in Chapter 4? In the absence of competitive elections, the model predicts that the Government always prefers to tax provided the costs of tax collection are less than the gains. While GPT collection was expensive, the best estimate is that collection cost about 40% of revenues, (equivalent to setting $\gamma = .6$ in the model). This leaves two possible equilibria: the government could choose either to tax coercively and provide few or no public goods, or to bargain with citizens and provide a higher level of public goods. Given the costs of coercion, the model predicts that, under a bargain, citizens would receive about 30% of total tax revenues in the form of public goods ($G^B = \frac{1-\gamma}{2}\gamma\tau$), and that the bargain can only be sustained if the government and citizens both sufficiently value the future.[5] For citizens, the model predicts that citizens must highly value each dollar spent on the public good for this to hold. This value (α in the model) is affected by both the degree to which the citizens value the public good and the per-unit costs of its production, and is critical for the success of the bargain. Given that Uganda is a rural country with very low population density, I argue that it would likely cost a district government more than 1 UGX to provide 1 UGX's worth of goods to each citizen. Take for example health care, a public good highly valued by Ugandans. Even a small rural clinic entails a large fixed cost, but may only be accessible to a small number of citizens. This implies that the government simply cannot spend enough on public goods to recompense citizens for their tax payments and maintain some rent extraction. The model therefore predicts that only coercive taxation will be feasible, and that few public goods will be provided—exactly the situation in Uganda in this period.

---

[5] In terms of the model, $\delta_G \geq \frac{1}{2}$ and $\delta_c \geq \frac{2}{2+.4\alpha}$.

7.3.2 The Fate of the Graduated Tax under Political Competition

By the presidential elections of 2001, the situation had changed. While political parties were still banned, opposition groups managed to coordinate in support of Dr. Kizza Besigye. Despite the fact that the GPT was a local tax, the power of the central government meant that Besigye was able to gather broader support among voters by promising to eliminate the Graduated Tax. As this movement gained momentum, President Museveni took ownership over the issue, promising to reduce the minimum GPT rate from 11,000 Ugandan Shillings (UGX) to only 3,000 UGX (Bahiigwa et al. 2004). At the same time, many politicians, both Parliamentary members and local officials, began telling their local constituents to simply not pay the GPT.[6] Overall, enforcement was much less coercive during the election year: total revenues from the GPT dropped from 103 billion UGX in 1999 to 69.7 billion UGX in 2001 (Sarzin 2007). While the GPT retained a number of bands for different income groups, in practice most individuals simply paid the low 3,000 UGX amount following the election. As Bahiigwa et al. (2004) reports, many Ugandans believed that President Museveni had "assessed them all in 2001." For the next five years, the GPT remained in place but compliance was substantially lower, making local governments more reliant on central transfers (Bahiigwa et al. 2004).

In 2005, a public referendum in Uganda restored multi-party politics (BBC News 2005), making the 2006 Presidential elections the first multi-party elections in contemporary Uganda. Faced with real electoral opposition by Besigye's newly legal political party, the Forum for Democratic Change (FDC), Museveni simply announced that the Graduated Tax was eliminated.[7] Given the real threat of losing power, the government stood to benefit if it could maintain support by reducing citizens' demands— eliminating taxation was one way to do this. Despite the GPT being a local tax, it was still a very costly policy decision for the national government, as the budget provided additional transfers to district governments for several years after the tax was eliminated. Once those additional transfers were eliminated, however, many districts saw significant budget shortfalls, and are still scrambling to find new sources of local revenues.

---

[6] This is consistent with Prichard (2018), which provides evidence for political budget cycles in which governments systematically lower tax enforcement in election years.

[7] This was part of a larger effort to maintain electoral support, one that included widespread clientelism.

While precise measurement is difficult, there is a widespread perception in Uganda that accountability is worse since the GPT was abolished. One journalist, Daniel Kalinaki, has repeatedly argued for the reinstatement of the Graduated Tax. In June 2012, he wrote in the *Daily Monitor* that:

> The biggest problem with the elimination of GT is that it has eroded the culture of accountability. Peasants are not invested in the State and see no need to demand for better services from the local and central governments; they take whatever is offered to them. –Daniel Kalinaki (2012)

The puzzle of the Graduated Tax is why citizens' discontent resulted in the GPT's abolition: why did the government reduce taxation rather than one of the other potential equilibria—coercion with some public goods provision or tax bargaining? In Chapter 4, I showed that introducing competitive elections could have different effects on taxation, depending on the underlying characteristics. First, in contrast to the case without elections, there is now an equilibrium in which the government, in the absence of a bargain, prefers no taxation to coercive taxation. A sufficient condition for this to be the equilibrium is that the inefficiencies of coercion are high enough that it is not possible to appease citizens' desire for public goods, even if the entire budget was dedicated to service provision.[8] This seems likely to hold in the case of the GPT, given how expensive tax collection was. Second, the government must prefer no taxation to tax bargaining. Even under elections, tax bargains are difficult to sustain when the value of money spent on public goods is low, and so bargaining is still not possible, as it is still too expensive to provide a unit of the public good to each citizen. Together, this suggests that, when tax bargaining is not feasible, the advent of political competition can make some forms of taxation less appealing to a government.

A similar pattern is found in the fate of a number of other direct taxes in Uganda. Prior to 1996 Ugandans paid schools fees for each term a child was enrolled in primary or secondary school; fees for using health centers; and property taxes on homes. Each of these taxes have since been abolished, and these cuts have each occurred just prior to an election. As part of the 1996 election campaign President Museveni announced Universal Primary Education, outlawing fees for public primary schools. This was a policy that Museveni had at first resisted as detrimental to the budget, but later

---

[8] Formally, $\gamma y \tau \leq G_\tau^*$.

embraced when his primary opponent, Paul Ssemogere, mobilized around it (Therkildsen 2006). While both enrollments and funding subsequently increased (Stasavage 2005), the years following UPE were marked by severe corruption in the education sector (Reinikka and Svensson 2005). In March 2001 health center fees were similarly abolished during the election campaign. Since then several studies have shown that, while utilization of health centers has increased, the centers are more likely to lack resources like drugs, increasing the out-of-pocket expenses patients face (Xu et al. (2005), Orem et al. (2011)).[9] Again, a reduction in taxation led to a corresponding drop in the quality of public goods received by poor citizens. Finally, in 2006 a bill was passed to abolish property taxes paid on owner-occupied houses. These taxes were primarily collected in urban areas and formed a significant portion of the local tax base; Sarzin (2007) argues that the abolition of the property tax "removes a key accountability link between taxpayers/voters and their elected councillors."[10] Like with the graduated tax, citizens saw the national government as ultimately responsible for taxation, and acted accordingly.

All of the taxes discussed in this section share two key characteristics. First, they are all direct taxes that were highly visible to citizens. The Graduated Tax had to be paid annually and a receipt for payment was supposed to be carried at all times; health and education user fees were paid each term or at each visit; and property taxes were paid annually. This meant that citizens felt their loss of income keenly, increasing their accountability demands as shown in the previous chapters. Second, all of these taxes were collected through coercion rather than quasi-voluntary compliance. The coercion of the GPT was the most extreme, but students could not attend school or patients receive care unless fees were paid. The property tax was likewise difficult to evade. Finally, all of these taxes were abolished as Uganda's political system liberalized, often to the detriment of local public goods provision and accountability. However, other taxes in Uganda had different fates. The following sections discuss taxes that were kept or even introduced during the same period, and uses the model to explain these outcomes.

---

[9] A 2001 WHO publication found that the previous *introduction* of health center user fees had led to better quality services and improved access to drugs (Kipp et al. 2001).

[10] All of these cases are in line with previous work that suggests that tax enforcement will be lower in the lead-up to elections (Hyde and O'Mahony 2010; McGuirk 2010; Prichard 2018). However, the implications here are stronger: in some cases a government will not only temporarily reduce tax effort, but eliminate taxes altogether.

7.4 Market Fees

In contrast to the Graduated Tax, taxes on agricultural market vendors have been resilient to elimination despite consistent demands for accountability from taxed vendors.[11] Ugandan municipalities typically have one or more markets that sell agricultural and other goods on a daily basis, and even small trading centers often have weekly or monthly markets. Markets are still formally governed by the Markets Act of 1942, which states that the local government shall control the markets and determine how they are administered, including "imposing stallages, rents or tolls and fixing the amount and providing for the collection thereof" (Government of Uganda 1942). In practice, the relevant local government is the municipality, the district, or the subcounty, and market fees have historically been an important source of revenue for these governments. During the colonial period market fees were set at 5% of sales, which Jamal (1978) estimates to be 10–15% of net income for most vendors; data are not available for local government budgets in this period. More recently, in 1992 Kampala City received 16% of its revenue from markets, and Owino market alone generated 23 million UGX a month in fees, or at the 1992 exchange rate about US$283,000 a year (Gombay 1994). In smaller municipalities market dues and other user fees comprised on average 10% of own revenue in rural areas and 21% in urban areas as of 2001.

Like the Graduated Tax, market taxation in Uganda was historically contentious and coercive. Through the 1980s and early 1990s, taxes were typically collected by government officials according to a complex schedule of fees; while in some cases these fees were codified into the official by-laws of each market, many were more informal (Uganda Law Reform Commission 2013). The most common tax is a set amount per unit either brought into the market ("offloading" fees) or sold; data from 2007 show these could range from 300 UGX for a tin of millet to 2,000 UGX for a cow (Magala and Rubagumya 2007).[12] However, market vendors often have to pay additional fees as well. A government survey of 16 urban and rural markets by a Ugandan government commission in 2013 found that fees could include

---

[11] While I refer to the market levy as a tax, it is legally a fee paid for access to the market, not a tax. However, revenues are deposited into general district funds, and as the largest source of local revenue, its function and effect on those who pay is indistinguishable from a tax.

[12] When compared to the contemporary selling prices, this is equivalent to a 1% tax on cows and a 5% tax on millet; the highest proportional taxes were on chickens (11%) and potatoes (10%).

"market dues, security fees, stall fees, pitch fees, garbage fees, sanitation fee, toilet fee, electricity fees, rental fees, off loading fees, loading fees, parking fees, membership to the market association, permit fees, ground rent, local service tax and trading license" (Uganda Law Reform Commission (2013), 72). Many of these fees have historically been collected daily, although the national government has in recent years pushed local governments to start collecting weekly or monthly instead. In a survey of market vendors I conducted in eight Ugandan districts in 2013, 85% of vendors reported paying market fees. Of these, 46% paid daily, 40% monthly, and the others at different intervals. Among those who paid, the median monthly fee was 6,000 UGX, but taxes ranged from 2,400 UGX (about US$1 at the time) to over 100,000 UGX for the largest vendors.

Most daily markets are relatively well organized, with permanent shops and stalls that are occupied by the same vendor each day, often with gates or walls that define the marketplace. This makes them relatively cheap and easy to tax—all taxpayers are confined to a single space, and markets with gates allow the authorities to exclude tax evaders more easily. Most sources agree that the collection of market fees has historically been coercive; local governments have extracted relatively high taxes from vendors, and those who refused to pay are denied access to markets that are critical to their livelihoods. In my own survey data, only 12.4% of vendors believed that they could individually evade market taxes successfully. Unsurprisingly, coercion has also led to widespread dissatisfaction by market vendors. This anger is in part driven by high tax burdens, but has been exacerbated by the poor services vendors often received in return. One of the striking aspects of markets is that vendors largely agree on a set of public goods that they desire in return for paying taxes, namely a clean, safe, and sanitary market. In my data collection, 47% of market vendors said that "building and maintaining markets" should be the primary use of tax funds, and another 10% listed it as the second-highest priority. When asked what proportion of market taxes they believed was actually spent on market upkeep, only 40% believed that it was "most" or "all," and these measures correlate strongly with self-reported satisfaction with the quality of market services. Critically, vendors can easily evaluate the quality of market services being provided, which is not the case for many other goods (such as roads) where technical knowledge is needed to evaluate the quality of service provision.

Even before the advent of competitive elections in Uganda, both the national and local governments attempted to change the nature of tax collection to appease vendors and induce quasi-voluntary compliance. Early changes seem to be designed primarily to move accountability demands away from the government and onto other individuals or bodies. In the 1980s and 1990s, many markets began to farm out tax collection to private tenderers, rather than have government officials collect taxes themselves. This was supposed to increase efficiency and reduce corruption (Magala and Rubagumya 2007), but a hoped-for side effect seems to be that anger over coercion or how fees were used would fall on the tenderer rather than the government, who could receive critical funds with one hand while using the other to make a pretense at chastising any abuses by private tenderers.

The shift did not have the desired effect, and the tenderering process was rife with corruption and abuse. When soliciting bids for tax collectors, the district government chooses a reserve price to be paid, with the tenderer keeping any surplus; this reserve price is supposed to allow for a 20% profit margin (Magala and Rubagumya 2007). In practice, reserve prices were often set egregiously low. For example, Magala and Rubagumya (2007) reports that in 2003 a market in Masaka District was tendered for 60,000 UGX per month (about US$30), but an estimated 394,000 UGX (US$197) was actually collected. While some observers argue that this disconnect is due to the difficulty of establishing the real revenue potential of a market, it seems more likely that low reserve prices are the result of corruption. Local officials are simply willing to forgo district revenue in return for personal kick-backs by tenderers, who anecdotally "have connections to the Councillors or members of the District Tender Board that award the tenders" (Magala and Rubagumya (2007), 10).

More generally, the tender process did not succeed either in decreasing corruption or in increasing vendors' satisfaction with taxation; if anything, it reduced willingness to pay taxes as tenderers had incentives to collect fees aggressively (as they kept any surplus over the reserve price), a practice which at times included the imposition of new fees or the confiscation of vendors' property. These last were possible because of the weak legal structure governing markets. A 2013 government report on markets cites vendor anger at the behavior of tenderers:

> In addition, tenderers were reportedly collecting a lot of money from the vendors with nothing given back for the development of markets. This argument was illustrated by a respondent who stated that "When the municipal used to give outsiders to collect revenue from the market, if you

delayed a bit they would confiscate your tools and even take you to court. They used to harass vendors when collecting revenue."

Uganda Law Reform Commission (2013)

Over time market vendors have frequently protested over the way taxes have been raised and spent, and vendors seem to blame their local government for problems even when tenderers are collecting dues. Market vendors associations (MVAs) have typically played a large role in these protests.[13] One of the major markets in Kampala, Owino Market, saw at least four rounds of riots between 2007 and 2011 over the way the market was managed, and has burned down more than once as a result (Goodfellow and Titeca 2012). In 2008, vendors at Nakawa Market in Kampala clashed with local government over how revenues were being used (New Vision 2008). In 2009 market vendors in Iganga town threatened protests over a lack of sanitation in the central market, and a contemporary media account explains that "[t]he vendors claim that they pay between shillings 1000 and 5000 to Iganga town council to maintain the market but nothing is done to improve its sanitary conditions" (Uganda Radio Network 2009). In 2012 vendors in Te-Obaya Market in Lira municipality staged protests over the lack of sanitation at their market; the market vendors association dumped pails of garbage on city hall, threatening to do the same to the mayor's house unless trash collection resumed (Uganda Radio Network 2012b).

The timing of these protests shows that problems have persisted even following political liberalization in Uganda. However, there is variation in the extent to which vendors are dissatisfied with taxation in different towns. This suggests that in some areas the equilibrium is coercive taxation with service provision: as predicted by the model, there is an equilibrium in which tax bargaining does not occur but taxation still increases government accountability. In the towns that have seen protests, one issue seems to be that local governments have been unable to credibly bargain with vendors. Market taxes generate substantial accountability pressures, as vendors demand clean and modern markets in return for tax payments. However, despite repeated promises, some local governments seem unwilling or unable to sustainably deliver these services, leading to continued conflict. At the same time, vendors do not appear to have sufficient power to exact serious consequences on local governments other than through protests. While market vendors

[13] 42% of vendors in my data report belonging to an MVA.

vote at high rates (86% of my sample voted, compared to 78% for the general Ugandan population), they cannot single-handedly threaten leaders with electoral losses, especially in any given district or municipality. As shown in the model, tax bargains may be difficult to maintain, especially when electoral pressures are weak and coercive taxation is relatively efficient.

There are, however, more recent signs of a shift towards a sustainable solution. First, the elimination of the GPT in 2006 has increased local governments' reliance on market revenues. While market fees formed on average 10–20% of locally generated revenue in the 2001/2 fiscal year, as of 2005/6 this had risen to almost 40% on average, due almost entirely to the loss of GPT revenues (Sarzin 2007). This may have made local leaders more anxious to eliminate the losses from tendering and increase market revenues and compliance. Second, market vendors have been able to successfully lobby the national government for assistance and protection. President Museveni is wary of any potential basis for an opposition movement, and the combined nation-wide opposition of well-organized market vendors could pose a potential threat; Museveni also does not benefit directly from market dues, making it "cheap" to change policy. In the lead-up to the 2006 elections Museveni decreed new policy guidelines for markets: rather than rely on tenderers, market vendors should themselves be put in charge of collecting revenues and administering markets (Uganda Law Reform Commission 2013). He also decreed that vendors should pay dues only monthly instead of daily; while this could be an effort to simplify the complex tax code governing most markets, it may also be an effort to reduce the visibility of taxation.

While some local governments did obey the presidential directive (which does not carry the force of law) to contract with market vendors to run the markets, and to collect dues only monthly, the overall system is still a patchwork of different approaches. In their 2013 report, the Ugandan Law Reform Commission found that among markets surveyed, market vendors collected revenue in approximately 10%, while in 30% of markets private tenderers controlled collection; in the remainder a local government was in control of collection. My own survey data shows that the local government collects market taxes in 43% of cases, while tenderers collect 45% and vendors 9%. In the ULRC report, the cases where the local government has tendered the market to the vendors themselves are instructive. In several instances, the contract allows vendors to keep a certain percentage (often 5% or 10%) of revenues raised to go towards market upkeep and other services, such as savings and loan associations, for the benefit of members. In these areas the local governments have at times organized elections for the heads of the MVAs, or put into place market management committees which include bureaucrats as well as MVA representatives. While these arrangements are not always perfect—for example, in Jinja town vendors complained of political interference and intimidation surrounding MVA elections (Uganda Radio Network 2012*a*)—the ULRC report confirms that vendors seem much happier running their own markets.

The ULRC report is ostensibly a precursor to new legislation governing markets, and based on the report's recommendations it seems likely that any attempt at new legislation will codify a system in which vendors collect revenues and keep some portion for upkeep. While current contracts seem to offer only 5–10% of revenues back to vendors, my own interviews suggest that vendors would prefer to keep at least 25%, and perhaps more when (as in many areas) new markets need to be constructed. In Kampala, Museveni has again personally intervened to push for such a system: in 2020 and again in 2021, he disbanded existing market leadership and suspended market dues until the Kampala government can implement new legislation governing markets: effectively demanding a formal, binding bargain in an attempt to end frequent unrest in Kampala's markets (The Independent 2021).

Again, this system seems designed to use tax bargaining to reduce pressures on government; if vendors are responsible for service provision, they have less leverage to protest when things go wrong. However, the general trend seems clear: from a coercive, contentious system, markets are slowly moving towards a tax bargain in which vendors have some formal power over collecting and spending revenues. This stands in stark contrast to the GPT, where protests led to abolition of the tax altogether. A few key differences can explain the different outcomes. First, in the wake of the abolition of the GPT, market dues are extremely important to local governments; this may make them less willing to accept further tax cuts by the central government. Second, market dues affect far fewer citizens than the GPT, making it less salient as a national election issue, again reducing the potential threat of keeping the tax should bargaining fail. Third, and perhaps most importantly, within each market vendors face low collective action costs and have very similar preferences over how taxes should be used. Most vendors place a high value on a sanitary and safe market, and this is a relatively cheap good to provide, as markets are geographically confined. In terms of the model, this means that the demands of citizens are relatively high, but because the public good is highly valued and efficiently produced (i.e. α is high), any bargain allows the government to keep a large percentage of any tax revenue: this is confirmed in the fact that existing bargains grant the vendors only 5–10% of revenues, even if they would like to keep more. Furthermore, the reservation payoff for both sides is fairly low, increasing the probability that the bargain will be kept. The local government stands to lose a substantial amount of necessary revenue, and vendors fear a return to coercive taxation combined with poor public goods provision. The ability of vendors to protest and disrupt local economic activity helps them to credibly commit to punishing the government if they deviate from the bargain. Critically, bargaining has been attempted for many years, but has only been successful more recently, in particular since elections have become more competitive. It is possible that the additional threats that vendors can now levy on local governments has made bargaining more sustainable on both sides.

7.5 Taxing Boda-Bodas

Market vendors represent a group with high collective action capacity that has been able to bargain with local governments for services in return for paying market fees. While these bargains have been at times difficult to maintain due to credible commitment problems on both sides, the general trend is one towards institutionalization of bargains in order to provide a steady revenue stream for government and modernized markets for vendors. On the surface, boda-boda riders (motorcycle taxi drivers) look like a similar group. They are also a key part of the Ugandan economy, are politically active, and are well organized. They also share a strong preference for the same public good, namely a good roads network: a full 70% of boda-bodas in a survey I ran in eight districts replied that roads should be one of the top two priorities for how taxes on boda-bodas were spent.[14] However, despite having even more homogeneous preferences than market vendors, taxation of boda-bodas has been surprisingly low: while 85% of market vendors in my sample report paying taxes, only 9.8% of boda-boda riders do. What explains different outcomes between market vendors and boda-boda riders? As the case of Kampala shows, there are two key factors. The first is the cost of

---

[14] In contrast, 58% of market vendors said that market upkeep should be a top priority for spending market taxes.

providing boda-bodas' preferred public services, and the second is the ability of boda-bodas to effectively threaten the government with punishment.

Kampala has grown rapidly over the past 20 years, leading to severe traffic congestion combined with a large workforce of young men. This has led to the explosion of the boda-boda industry; as of 2012 the estimated number of boda-bodas in the city was over 100,000. Boda-boda riders are almost all men, making their living zipping between cars to ferry Ugandans to and from meetings, work, and school. Given the needs of a growing city, the Kampala City Government tried for almost a decade to levy registration taxes on boda-boda riders; in 2003 it was estimated that such a tax could raise 700 million UGX (US\$304,000) a year (Goodfellow and Titeca 2012). The elected Kampala City Council (KCC) first attempted to mandate a licensing fee of 10,000 UGX a month for all boda-boda riders in 2003 (Goodfellow and Titeca 2012, New Vision 2004). However, boda-boda riders resisted the new tax. Despite the fact that many boda-boda riders support opposition parties, they jointly appealed to the national government, and to President Museveni himself, to free them from the tax.[15] In June 2004 Museveni did just that, and "taxation was blocked by the Kampala Resident District Commissioner, Mr Stanley Kinyata, who claimed to have been asked to do so by President Yoweri Museveni" (Daily Monitor 2006).

In 2006, after a protracted lawsuit, the tax was ruled unconstitutional. The court argued that "If there is no authority of an Act of Parliament to levy and collect a particular tax, then that tax is illegal" (Daily Monitor 2006). However this justification is suspect, given that many local governments have successfully implemented new taxes without acts of Parliament to justify the imposition. The failure of the tax can instead be explained through the politics of Kampala and Uganda. Kampala is an opposition stronghold, and the mayor has typically been a member of the opposition, even before multi-party elections were formally allowed; John Ssebaana Kizito, the mayor who attempted to implement a boda-boda tax, is a member of the Democratic Party. Observers have argued that President Museveni, worried about any area that could serve as a basis for a national opposition movement, has consistently tried to weaken Kampala's government (Lambright 2014). Eliminating the boda-boda tax was a way for Museveni to both weaken the mayor and to gain support of the riders, who have since been

---

[15] During the 2001 elections, Museveni famously rode a boda-boda to his nomination, gaining support of the group and painting himself as a "common man's candidate" (The Observer 2009).

instrumental in delivering patronage and clientelism in multiple elections.[16] The mayor could stay in power without the boda-boda's support, but without the tax revenue his ability to develop the city and improve his reputation was limited. In Kampala, therefore, the equilibrium was one of no taxation rather than coercive taxation, due to the threat boda-bodas posed to the ruling coalition. However, note that tax bargaining likewise did not take place; this is discussed further below.

In 2009, Kampala's political landscape underwent a radical change. On the pretext of reducing corruption and improving city management, the NRM-controlled Parliament passed the Kampala City Act, which essentially turned Kampala into a subnational autocracy. As described by (Lambright 2014, s52):

> The Act sought to 'moderate' the powers of locally elected politicians and in essence it strips them of the authority they previously held. The mayor, termed Lord Mayor, is ceremonial rather than the executive head of the city administration, while the law also eliminates the executive committee. Executive power is now vested in an Executive Director (ED) directly appointed by and accountable to the President. The ED serves as the head of the public service, head of the administration, and the accounting officer for the authority. . . . The Act also created a new ministerial position, Minister of Kampala, with the authority to veto or rescind decisions and actions of the new KCCA, as well as give directives to the authority that it must follow.

As President Museveni has previously won election despite low support from Kampala, it seems unlikely that the city's residents will be able to put any serious electoral pressure on Museveni. This can therefore be seen as a striking roll-back of democracy and democratic accountability. After taking office in 2011 Kampala's appointed Executive Director, Jennifer Musisi, exerted her power in a number of ways.[17] While services in the city seem to have improved (possibly in a bid to regain residents' support for the NRM), the city also used police to confine opposition supporter Lord Mayor Lukwago to house arrest in 2013, making clear the limits of the elected city

---

[16] Delivering quite literally in some cases, as boda-boda drivers are at times tasked with handing out cash to potential voters.

[17] Musisi resigned in 2018; since 2020 the new ED is Dorothy Kisaka.

council's power (Daily Monitor 2014*b*). The central government's relationship with boda-bodas also soured. Rather than being seen as a source of potential electoral strength, boda-boda riders are seen as a potential source of urban riots, something the central government is increasingly concerned about as Uganda once again restricts the space for meaningful democratic competition.

In this new, non-democratic context, Executive Director Musisi successfully implemented a tax on boda-boda riders for the first time. The taxes, announced in 2013, include several permit fees as well as the purchase of special jackets and helmets; these last make evasion difficult, as those who have paid their tax are easily identified. The total cost of the taxes is 240,000 UGX per year, or about US$100 (Insider 2013). Given that boda-bodas make 10,000–20,000 UGX a day in profits, this amounts to almost a month's wages for many. The announcement of the taxes spurred numerous protests; one news article describes an association of boda-bodas "storming" city offices, with one boda-boda representative saying that "they will protest the new taxes and vow to fight any KCCA law enforcer who comes to collect these taxes from them" (Insider 2013). In September 2013, when the registration of boda-bodas was scheduled to begin, riders rioted, leading to police "using teargas to disperse them, arresting over 80 cyclists." At least one boda-boda rider was shot dead by the police (Kenya 2013).

Despite this opposition, the tax was employed with surprising success. By the end of the registration period over 60,000 boda-bodas had submitted to the new taxes (Daily Monitor 2014*a*). While this is still far from full compliance, it still represents the first time that boda-bodas have been taxed by the Kampala government. Given the resistance of the boda-boda associations, this is clearly a coercive tax. While Kampala's government did attempt to bargain with the riders over the new taxes, these attempts were ultimately unsuccessful.

In some ways this case is very similar to that of the Graduated Tax. Taxation of boda-bodas was not feasible under electoral competition, but could be successfully implemented in the absence of a democratic city government. This reversion to non-democratic politics cannot, however, explain why tax bargaining failed in this case. On the surface, boda-bodas look like an excellent candidate for tax bargaining: they are a highly organized, politically active group of citizens who all work in a defined geographic area. Most riders belong to organized stages, where each stage has a chairman and these chairmen in turn form regional councils. Furthermore, boda-bodas largely agree on a couple of public goods that they would like in return for taxation, namely good roads (the desire for which should be self-evident) and better health care. Boda-bodas are frequently involved in serious accidents, to the extent that Kampala's Mulago hospital has a ward devoted to boda-boda injuries. Survey evidence confirms that boda-bodas have similar interests; in my own survey data a full 70.8% of boda-bodas agree that roads should be a top priority when spending boda taxes. Kampala's government did indeed attempt to generate quasi-voluntary compliance by promising that boda registration taxes would be spent on roads and on health care for those involved in accidents; however, these attempts were ultimately unsuccessful.

I argue that the key difference between spending on markets and spending on roads is the (in)efficiency of producing the desired public goods. Market upkeep is relatively cheap and centralized; providing toilets in one location in the market serves all vendors, as does trash pickup. In contrast, providing good roads is expensive. Kampala is a sprawling metropolis, and improving roads in one section of town is of little benefit to those who operate elsewhere. Building new roads is also extremely resource-intensive, making it unlikely that the new revenue could support a sufficient amount of roads investment. For example, in Fiscal Year 2013/14 in Kampala, 51.88 billion UGX was spent building 21.3 miles of paved roads, for a cost of 2.44 billion UGX per mile of road (Kampala City Council Authority 2014). If this is indicative of the costs faced by the city, the fees raised from registering 60,000 boda-bodas are only enough to build an additional 6 miles of roads. This illustrates one of the limitations of tax bargaining: even when a group is well organized and relatively easy to tax, bargaining may simply not be possible based on the policies favored by the potential taxpayers. These findings are borne out by the experience of boda-bodas outside of Kampala, where very few (less than 8% of those surveyed) pay any taxes to local government at all, indicating that it is only when democratic accountability is reduced that coercive taxation of boda-bodas is possible.

7.6 The Social Media Tax

Reducing democracy in Kampala preceded a broader move towards autocracy in Uganda. Over the past decade, Uganda's political space has become increasingly closed. In 2013, Parliament passed the Public Order Management Act, which put into place sharp restrictions on civic engagement. Prior police approval was now required for all protests or public gatherings, and violations carried steep fines and jail time. As the police have wide latitude to deny permission to any protest or gathering that they deemed likely to breach the peace, this translated into a de facto ban not only on most protests, but also on many opposition campaign rallies and meetings. The Act allowed the ruling party to crack down during the 2016 election, and violent repression was even more evidence in the 2021 election (UN News 2021).

As part of this more general push to stifle the opposition, Museveni successfully pushed for a new tax on social media use. Under the 2018 tax bill, Ugandans had to pay a fee of 200 UGX per day (about $0.05 at contemporary exchange rates) to access WhatsApp, Facebook, Twitter, and a host of other social media sites (The East African 2018). In contrast to most new taxes, which originate in the Ministry of Finance, this tax on "Over-the-top" (OTT) services originated in a directive from Museveni's office (Guardian 2019). The president is on record as saying that the tax, in addition to raising needed revenue, would discourage "gossip" (Guardian 2019).

The new tax came into effect on July 1, 2018, and was quickly followed by large-scale protests. Member of Parliament Robert Kyagulanyi, better known as singer Bobi Wine, helped organize large street protests in the following weeks; police reacted by declaring the protests illegal, arresting participants, and using tear gas and bullets against protesters (Reuters 2018).

While the tax initially generated significant revenues, Ugandans quickly realized that they could bypass the tax by using a Virtual Private Network (VPN). By February 2019, revenues from the social media tax had plummeted (Guardian 2019). One year after introduction, the tax had only raised 17% of expected revenues (The East African 2019). Still, the government persisted in supporting the tax through both significant protests and declining revenues. It was not until 2021 that the tax was repealed and replaced.

In a 2021 tax bill, the government officially repealed the social media tax and replaced it with a 12% tax on the price of internet data (CIPESA 2021). Most Ugandans use pay-as-you-go phone plans in which data and airtime are purchased piecemeal. Data is typically offered in "bundles" of so many megabytes that are valid for a certain length of time. After the tax was introduced, several telecom companies announced higher data prices, evidence that the new tax was being passed on to consumers. In contrast to the social media tax, the new tax affected all Ugandans who used data, not only those who used social media. It also had significant implications on the internet costs for businesses. Yet, as discussed further below, the government clearly believed that a broad-based tax that in some ways "bit" more deeply into the subsistence costs of poorer Ugandans was more palatable than the social media tax.

7.6.1 Analysis

How does the rise—and fall—of the social media tax fit into the broader tale of taxation and accountability in Uganda? In many ways, the government's strategy seems almost "off-path" in game-theoretic terms: more simply put, it looks like the government made a mistake. The social media tax was essentially a direct tax on almost all internet users. It was highly visible, as it had to be actively paid on any day when a citizen accessed social media sites. And, its clear intention of stifling online political discussion made it an obvious target for a young, charismatic leader like Bobi Wine to use as a focal point for youth protest. The government may simply have underestimated how contentious the tax would be. Likewise, the government may have underestimated how easily tech-savvy Ugandans could avoid the tax through using VPN. The coercive capacity of the tax was simply too low, as it is extremely difficult to monitor who is posting in a private WhatsApp group without paying the tax. However, the use of VPN may also have kept the tax from staying salient as a political issue: after the initial round of protests, Ugandans who were opposed to the tax could simply avoid it, rather than being coerced into paying it. This may have muted the long-term political effects of the tax.

The end of the tax is also instructive. Rather than simply abolish the tax, as the regime did with other contentious taxes, Parliament replaced it with a 12% tax on internet data more generally. From the government's perspective, this had several advantages. First, as an indirect tax it was much more difficult to evade: the tax was charged to telecom companies, who then only indirectly charge consumers via higher data charges. This means that revenues are significantly higher, compared to the previous tax. Second, for similar reasons the new tax is much less visible, compared to the social media tax which was explicitly paid on a daily basis. We should expect this to dampen citizen protest and tax-related accountability pressures more generally. It also still accomplishes the government's goal of reigning in the opposition, by increasing the costs of online organizing and protest, but doing so less explicitly. Thus, from the government's perspective the new tax was strictly superior.

The government also took steps to ensure that there was not a repeat of the 2018 protests. The data tax was introduced on July 1, 2021; several days earlier, Museveni announced a 45-day COVID lockdown that made protest virtually impossible (Reuters 2019). There are also rumors that the police were told to ensure no protests occurred. By the time the lockdown was lifted, the tax was firmly in place.

While the new tax on data is, by revealed preference, more politically palatable to Museveni's regime, it is also less desirable from an economic standpoint. The new tax poses a significant challenge to expanding Uganda's economy. The economic burden for poor Ugandans is sufficient to drastically curtail internet use by many low-income citizens. It also significantly raises the costs many small businesses face, without clearly giving them a benefit. The tax is still new, and so more time will be needed to see if it is sustainable, or if alternatives must yet again be found.

7.7 Indirect Taxation in Uganda

Almost all of the taxes discussed so far are *direct* taxes: they are paid by citizens directly to the government. The exception is the tax on internet data discussed in the previous section. As I showed in Chapters 5 and 6, less visible indirect taxes are less likely to generate strong accountability demands from citizens, and may mute the effects of taxation on governance (de la Cuesta et al. 2020). Take for example taxes that are incorporated into the purchase price of a good—sales tax, valued-added tax (VAT), or excise taxes. If the base price plus the tax is less than the utility a rational citizen expects to gain from a purchase, he or she will simply avoid the purchase altogether.[18] By definition, then, indirect taxes are unlikely to activate loss aversion, and thus should be less likely to stimulate accountability demands by citizens. They are also relatively easy to collect coercively, as taxes are often collected from businesses with fixed locations, rather than from more mobile individuals.

If a government is concerned about increasing citizens' demands for accountability, it may therefore be more likely to raise revenue primarily

---

[18] This logic is the basis for so-called "vice" taxes on goods like cigarettes or alcohol.

using indirect taxes. This is also in line with the finding in Chapter 6 that low-income democracies have higher indirect taxes than autocracies, but not higher direct taxes. This pattern is well represented by Uganda. In 1996, the same year that primary education fees were eliminated, Uganda introduced a value-added tax (VAT). The introduction of VAT was not without opposition—citizens knew that they would face an 18% surcharge on many purchases, but the primary organized resistance was not by citizens, but by traders who believed that higher prices would reduce their business; they felt the losses from taxation more than citizens did (Gloppen and Rakner 2002). The limited degree of citizen opposition was likely because most food and other staple goods used by the poor were exempt or zero-rated; even within this single form of taxation, the government organized the tax to minimize popular pressure (Gloppen and Rakner 2002).

Similar patterns are evident in more recent changes to indirect taxation. Both the 2018 legislation that established the social media tax, and the 2021 legislation that replaced it with the internet data tax, included a number of other provisions that either introduced new indirect taxes, or increased existing ones. The 2018 bill increased or introduced excise taxes on several types of alcohol; put a 15% tax on powdered juice drinks; instituted a 200 UGX per liter tax on cooking oil; and increased the tax on gasoline from 950 UGX to 1200 UGX per liter (PriceWaterhouseCooper 2018). It also mandated a 200,000 UGX tax to be paid upon the first registration of a motorcycle. The 2021 legislation again increased excise taxes on several types of alcohol; increased the tax on gasoline by another 100 UGX per liter; and introduced an excise tax on "plastic product" (PriceWaterhouse-Cooper 2021). It also introduced a 1% tax on mobile money transfers (PriceWaterhouseCooper 2021).[19]

While some of these taxes closely resemble the "sin taxes" that many governments use, and that citizens often see as justified, others seem on the surface like they would be more contentious. The 2018 and 2021 increases in the tax on gasoline hurts not only drivers, who are typically wealthier, but also those who rely on minibuses and motorcycle taxis for transport. Likewise, the 2018 tax on cooking oil increased the price of a staple good for many Ugandans. And yet, there are no reports of protests against these tax increases, either in 2018 or 2021. The social media tax protests were, based on

---

[19] Mobile money is a phone-based banking alternative that has significantly increased access to financial services in many African countries.

media reports, solely focused on that tax and no others. The mobile money tax did generate initial outrage, but within days was reduced in scope to a 0.5% tax on a smaller range of transfer types (Lees and Akol 2021); it has since been much less contentious, despite its significant impact on the cost of financial services.[20]

The lack of protest has several possible causes. First, the taxes all involved small increments that, while they affected purchasing power, may not have generated sufficiently high losses to activate loss aversion.[21] The taxes that, ex ante, would seem most contentious are those on gasoline and cooking oil, as these are staple goods. However, it is not clear whether citizens fully understood that price increases in these goods was actually the result of taxation: they may have attributed them to general inflation and price fluctuation. Effectively, visibility was low even for these newly introduced taxes.

Crucially, the 2021 tax bill originally proposed one potentially more contentious tax that was ultimately dropped: a proposed annual registration fee for all motor vehicles (PriceWaterhouseCooper 2021). The motor vehicle registration would have been 200,000 UGX (approximately USD$57) for cars, and 50,000 UGX (US$15) for motorcyles (KPMG 2018). This large, lump-sum annual payment would have represented a significant burden even for middle-class Ugandans, and had the potential to focus discontent and citizen pressures. The tax was eventually replaced with the 100 UGX increase in the excise tax on fuel: a much more regressive, widespread tax but one that was more difficult to see in a world of fluctuating fuel prices, and one that was paid in a much smaller increment.

7.7.1 Analysis

Since 2018, the Ugandan government has therefore been able to significantly increase tax revenues through the introduction or increase of regressive indirect taxes. This has occurred at the same time as Uganda's national political environment has recently become much less democratic. While there are still technically multi-party elections, most observers agree that Uganda is

---

[20] It appears most likely that the initial tax structure was simply a government miscalculation in a rush to implement the tax; even many simple transactions ended up paying the 1% levy at four points, making it effectively a 4% tax on receiving and withdrawing money.

[21] Recall that loss aversion seems to be most prevalent for large losses (Gal and Rucker 2018).

essentially an electoral autocracy. Opposition leaders are frequently harassed and arrested, and there are widespread fears that elections have been rife with vote-buying and corruption.

One potential factor confounding the relationship between regime type and taxation is foreign aid. Uganda has seen significant drops in foreign aid over the past ten years. In December 2012 it came to light that US$20 million in aid funding had been stolen from the Office of the Prime Minister; this led donors to collectively cut US$300 million in the following fiscal year, representing a substantial loss to the budget. In 2014, a draconian anti-homosexuality law passed, leading donors to cut over US$140 million in additional funding (IRIN 2014). Initially, this drop in aid money led to the government proposing a slew of new taxes and eliminating some tax exemptions, for example reinstating VAT on hotels and on piped water to homes. However, since that time the drop in aid has partially recovered, and the government has also received significant amounts of money from selling the right to drill for oil in Western Uganda. Thus, it is not clear that the drop in aid has led to higher revenue pressures overall. Rather, the increasingly autocratic government has been able to levy higher taxes on a recalcitrant population.

In some cases, the central government has increased its own revenues at the expense of local governments by taking over several sources of local revenues. In interviews I conducted with district-level officials, one bureaucrat explained that they used to receive 2 billion UGX in tax revenue from fisheries, but that these were now collected by the national government. The same official described recent changes to the way that taxes on land sales were collected; the central government had opened new land offices that are supposed to streamline the system, but the district feared that this was an attempt to take land tax revenue back to the Center. Subsequent visits confirmed that this is exactly what happened. Officials in multiple districts also reported that the central government had failed to remit Local Service Tax—which is supposed to be withheld from bureaucrats' salaries and passed on to local governments—in recent years, suggesting that these revenues are now being kept by the central government. In 2022, district governments complained that the central government was keeping *all* tax revenues remitted by local governments and failing to send any back to help fund local governments (Daily Monitor 2022).

The taxes that are (at least anecdotally) being taken away from local government are all those that are relatively easy and lucrative to collect, and which generate few accountability demands. The Local Service Tax was supposed to replace the graduated tax for salaried workers, but in reality is primarily paid by bureaucrats who cannot easily protest the government without losing their jobs. Taxes on fisheries and land taxes are both fee-for-service, viewed as a cost of doing business rather than a tax. The taxes that remain for local governments to collect are those that are more contentious, such as market fees: the local government is left to negotiate with citizens or coerce them into paying the taxes that are hardest to collect.

7.8 Discussion

Taxation in Uganda has undergone substantial changes over the past 20 years. While some taxes have been created and others abolished, the general trends are clear: where taxation generates increased citizen demands for accountability, the government has generally preferred to eliminate taxation altogether rather than improve public goods provision. A key aspect of many abolished taxes is that citizens and government could not reach or keep a tax bargain; this lack of bargain was often due to the high cost of providing public services to these groups, relative to the amount of tax revenue that could be raised. This points to the limitations of tax bargaining as a method of increasing accountability in sub-Saharan Africa, and the difficulty of extending the government's reach into sparsely populated rural areas.

Where tax bargaining does succeed, it will likely be with groups like market vendors, who are geographically concentrated and who share a preference for a public good that is relatively cheap and easy to provide. However, governments in these cases may need to grant such citizens additional institutional concessions—such as a voice on local commissions—in order to make bargains credible in weakly institutionalized settings where corruption is rampant. Finally, the case of the market vendors points to the fact that such bargains are not struck overnight, but might require several adjustments before all sides can find a bargain that works.

More generally, this chapter suggests that even rent-seeking governments who rely on taxation can shape policy to minimize accountability demands. As the recent foreign aid cuts show, the Ugandan government is very unwilling to impose direct taxes when it can instead use excise taxes and other indirect taxation measures that are less visible to citizens. What seems most probable is that local governments in Uganda will be more likely than the national government to implement direct taxes, such as those on market vendors, to raise revenue where possible, and these types of taxes may increase accountability. My own interviews in several districts suggest that district officials are indeed actively looking for new sources of tax revenue, and in the presence of competitive elections these may encourage strong, accountable governments at the local level. However, these same interviews reveal that it is bureaucrats who want to increase taxes: politicians are, as my theory predicts, much less willing to do so.

8

Conclusion

Taxation is a fundamental part of state development. Without the capacity to raise revenue, governments will not be able to protect citizens, promote economic development, or provide citizens with the public goods and services they need to thrive. Yet, fiscal capacity remains low in many developing countries, even as economic development has taken off. This state of affairs has persisted despite expressed willingness of citizens in many countries to pay more taxes, especially if revenues funded critical infrastructure and valued public goods like healthcare and education. Existing theories of taxation and state development have not been able to satisfactorily account for this puzzle.

This book argues that persistent low state capacity is due to a paradox of accountability. Taxation has typically been viewed as good for accountability, leading to more responsive governments that are beholden to taxpayer preferences. Consistent with this view, this book shows that taxation increases the demands that leaders face from citizens. However, these same demands can make taxation less appealing to political leaders, especially when elections give citizens a credible threat against rent-seeking governments. If state capacity is high, governments can effectively control rent-seeking and efficiently provide citizens with valued public goods. In these cases a high-tax, high-accountability outcome is likely. However, when state capacity is low, it may be too costly to provide citizens' desired public goods. This can lead governments to systematically underinvest in fiscal capacity rather than tax and increase accountability. My theoretical model suggests that in such states democracy, rather than increasing accountability, can instead simply lead to lower taxation.

A wide range of evidence supports this argument. As predicted, taxation does increase citizens' accountability demands, especially when taxes are visible and so "bite" harder. This holds in laboratory experiments in Ghana and Uganda, and is supported by related survey experiments and observational data on taxation and political action. More recent work further supports this

Strategic Taxation: Fiscal Capacity and Accountability in African States. Lucy E. S. Martin.
Oxford University Press. © Oxford University Press 2023. DOI: 10.1093/oso/9780197672631.003.0008

account (Weigel 2020). Taxed citizens are simply less tolerant of, and more likely to punish, poor government performance.

The empirical evidence also supports the claim that low-capacity democracies may be especially unlikely to tax. In a cross-national panel dataset, a positive effect of democracy on taxation primarily holds for high-income countries. This effect is small or even negative for low-income, low-capacity countries. Indeed, for these countries democratization is associated with lower taxation in subsequent years, and with a smaller tax net. Case studies from Uganda showed how these dynamics work in practice. As Uganda's political environment became more democratic, the government chose to eliminate a number of taxes rather than reduce rent seeking and increase public goods provision. As democratic backsliding has occurred, the trend has reversed. New taxes are being introduced, including some (like the tax on boda-boda riders) that were not feasible under competitive elections.

This book has methodological and substantive implications for the study of accountability, state development, and taxation. Perhaps most importantly, it suggests that efforts to increase state capacity, and particularly fiscal capacity, need to consider the political incentives of elected leaders. Efforts to increase state capacity through strengthening bureaucracies may fail to increase revenues unless we also consider the political barriers to taxation. If politicians fear that higher taxation will lead to demands that will constrain their access to rents or threaten their tenure in office, taxation will simply not succeed.

This does not mean that all is hopeless. Chapter 7 showed that taxation is possible under certain conditions. By focusing on efficient tax collection, it may be possible to reach a state where governments can meet citizen demands with available revenues. Likewise, it may be possible to help governments and citizens bargain on public goods that are feasible given revenues, and perhaps to help support those bargains. In ongoing work with Brigitte Seim, Simon Hoellerbauer, and Luis Camacho, we use a field experiment to successfully jump-start tax bargaining in Malawian markets, increasing tax compliance and vendor satisfaction with government. However, this approach required an initial investment in local public goods to help local governments escape a low-taxation equilibrium.

This book also suggests that, in settings where taxation is politically feasible, it can help promote government accountability. Governments and donors who are attempting to improve accountability could consider the role of taxation and informal community contributions when designing development interventions. Adding community contributions to aid programs could give beneficiaries more ownership over projects and make them more likely to hold local leaders accountable for how funds are spent. The fact that Chapter 5 shows that taxation has the strongest effect on those citizens with a low propensity to punish political leaders also suggests that taxation might have the most impact in groups who are traditionally less involved with politics.

8.1 Scope Conditions

The theory and evidence presented in this book are drawn from extensive fieldwork and data collection in Uganda. While the cross-national evidence in Chapter 6 draws on a worldwide sample, it is important to consider how broadly applicable the theory and its implications are. Two important scope conditions to consider are the types of taxes, and taxpayers, for whom the theory is most applicable, and the types of governments for which it can apply.

8.1.1 Types of Taxes and Taxpayers

Despite the simplicity of most models of taxation, including the one presented in Chapter 4, taxation is rarely if ever a single proportional levy on income. Instead, governments rely on a mix of potential tax instruments that vary in a number of ways. Direct taxes include not only income tax but also taxes on property, capital gains, and inheritance. Indirect taxes are even more varied, encompassing the value added tax (VAT) as well as import taxes, export taxes, and excise taxes, each of which in turn can be applied to a huge number of possible goods and services.

Both in this book and in coauthored work, I argue that taxes are most likely to increase citizens' accountability demands when they are *visible* (de la Cuesta et al. 2020); this also accords with work arguing that tax salience is important for accountability demands (Prichard 2015). While tax type and visibility are not perfectly aligned, in general I follow previous work in expecting direct taxes to be more visible (Moore 2004; Bräutigam, Fjeldstad, and Moore 2008). However, indirect taxes may still be highly visible when they are first introduced, as they have a significant effect on citizens' purchasing power in ways that can activate loss aversion (de la Cuesta et al. 2020). Over time as citizens adjust to higher prices, the tax becomes less salient and visible.

Thus, the theory presented here is most applicable for direct taxes. However, it still has implications for indirect taxes: governments concerned with the accountability effects of taxation will prefer to tax consumer goods rather than increase direct taxes. This is seen in Uganda, where recent tax bills increase excise taxes on a number of goods (see Chapter 7). This is also borne out more generally: even in OECD countries with strong welfare states, reliance on indirect taxation is high despite its regressive nature.

The other source of variation in taxes is the identity of the taxpayers. Taxes like VAT are broad-based, affecting nearly all citizens, while other taxes have much narrower tax bases. Income taxes can theoretically apply to everyone, but in practice may be narrow: tax brackets in Uganda suggest that less than 10% of earners are actually subject to income tax requirements. Other taxes, particularly at the local level, may be levied only on certain groups, as in the case of market taxes or taxes on fisheries.

There may be tradeoffs between the size of a tax base and the degree to which it can generate accountability dividends. For example, a broad, highly visible tax has the potential to mobilize accountability demands across a wide range of citizens. In theory, this could have significant benefits for governance. However, that same broad base can also make it more difficult to meet citizens' demands. Unless revenues are sufficient to meet the demands of, if not all, then at least a large fraction of taxpayers, the government might be better of not taxing at all. In such cases, the potential benefits of taxation are high, but so are the potential pitfalls. When a tax has a narrow base, it is less likely that taxpayers have sufficient political clout to impose costs on leaders. However, such citizens may also be much easier to strike a bargain with, especially if they are geographically consolidated and share preferences, as in the case of market vendors. Which effect will predominate will depend on the individual case.

8.1.2 Types of Governments

The other type of scope conditions to consider are the types of governments for which the theory should hold. This in turn can vary along several potential axes, including whether government is local or national; its level of development and capacity; and its history and geographic region. In some ways, the theory and findings presented in this book are very general. I expect that all kinds of governments will need to worry about the effects of taxation on the citizen pressures they face and respond accordingly. However, it is possible that some governments will feel these pressures more strongly than others, or have different tools at their disposal to address potential accountability demands.

While this volume has focused on national governments, local governments may be particularly sensitive to the accountability effects of taxation. Those who pay local taxes are almost by definition confined to a relatively small geographic area, and so face fewer collective action costs than the same citizens would trying to put pressure on a national government. Political competition may also be higher. While President Museveni maintains a strong grip on power at the national level in Uganda, many local elections are more competitive, effectively raising the risks to local leaders of taxing without providing citizens' desired policies. However, local governments may also be lower capacity than national governments. In developing countries, local politicians in particular may have low levels of education and struggle to control bureaucrats (Raffler 2022). This raises the possibility that taxation will be particularly difficult to sustain at the local level, if politicians do not feel that they can guarantee that they will meet citizens' demands. Indeed, in my own interviews local bureaucrats in Uganda frequently expressed frustration, saying that they knew exactly how to increase tax revenues but that politicians would not allow it.

The particular historical factors in different regions of the world may also affect the types of tax equilibria that emerge. Even among countries that were subject to colonization in the nineteenth and twentieth century, colonial powers implemented a wide range of financial and economic systems, and independence transitions likewise varied widely. In particular, Latin American countries are often supposed to be subject to different incentives due to the longer independence history and the conflicts of the nineteenth century (Centeno 1997). However, I do not expect these differences to change the underlying logic and constraints that face governments when they decide whether and how to tax. Different equilibria may emerge, but this is due to differing conditions that can be explained through the model's parameters.

8.2 Directions for Future Research

Scholarly work on taxation has boomed in the past ten years, and we are constantly learning more about the best ways to support fiscal capacity in developing states while protecting citizens. Yet, there is still much more to learn, both about how taxation affects citizen-government relations, and about when taxation will be successful.

8.2.1 Understanding Citizen Behavior

More work is needed to fully understand the ways in which taxation affects citizen behavior. First, while existing evidence has focused on taxation's effects on individuals, many forms of political engagement are collective. This suggests the need to study how taxation affects citizens' ability to overcome the collective action problem. Taxation may help foster collective action either by increasing the private expressive benefits citizens receive from such actions, or by making citizens believe that others are also more likely to take action, raising the perceived probability of an action's success. Both increase the expected private payoff a citizen receives from taking action, which Olson (1965) argues should help citizens overcome free-riding. Testing this would require both showing that the behavioral effect of taxation persists in the presence of collective action problems and that taxation alters individuals' beliefs about the likelihood that their fellow citizens will take part in collective action. This would then serve as a coordination device such that taxation decreases the collective action problem for citizens.

We also need a better understanding of the long-run effects of taxation. Many tax protests occur when a tax is first introduced, and the experimental evidence on taxation likewise examines a real or simulated new tax (Prichard 2015; de la Cuesta et al. 2022; Weigel 2020; Paler 2013). However, in ongoing work in de la Cuesta et al. (2020), we argue that citizens may actually acclimate to some taxes over time, making them less visible and salient. While some evidence is consistent with this process, it has not been observed directly, and needs to be better studied. More work is also needed to test whether it is possible to increase the visibility and salience of hidden taxes in ways that can increase political engagement.

8.2.2 Understanding Policy Outcomes

At a broader level, we need more research into how best to overcome political resistance to taxation, and how to encourage high-accountability equilibria while protecting citizens from over-extraction. One possibility is that local governments will have an easier time raising taxes than national governments, for the reasons detailed above. If this is true, then fiscal decentralization could significantly improve state capacity. However, this may be difficult for poorer areas of a country, and so more work is needed on how to ensure central transfers are well spent, especially when local taxation is difficult to sustain.

We also need a better understanding of the potential tradeoffs between a tax's economic and political effects. Economists often favor broad-based taxes like VAT due to the lower capacity needed and, in many cases, the smaller economic inefficiencies. However, it is also likely that these taxes have fewer accountability dividends. If a more economically "inefficient" tax is more likely to be spent on public goods that can improve future economic growth, policymakers must properly understand these tradeoffs to determine which taxes are best suited to particular situations. It is also possible that taxes targeted at particular economic groups, while appearing more inefficient than broad-based taxes, are actually easier to sustain.

Overall, this suggests that we still lack evidence on how governments in developing countries can best structure taxation to make it politically feasible and generate higher levels of accountability and state development. Taxation can be a critical part of building state capacity, but only if we understand when it will be sustainable and help citizens rather than simply allowing leaders to extract from their populace.

References

Abeler, Johannes, Armin Falk, Lorenz Goette, and David Huffman. 2011. "Reference Points and Effort Provision." *American Economic Review* 101(2):470–492.

Acemoglu, Daron and James A. Robinson. 2006. *Economic Origins of Dictatorship and Democracy*. Cambridge University Press.

Afrobarometer Data, Round 5. 2011. Available at http://www.afrobarometer.org.

Aidt, Toke S. and Peter S. Jensen. 2009*a*. "Tax Structure, Size of Government, and the Extension of the Voting Franchise in Western Europe, 1860–1938." *International Tax and Public Finance* 16(3):362–394.

Aidt, Toke S. and Peter S. Jensen. 2009*b*. "The Taxman Tools Up: An Event History Study of the Introduction of the Personal Income Tax." *Journal of Public Economics* 93(1):160–175.

Alesina, Alberto, William Easterly, and Janina Matuszeski. 2011. "Artificial States." *Journal of the European Economic Association* 9(2):246–277.

Allingham, Michael G. and Agnar Sandmo. 1972. "Income Tax Evasion: A Theoretical Analysis." *Journal of Public Economics* 1:323–338.

Atkinson, Ronald R. 2004. *The Roots of Ethnicity*. University of Pennsylvania Press.

Aytaç, S. Erdem and Susan C. Stokes. 2019. *Why Bother?: Rethinking Participation in Elections and Protests*. Cambridge University Press.

Bahiigwa, Godfrey, Frank Ellis, Odd-Helge Fjeldstad, and Vegard Iversen. 2004. *Rural Taxation in Uganda: Implications for Growth, Income Distribution, Local Government Revenue and Poverty Reduction*. Economic Policy Research Centre.

Ballard-Rosa, Cameron. 2020. *Democracy, Dictatorship, and Default: Urban-Rural Bias and Economic Crises across Regimes*. Cambridge University Press.

Baskaran, Thushyanthan and Arne Bigsten. 2013. "Fiscal Capacity and the Quality of Government in Sub-Saharan Africa." *World Development* 45:92–107.

Bastiaens, Ida and Nita Rudra. 2018. *Democracies in Peril*. Cambridge University Press.

Bates, Robert. 1981. "States and Markets in Tropical Africa: The Political Basis of Agricultural Policy." University of California Press.

Bates, Robert H. 2015. *When Things Fell Apart*. Cambridge University Press.

Bates, Robert H. and Da-Hsiang Donald Lien. 1985. "A Note on Taxation, Development, and Representative Government." *Politics and Society* 14(1):53–70.

BBC News. 2005. "Uganda backs multi-party return." **URL:** *http://news.bbc.co.uk/2/hi/africa/4726419.stm*.

Beramendi, Pablo, Mark Dincecco, and Melissa Rogers. 2019. "Intra-Elite Competition and Long-run Fiscal Development." *The Journal of Politics* 81(1):49–65.

Bermeo, Sarah Blodgett. 2015. "Aid Is Not Oil: Donor Utility, Heterogeneous Aid, and the Aid-Democratization Relationship." *International Organization* pp. 1–32.

Besley, Timothy and Torsten Persson. 2014. "Why Do Developing Countries Tax So Little?" *Journal of Economic Perspectives* 28(4):99–120.

Bird, Richard M., Jorge Martinez-Vazquez, and Benno Torgler. 2008. "Tax Effort in Developing Countries and High Income Countries: The Impact of Corruption, Voice and Accountability." *Economic Analysis and Policy* 38(1):55–71.

Blair, Robert A. and Philip Roessler. 2021. "Foreign Aid and State Legitimacy: Evidence on Chinese and US Aid to Africa from Surveys, Survey Experiments, and Behavioral Games." *World Politics* 73(2):315–357.

Bodea, Cristina and Adrienne LeBas. 2016. "The Origins of Voluntary Compliance: Attitudes toward Taxation in Urban Nigeria." *British Journal of Political Science* 46(1):215–238.

Boix, Carles. 2001. "Democracy, Development, and the Public Sector." *American Journal of Political Science* 45:1–17.

Bordo, Michael D. and Eugene N. White. 1991. "A Tale of Two Currencies: British and French Finance During the Napoleonic Wars." *The Journal of Economic History* 51(2):303–316.

Bräutigam, D.A. and Knack, S., 2004. Foreign aid, institutions, and governance in sub-Saharan Africa. *Economic development and cultural change*, 52(2), pp. 255–285.

Bräutigam, D., O. H. Fjeldstad, and M. Moore. 2008. *Taxation and State-Building in Developing Countries: Capacity and Consent*. Cambridge University Press.

Brewer, John. 2002. *The Sinews of Power: War, Money and the English State 1688–1783*. Routledge.

Brollo, Fernanda, Tommaso Nannicini, Roberto Perotti, and Guido Tabellini. 2013. "The Political Resource Curse." *American Economic Review* 103(5):1759–1796.

Castro, Lucio and Carlos Scartascini. 2015. "Tax Compliance and Enforcement in the Pampas: Evidence from a Field Experiment." *Journal of Economic Behavior & Organization* 116:65–82.

Centeno, Miguel Angel. 1997. "Blood and Debt: War and Taxation in Nineteenth-Century Latin America." *American Journal of Sociology* 102(6):1565–1605.

Cheibub, José Antonio. 1998. "Political Regimes and the Extractive Capacity of Governments: Taxation in Democracies and Dictatorships." *World Politics* 50(3): 349–376.

Chowdhury, Arjun. 2017. *The Myth of International Order: Why Weak States Persist and Alternatives to the State Fade Away*. Oxford University Press.

CIPESA. 2021. "Uganda Abandons Social Media Tax but Slaps New Levy on Internet Data." **URL:** *https://cipesa.org/2021/07/uganda-abandons-social-media-tax-but-slaps-new-levy-on-internet-data/*.

Coleman, Stephen. 1996. "The Minnesota Income Tax Compliance Experiment: State Tax Results." Minnesota Department of Revenue as publisher. **URL:** *https://www.revenue.state.mn.us/sites/default/files/2011-11/research_reports_content_complnce.pdf*.

Daily Monitor. 2006. "Shs10,000 Boda-Boda Tax is Illegal—Court." **URL:** *http://allafrica.com/stories/200611030853.html*.

Daily Monitor. 2014*a*. "KCCA to Push its Plans Despite Criticism—Musisi." **URL:** *http://www.monitor.co.ug/News/National/-/688334/2165730/-/4twfya/-/index.html*.

Daily Monitor. 2014*b*. "Namboozе Arrested, Lukwago Blocked from Accessing Office." **URL:** *http://www.monitor.co.ug/News/National/Namboozе-arrested-Lukwago-blocked-from-accessing-office/-/688334/2146304/-/uwcpoyz/-/index.html*.

Daily Monitor. 2022. "Districts Urge Govt to Reverse Directive on Remitting Taxes." **URL:** *https://www.monitor.co.ug/uganda/news/national/districts-urge-govt-to-reverse-directive-on-remitting-taxes-3739506*.

de Kadt, Daniel and Evan S. Lieberman. 2020. "Nuanced Accountability: Voter Responses to Service Delivery in Southern Africa." *British Journal of Political Science*, 50(1), 185–215.

de la Cuesta, Brandon, Helen V. Milner, Daniel L. Nielson, and Stephen F. Knack. 2019. "Oil and Aid Revenue Produce Equal Demands for Accountability as Taxes in Ghana and Uganda." *Proceedings of the National Academy of Sciences* 116(36):17717–17722.

de la Cuesta, Brandon, Lucy Martin, Helen V. Milner, and Daniel L. Nielson. 2020. "Do Indirect Taxes Bite? How Hiding Taxes Erases Accountability Demands from Citizens." Working Paper. **URL:** *https://drive.google.com/file/d/1tar4Fb2uYnwkqDhVPo2Byd9KfU-dsvSi/view.*

de la Cuesta, Brandon, Lucy Martin, Helen V. Milner and Daniel L. Nielson. 2021. "Foreign Aid, Oil Revenues, and Political Accountability: Evidence from Six Experiments in Ghana and Uganda." *The Review of International Organizations* 16(3): 521–548.

de la Cuesta, Brandon, Lucy Martin, Helen V. Milner, and Daniel L. Nielson. 2022. "Owning It: Accountability and Citizens' Ownership over Oil, Aid, and Taxes." *The Journal of Politics* 84(1):304–320.

Del Carpio, Lucia. 2013. "Are the Neighbors Cheating? Evidence from a Social Norm Experiment on Property Taxes in Peru." Unpublished Manuscript. **URL:** *https://www.eief.it/files/2014/01/02-jmp_del-caprio.pdf.*

Djankov, Simeon, Rafael La Porta, Florencio Lopez-de Silanes, and Andrei Shleifer. 2008. "The Law and Economics of Self-Dealing." *Journal of Financial Economics* 88(3): 430–465.

Dunning, T. 2005. "Resource Dependence, Economic Performance, and Political Stability." *Journal of Conflict Resolution* 49(4):451–482.

Dunning, Thad, Guy Grossman, Macartan Humphreys, Susan Hyde, Craig McIntosh, and Gareth Nellis. 2019. *Information, Accountability, and Cumulative Learning: Lessons from Metaketa I.* New York: Cambridge University Press.

Dynes, Adam M. and Lucy Martin. 2019. "Revenue Source and Electoral Accountability: Experimental Evidence from Local US Policymakers." *Political Behavior* 43:1113–1136.

Easterly, William and Sergio Rebelo. 1993. "Fiscal Policy and Economic Growth." *Journal of Monetary Economics* 32(3):417–458.

Eubank, Nicholas. 2012. "Taxation, Political Accountability and Foreign Aid: Lessons from Somaliland." *Journal of Development Studies* 48(4):465–480.

Fauvelle-Aymar, Christine. 1999. "The Political and Tax Capacity of Government in Developing Countries." *Kyklos* 52(3):391–413.

Fearon, James D. 1999. "Electoral Accountability and the Control of Politicians: Selecting Good Types versus Sanctioning Poor Performance." In *Democracy, Accountability, and Representation*, ed. Adam Przeworski, Susan C. Stokes, and Bernard Manin. New York: Cambridge University Press, pp. 55–97.

Fehr, E. and S. Gächter. 2002. "Costly Punishment in Humans." *Nature* 415:137–140.

Fehr, Ernst and Klaus M. Schmidt. 1999. "A Theory of Fairness, Competition, and Cooperation." *The Quarterly Journal of Economics* 114(3):817–868.

Fehr, Ernst, Oliver Hart, and Christian Zehnder. 2011. "Contracts as Reference Points: Experimental Evidence." *American Economic Review* 101(2):493–525.

Fehr, Ernst and Simon Gächter. 2000. "Cooperation and Punishment in Public Goods Experiments." *American Economic Review* 90(4):980–994.

Fehr, Ernst and Urs Fischbacher. 2004. "Third-Party Punishment and Social Norms." *Evolution and Human Behavior* 25(2):63–87.

Fiorina, Morris P. 1981. "Retrospective Voting in American National Elections." New Haven: Yale University Press.

Fisman, Raymond and Roberta Gatti. 2002. "Decentralization and Corruption: Evidence from US Federal Transfer Programs." *Public Choice* 113(1–2):25–35.

Fjeldstad, Odd-Helge and Mick Moore. 2009. "Revenue Authorities and Public Authority in Sub-Saharan Africa." *Journal of Modern African Studies* 47(1):1–18.

Flora, Peter, Jens Alber, and Franz Kraus. 1983. *State, Economy, and Society in Western Europe 1815–1975: The Growth of Mass Democracies and Welfare States*. Vol. 1. Frankfurt, London, Chicago: St James Press.

Flores-Macias, Gustavo. 2019. *The Political Economy of Taxation in Latin America*. Cambridge: Cambridge University Press.

Frizell, Jakob. 2021. "War and Modern Taxation." *Global Taxation: How Modern Taxes Conquered the World*. Oxford: Oxford University Press, p. 43.

Gadenne, Lucie. 2017. "Tax Me, But Spend Wisely? Sources of Public Finance and Government Accountability." *American Economic Journal: Applied Economics*, 9(1): 274–314.

Gal, David and Derek D. Rucker. 2018. "The Loss of Loss Aversion: Will It Loom Larger Than its Gain?" *Journal of Consumer Psychology* 28(3):497–516.

Gardner, Leigh A. 2010. "Decentralization and Corruption in Historical Perspective: Evidence from Tax Collection in British Colonial Africa." *Economic History of Developing Regions* 25(2):213–236.

Gardner, Leigh A. 2012. *Taxing Colonial Africa: The Political Economy of British Imperialism*. Oxford: Oxford University Press.

Gleditsch, Nils Petter; Peter Wallensteen, Mikael Eriksson, Margareta Sollenberg & Håvard Strand. 2002. "Armed Conflict 1946–2001: A New Dataset', *Journal of Peace Research* 39(5):615–637.

Gloppen, Siri and Lise Rakner. 2002. "Accountability through Tax Reform? Reflections from Sub-Saharan Africa." *IDS Bulletin* 33(3):1–17.

Gombay, Christie. 1994. "Eating Cities: Urban Management and Markets in Kampala." *Cities* 11(2):86–94.

Goodfellow, Tom and Kristof Titeca. 2012. "Presidential Intervention and the Changing 'Politics of Survival' in Kampala's Informal Economy." *Cities* 29(4):264–270.

Gottlieb, Jessica. 2016. "Greater Expectations: A Field Experiment to Improve Accountability in Mali." *American Journal of Political Science* 60(1):143–157.

Government of Uganda. 1942. "Markets Act 1942." **URL:** *http://www.ulii.org/ug/legislation/consolidated-act/94*.

Government of Uganda. 2014. "Budget Speech Fiscal Year 2014/15." **URL:** *http://www.statehouse.go.ug/media/news/2014/06/12/budget-speech-financial-year-201415-delivered-meeting-4th-session-9th-parliame*.

Government of Uganda. 2022. "Budget Speech Fiscal Year 2022/2023." **URL:** *https://budget.finance.go.ug/sites/default/files/National%20Budget%20docs/FY%202022-23%20Budget%20Speech.pdf*.

Grossman, Guy. 2014. "Do Selection Rules Affect Leader Responsiveness? Evidence from Rural Uganda." *Quarterly Journal of Political Science* 9(1):1–44.

Guardian. 2019. "Millions of Ugandans quit internet services as social media tax takes effect." **URL:** *https://www.theguardian.com/global-development/2019/feb/27/millions-of-ugandans-quit-internet-after-introduction-of-social-media-tax-free-speech*.

Habyarimana, James, Macartan Humphreys, Daniel N. Posner and Jeremy M. Weinstein. 2009. *Coethnicity: Diversity and the Dilemmas of Collective Action*. New York: Russell Sage Foundation.

Henrich, Joseph, Richard McElreath, Abigail Barr, Jean Ensminger, Clark Barrett, Alexander Bolyanatz, Juan Camilo Cardenas, Michael Gurven, Edwins Gwako, Natalie Henrich, et al. 2006. "Costly Punishment Across Human Societies." *Science* 312(5781):1767–1770.

Herbst, Jeffrey. 2000. *States and Power in Africa*. Princeton: Princeton University Press.

Hyde, Susan D. and Angela O'Mahony. 2010. "International Scrutiny and Pre-electoral Fiscal Manipulation in Developing Countries." *The Journal of Politics* 72(3):690–704.

ICTD/UNU-WIDER. 2020. "Government Revenue Dataset." Technical report.

Iliffe, John. 2017. *Africans: The History of a Continent*. Vol. 137. Cambridge: Cambridge University Press.

Insider, The. 2013. "Kampala Boda-Boda Cyclists Have Opposed New KCCA Taxes." **URL:** *http://www.theinsider.ug/kampala-boda-boda-cyclists-have-opposed-new-kcca-taxes/*.

Inter-Parliamentary Union. 2015. "Uganda: Elections Held in 1996." **URL:** *http:// www.ipu.org/parline-e/reports/arc/2329_96.htm*.

IRIN. 2014. "Briefing: Punitive Aid Cuts Disrupt Healthcare in Uganda." **URL:** *http:// www.irinnews.org/printreport.aspx?reportid=99878 2/3*.

Jamal, Vali. 1978. "Taxation and Inequality in Uganda, 1900–1964." *The Journal of Economic History* 38(2):418–438.

Kahneman, Daniel and Amos Tversky. 1979. "Prospect Theory: An Analysis of Decision under Risk." *Econometrica* 47(2):263–291.

Kalinaki Daniel. 2012. "One Thing Kiwanuka Forgot to Put in Her New Budget— Graduated Tax." **URL:** *http://www.monitor.co.ug/OpEd/OpEdColumnists/Daniel Kalinaki/Kiwanuka-forgot-to-put-in-her-new-budget-Graduated-Tax/-/878782/ 1437450/-/v1mk5/-/index.html*.

Kampala City Council Authority. 2014. "Ministerial Policy Statement for Fiscal Year 2014/15."

Kasara, Kimuli. 2007. "Tax Me if You Can: Ethnic Geography, Democracy, and the Taxation of Agriculture in Africa." *American Political Science Review* 101(1):159–172.

Kenya, News24. 2013. "Boda Boda Registration Kicks Off in Kampala City." **URL:** *http:// m.news24.com/kenya/MyNews24/Boda-boda-registration-kicks-off-in-Kampala-city-20130913*.

Kipp, Walter, Jimmy Kamugisha, Phil Jacobs, Gilbert Burnham, and Tom Rubaale. 2001. "User Fees, Health Staff Incentives, and Service Utilization in Kabarole District, Uganda." *Bulletin of the World Health Organization* 79(11):1032–1037.

Kisangani, Emizet F. and Jeffrey Pickering. 2014. "Rebels, Rivals, and Post-colonial State-building: Identifying Bellicist Influences on State Extractive Capability." *International Studies Quarterly* 58(1):187–198.

Kiser, Edgar and Steven M. Karceski. 2017. "Political Economy of Taxation." *Annual Review of Political Science* 20(1):75–92.

Klein, Richard A., Kate A. Ratliff, Michelangelo Vianello, Reginald B. Adams, Jr, Štěpán Bahník, Michael J. Bernstein, Konrad Bocian, Mark J. Brandt, Beach Brooks, Claudia Chloe Brumbaugh, et al. 2014. "Investigating Variation in Replicability: A "Many Labs" Replication Project." *Social Psychology* 45(3):142.

Klein, Richard A., Michelangelo Vianello, Fred Hasselman, Byron G. Adams, Reginald B. Adams, Jr, Sinan Alper, Mark Aveyard, Jordan R. Axt, Mayowa T. Babalola, Štěpán Bahník, et al. 2018. "Many Labs 2: Investigating Variation in Replicability across Samples and Settings." *Advances in Methods and Practices in Psychological Science* 1(4):443–490.

Kőszegi, Botond and Matthew Rabin. 2006. "A Model of Reference-Dependent Preferences." *The Quarterly Journal of Economics* 121(4):1133–1165.

KPMG. 2018. "Tax Alert: Uganda Issues 2021 Tax Amendment Bills." **URL:** *https://assets.kpmg/content/dam/kpmg/ke/pdf/tax/KPMG%20Tax%20Alert-%20Uganda%20Issues%202021%20Tax%20Amendment%20Bills.pdf.*

Kuran, Timur. 1997. *Private Truths, Public Lies: The Social Consequences of Preference Falsification.* Cambridge, MA: Harvard University Press.

Lambright, Gina. 2014. "Opposition Politics and Urban Service Delivery in Kampala, Uganda." *Development Policy Review* 32(s1):s39–s60.

Lees, Adrienne and Doris Akol. 2021. "There and Back Again: The Making of Uganda's Mobile Money Tax." International Centre for Tax and Development, Working Paper 123.

Levi, Margaret. 1989. *Of Rule and Revenue.* Berkeley: University of California Press.

Levi, Margaret, Audrey Sacks, and Tom Tyler. 2009. "Conceptualizing Legitimacy, Measuring Legitimating Beliefs." *American Behavioral Scientist* 53(3):354–375.

Livingstone, Ian and Roger Charlton. 1998. "Raising Local Authority District Revenues through Direct Taxation in a Low-Income Developing Country: Evaluating Uganda's GPT." *Public Administration and Development* 18(5):499–517.

Local Government Finance Commission. 2001. "A Case for Continued Collection of Graduated Tax." Republic of Uganda.

Magala, Charles and Alphonse Rubagumya. 2007. *Why Pay?: Motivators for Payments of Local Market Dues in Rwanda and Uganda.* SNV Netherlands Development Organisation.

Mamdani, Mahmood. 1996. *Citizen and Subject: Contemporary Africa and the Legacy of Late Colonialism.* Princeton: Princeton University Press.

Mares, Isabela and Didac Queralt. 2015. "The Non-Democratic Origins of Income Taxation." *Comparative Political Studies* 48(14):1974–2009.

Martin, Isaac and Nadav Gabay. 2018. "Tax Policy and Tax Protest in 20 Rich Democracies, 1980–2010." *The British Journal of Sociology* 69(3):647–669.

McGuirk, Eoin F. 2010. "The Illusory Leader: Natural Resources, Taxation and Accountability." *Public Choice* 154:285–313.

Mehlum, Halvor, Karl Moene, and Ragnar Torvik. 2006. "Institutions and the Resource Curse." *The Economic Journal* 116:1–20.

Meltzer, Allan H. and Scott F. Richard. 1981. "A Rational Theory of the Size of Government." *Journal of Political Economy* 89(5):914–927.

Ministry of Finance, Uganda. 2022. "Background to the Budget, 2022/2023 Fiscal Year." *https://www.finance.go.ug/sites/default/files/Publications/Background%20to%20the%20Budget%20FY%202022-23.pdf.*

Ministry of Local Government. 2014. "Decentralization and Local Development in Uganda." **URL:** *https://molg.go.ug/mo/docs/2014/12/LOCAL-GOVENMENT-HANDBOOK-2014-lite.pdf.*

Moore, Mick. 2004. "Revenues, State Formation, and the Quality of Governance in Developing Countries." *International Political Science Review* 25(3):297–319.

Morrison, Kevin M. 2009. "Oil, Nontax Revenue, and the Redistributional Foundations of Regime Stability." *International Organization* 63(1):107–38.

Morrison, Kevin M. 2015. Natural Resources and Development. In *Emerging Trends in the Social and Behavioral Sciences*, ed. Robert Scott and Stephen Kosslyn. Hoboken, NJ: John Wiley & Sons, Inc., pp. 1–15.

Mulligan, Casey B., Ricard Gil. and Xavier Sala-i Martin. 2004. "Do Democracies Have Different Public Policies Than Nondemocracies?" *Journal of Economic Perspectives* 18(1):51–74.

Murphy, Liam and Thomas Nagel. 2002. *The Myth of Ownership*. Oxford: Oxford University Press.

New Vision. 2004. "Kampala Insist On Cyclist Tax." **URL:** *http://allafrica.com/stories/200406080161.html.*

New Vision. 2008. "KCC, Nakawa Vendors Clash." **URL:** *http://allafrica.com/stories/200808210349.html.*

North, Douglass C. and Barry R. Weingast. 1989. "Constitutions and Commitment: The Evolution of Institutions Governing Public Choice in Seventeenth-Century England." *The Journal of Economic History* 49(4):803–832.

Ojambo, Fred, and Burkhardt, Paul. 2022. "Uganda's $10 Billion Oil Development Finally Gets Go-Ahead." **URL:** *https://www.bloomberg.com/news/articles/2022-02-01/totalenergies-reaches-final-decision-on-10-billion-uganda-oil.*

Olson, Mancur. 1965. *The Logic of Collective Action*. Cambridge, MA: Harvard University Press.

Olson, Mancur. 1993. "Dictatorship, Democracy, and Development." *American Political Science Review* 87(3):567–576.

Orem, Juliet Nabyonga, Frederick Mugisha, Christine Kirunga, Jean Macq and Bart Criel. 2011. "Abolition of User Fees: The Uganda Paradox." *Health Policy and Planning* 26(suppl 2):ii41–ii51.

Paler, Laura. 2013. "Keeping the Public Purse: An Experiment in Windfalls, Taxes, and the Incentives to Restrain Government." *American Political Science Review* 107(4): 706–725.

Pearlman, Wendy. 2013. "Emotions and the Microfoundations of the Arab Uprisings." *Perspectives on Politics* 11(2):387–409.

Picur, Ronald D. and Ahmed Riahi-Belkaoui. 2006. "The Impact of Bureaucracy, Corruption and Tax Compliance." *Review of Accounting and Finance* 5(2):1–7.

Piketty, Thomas. 2013. *Capital in the 21st Century*. Cambridge, MA: Harvard University Press.

Plümper, Thomas, Vera E. Troeger, and Philip Manow. 2005. "Panel Data Analysis in Comparative Politics: Linking Method to Theory." *European Journal of Political Research* 44(2):327–354.

Powell Jr, Bingham and Guy Whitten. 1993. "A Cross-National Analysis of Economic Voting: Taking Account of the Political Context." *American Journal of Political Science* 37(2):391–414.

PriceWaterhouseCooper. 2018. "Uganda Tax Watch 2018." **URL:** *https://www.pwc.com/ug/en/assets/pdf/ug-tax-watch2018.pdf/.*

PriceWaterhouseCooper. 2021. "Tax Amendments FY2021/22." **URL:** *https://www.pwc.com/ug/en/assets/pdf/tax-amendments-2021-presentation.pdf.*

Prichard, Wilson. 2015. *Taxation, Responsiveness and Accountability in Sub-Saharan Africa: The Dynamics of Tax Bargaining*. Cambridge: Cambridge University Press.

Prichard, Wilson. 2018. "Electoral Competitiveness, Tax Bargaining and Political Incentives in Developing Countries: Evidence from Political Budget Cycles Affecting Taxation." *British Journal of Political Science* 48(2):427–457.

Prichard, Wilson and David K. Leonard. 2010. "Does Reliance on Tax Revenue Build State Capacity in Sub-Saharan Africa?" *International Review of Administrative Sciences* 76(4):653–675.

Profeta, Paola, Riccardo Puglisi, and Simona Scabrosetti. 2013. "Does Democracy Affect Taxation and Government Spending? Evidence from Developing Countries." *Journal of Comparative Economics* 41(3):684–718.

Queralt, Didac. 2022. *Pawned States: State Building in the Era of International Finance.* Vol. 109. Princeton: Princeton University Press.

Raffler, Pia. 2022. Does Political Oversight of the Bureaucracy Increase Accountability? Field Experimental Evidence from a Dominant Party Regime. *American Political Science Review,* 116(4):1443–1459.

Reinikka, Ritva and Jakob Svensson. 2005. "Fighting Corruption to Improve Schooling: Evidence from a Newspaper Campaign in Uganda." *Journal of the European Economic Association* 3(2–3):259–267.

Reuters. 2018. "Uganda Police Use Teargas to Disperse Protest against Social Media Taxes." URL: *https://www.reuters.com/article/us-uganda-socialmedia-protests/uganda-police-use-teargas-to-disperse-protest-against-social-media-taxes-idUSKBN1K121S.*

Reuters. 2019. "Uganda Partially Eases COVID-19 Containment measures." URL: *https://www.reuters.com/world/africa/uganda-partially-eases-covid-19-containment-measures-2021-07-30/.*

Rieger, Marc Oliver, Mei Wang, and Thorsten Hens. 2011. "Prospect Theory around the World." NHH Dept. of Finance & Management Science Discussion Paper (2011/19).

Rodden, Jonathan A. 2005. *Hamilton's Paradox: The Promise and Peril of Fiscal Federalism.* Cambridge: Cambridge University Press.

Rodríguez-Franco, Diana. 2016. "Internal Wars, Taxation, and State Building." *American Sociological Review* 81(1):190–213. URL: *https://doi.org/10.1177/0003122415615903.*

Ross, Michael. 1999. "The Political Economy of the Resource Curse." *World Politics* 51(2):297–322.

Ross, Michael L. 2001. "Does Oil Hinder Democracy?" *World Politics* 53(3): 325–361.

Ross, Michael L. 2004. "Does Taxation Lead to Representation?" *British Journal of Political Science* 34(2):229–249.

Ross, Michael L. 2012. *The Oil Curse: How Petroleum Wealth Shapes the Development of Nations.* Princeton: Princeton University Press.

Sánchez De La Sierra, Raúl. 2020. "On the Origins of the State: Stationary Bandits and Taxation in Eastern Congo." *Journal of Political Economy* 128(1):32–74.

Sandbu, Martin E. 2006. "Natural Wealth Accounts: A Proposal for Alleviating the Natural Resource Curse." *World Development* 34(7):1153–1170.

Sandbu, Martin E. 2012. "Direct Distribution of Natural Resource Revenues as a Policy for Peacebuilding." In *High-Value Natural Resource and Post-conflict Peacebuilding,* ed. P. Lujala and S. A. Rustad. Vol. 1. New York: Routledge, pp. 275–290.

Sarzin, Zara. 2007. "Local Government Revenue Policies and Their Impacts: A Model for Tanzania and Uganda." Washington, DC: World Bank.

Scheve, Kenneth and David Stasavage. 2010. "The Conscription of Wealth: Mass Warfare and the Demand for Progressive Taxation." *International Organization* 64(4):529–561.

Scheve, Kenneth and David Stasavage. 2016. *Taxing the Rich*. Princeton: Princeton University Press.

Schumpeter, Joseph A. 1991. "The Crisis of the Tax State." In *The Economics and Sociology of Capitalism*, ed. Richard Swedberg. Princeton: Princeton University Press, pp. 99–141.

Seelkopf, Laura, Moritz Bubek, Edgars Eihmanis, Joseph Ganderson, Julian Limberg, Youssef Mnaili, Paula Zuluaga, and Philipp Genschel. 2021. "The Rise of Modern Taxation: A New Comprehensive Dataset of Tax Introductions Worldwide." *The Review of International Organizations* 16(1):239–263.

Stasavage, David. 2005. "The Role of Democracy in Uganda's Move to Universal Primary Education." *The Journal of Modern African Studies* 43(1):53–73.

Stasavage, David. 2011. *States of Credit*. Princeton: Princeton University Press.

Suryanarayan, Pavithra. 2021. "Status Politics Hollows Out the State: Evidence from Colonial India." Baltimore: Johns Hopkins University. URL: *https://pavisuridotcom. files.wordpress.com/2021/02/suryanarayan2021_hollowing_out_the_state.pdf*.

Tarus, Isaac Kipsang. 2004. "A History of the Direct Taxation of the African People of Kenya, 1895–1973." PhD thesis Rhodes University.

The East African. 2018. "WhatsApp Users in Uganda to Pay $0.05 daily tax." URL: *https://www.theeastafrican.co.ke/tea/business/whatsapp-users-in-uganda-to-pay-0-05-daily-tax-1395032*.

The East African. 2019. "Uganda Social Media Tax Fails to Raise Expected Amount." URL: *https://www.theeastafrican.co.ke/business/Uganda-social-media-tax-fails-to-raise-expected-amount/2560-5198446-format-xhtml-2atmorz/index.html*.

The Independent. 2021. "Lukwago, CEC Want Military Out of City Markets." URL: *https://www.independent.co.ug/lukwago-cec-want-military-out-of-city-markets/*.

The Observer. 2009. "Buganda Riots behind Boda Boda Clampdown?" URL: *http:// www.observer.ug/index.php?option=com_content&view=article&id=5716:buganda-riots-behind-boda-boda-clampdown&catid=34:news&Itemid=114*.

The C.I.A. World Factbook. 2014. https://www.cia.gov/library/publications/the-world-factbook/geos/ug.html.

Therkildsen, O. 2006. *The Rise and Fall of Mass Taxation in Uganda 1900–2005*. Danish Institute for International Studies (DIIS).

Thies, Cameron G. 2005. "War, Rivalry, and State Building in Latin America." *American Journal of Political Science* 49(3):451–465.

Thies, Cameron G. 2007. "The Political Economy of State Building in Sub-Saharan Africa." *The Journal of Politics* 69(3):716–731.

Tilly, Charles. 1992. *Coercion, Capital, and European States, AD 990–1992*. Hoboken, NJ: Wiley-Blackwell.

Timmons, Jeffrey F. 2005. "The Fiscal Contract: States, Taxes, and Public Services." *World Politics* 57(4):530–567.

Torgler, Benno. 2007. *Tax Compliance and Tax Morale: A Theoretical and Empirical Analysis*. Cheltenham: Edward Elgar Publishing.

Tversky, Amos and Daniel Kahneman. 1991. "Loss Aversion in Riskless Choice: A Reference-Dependent Model." *The Quarterly Journal of Economics* 106(4): 1039–1061.

Uganda Law Reform Commission. 2013. "A Report of the Review of the Markets Act, Cap 94 in Uganda." Ministry of Local Government.

Uganda Radio Network. 2009. "Iganga Market Vendors Plan Boycott." URL: *http:// ugandaradionetwork.com/a/story.php?s=25253*.

Uganda Radio Network. 2012a. "Jinja Central Market Closed." **URL:** *http:// ugandaradionetwork.com/a/story.php?s=40622.*

Uganda Radio Network. 2012b. "Vendors Dump Garbage at Lira Municipal Chambers." **URL:** *http://ugandaradionetwork.com/a/story.php?s=42864.*

UN News. 2021. "Rights Experts Sound Alarm over Uganda 'Brutal' Election Crackdown." **URL:** *https://news.un.org/en/story/2021/04/1089642.*

Van de Walle, Nicolas. 2001. *African Economies and the Politics of Permanent Crisis, 1979–1999.* New York: Cambridge University Press.

Weigel, Jonathan L. 2020. "The Participation Dividend of Taxation: How Citizens in Congo Engage More with the State When It Tries to Tax Them." *The Quarterly Journal of Economics* 135(4):1849–1903.

Wilensky, Harold L. 2002. *Rich Democracies.* Berkeley: University of California Press.

World Bank. 2012. *World Development Indicators 2012.* The World Bank. **URL:** *http:// EconPapers.repec.org/RePEc:wbk:wbpubs:6014.*

World Bank. 2020. *"World Development Indicators."*

Xu, Ke, David B. Evans, Patrick Kadama, Juliet Nabyonga, Peter Ogwang Ogwal, and Ana Mylena Aguilar. 2005. "The Elimination of User Fees in Uganda: Impact on Utilization and Catastrophic Health Expenditures." World Health Organization.

Yechiam, Eldad. 2019. "Acceptable Losses: The Debatable Origins of Loss Aversion." *Psychological Research* 83(7):1327–1339.

Yechiam, Eldad and Guy Hochman. 2013. "Losses as Modulators of Attention: Review and Analysis of the Unique Effects of Losses over Gains." *Psychological Bulletin* 139(2):497.

Index

Printed in the USA/Agawam, MA
February 6, 2024

860710.011